D1393924

England's Citizenship Education Experiment

State, School and Student Perspectives

Lee Jerome

B L O O M S B U R Y

LONDON • NEW DELHI • NEW YORK • SYDNEY

Bloomsbury Academic

An imprint of Bloomsbury Publishing Plc

50 Bedford Square
London
WC1B 3DP
UK

175 Fifth Avenue
New York
NY 10010
USA

www.bloomsbury.com

First published 2012

British Library Cataloguing-in-Publication Data
A catalogue record for this book is available from the British Library.

ISBN: HB: 978-1-4411-2224-7
PDF: 978-1-4411-0487-8
ePub: 978-1-4411-8116-9

Library of Congress Cataloging-in-Publication Data
A catalog reference for this book is available from the Library of Congress.

Typeset by Fakenham Prepress Solutions, Fakenham, Norfolk NR21 8NN
Printed and bound in Great Britain

Contents

Acknowledgements

I would like to record my thanks to the people I met at the two schools where I conducted my research. The teachers were all enthusiastic about Citizenship and were playing a significant part in making the subject successful in their schools – it was a privilege to work with them for this short time. Whilst working hard to ensure the subject was successful in their schools they were also very generous in giving me their time and organising opportunities for me to work with students, for which I am immensely grateful.

The students were a joy to work with. Whilst I hope the serious intent of this research is evident, the young people made the research enjoyable and entertaining. They embraced their roles as co-researchers with enthusiasm and brought insights to the research that have enriched my understanding. I felt it was necessary to embrace student voice as a part of my research, simply because it is an important principle, but the young people I met transformed this sense of duty into a thoroughly enjoyable experience. As the research process wore on through the years, my meetings with my co-researchers turned into the highlights of my schedule and I am grateful for the openness, diligence and sense of fun they brought to the task.

Several colleagues have helped me to develop my thinking about the nature of Citizenship and curriculum reform and I would like to thank Gary Clemitshaw with whom I collaborated on a project exploring Britishness and Citizenship; our discussions helped me to develop my thinking about community and identity, themes which are explored in this book. I would also like to thank Jeremy Hayward for collaborating on a paper looking at the implications of Citizenship becoming a curriculum subject; chapter 5 includes material that was first published in Hayward, J. and Jerome, L. (2010) 'Staffing, status and subject knowledge: what does the construction of citizenship as a new curriculum subject in England tell us about the nature of school subjects?' in the *Journal of Education for Teaching*, 36 (2). I am grateful to colleagues at citizED who provided the means to support the project with Gary and the invitation to present a joint paper with Jeremy.

I would also like to thank colleagues at the Association for Citizenship Teaching (ACT), who ensured I have always enjoyed stimulating conversations over the years to keep my thinking fresh about the subject. Thanks are also due to Liz Moorse who has consistently supported the subject at the Qualifications and Curriculum Authority (QCA), the Citizenship Foundation and in Democratic Life – her understanding of curriculum and assessment has helped me to understand the processes that underpin curriculum construction and I am grateful for comments she made on several chapters. Marcus Bhargava has also been a source of inspiration and ideas over the years of our association and I would particularly like to thank him for helping me to identify my case study schools and helping me shape some of the chapters in this book. Bhavini Algarra also gave wise advice on some of the draft chapters and has been influential on the thinking here over the many years since we trained to teach Social Studies at the Institute of Education in London. Maria Dominguez provided invaluable support getting the student questionnaires into a usable electronic format and I am grateful for the painstaking attention she paid to detail – all the grammatical and spelling errors in students' responses have been faithfully transcribed from some almost illegible questionnaires.

Finally I would like to thank two people for their patience over the years I have been working on this project. My PhD supervisor, Professor Hugh Starkey, has been unfaltering in his support and thorough in his feedback, and has applied gentle pressure when he thought I could handle it, for which I thank him. My partner, Robert, has tolerated my musings on the subject for a very long time and I thank him for his support and forbearance.

List of Tables and Figures

Abbreviations

ACT	Association for Citizenship Teaching
ASBOS	Anti-Social Behavioural Orders
BME	Black and Minority Ethnic
BYC	British Youth Council
CELS	Citizenship Education Longitudinal Study
CIVED	International Civic Education study
CVA	Contextual Value Added
DCLG	Department for Communities and Local Government (established as a central government department in 2006)
DCSF	Department for Children, Schools and Families (government department with responsibility for schools and curriculum, 2007–10)
DFE	Department for Education (government department with responsibility for schools and curriculum, 1992–5 and 2010–)
DFEE	Department for Education and Employment (government department with responsibility for schools and curriculum, 1995–2001)
DFES	Department for Education and Skills (government department with responsibility for schools and curriculum, 2001–7)
GCSE	General Certificate of Secondary Education (the most common examination taken by school-leavers at the age of 16 in England)
GTP	Graduate Training Programme (school-based initial teacher training)
HS	The Heath School
ICCS	International Civic and Citizenship Education Study

IEA	International Association for the Evaluation of Educational Achievement
IMF	International Monetary Fund
KS	Key Stage (KS1/2 = primary education and KS3/4 = secondary)
NCS	National Citizen Service
NCSR	National Centre for Social Research
NFER	National Foundation for Educational Research
NGO	Non-Governmental Organisation
NHS	National Health Service
OECD	Organisation for Economic Cooperation and Development
OFSTED	Office for Standards in Education, Children's Services and Skills
OP	Oak Park
PE	Physical Education
PGCE	Post Graduate Certificate in Education (the most common route for initial teacher training)
PMSU	Prime Minister's Strategy Unit (2002–10)
PSHE	Personal, Social and Health Education
QCA	Qualifications and Curriculum Authority
QTS	Qualified Teacher Status
RE	Religious Education
RRSA	Rights Respecting Schools Award
SACRE	Standing Advisory Council for Religious Education
SPSS	Statistical Package for the Social Sciences (computer software)
SSAT	Specialist Schools and Academies Trust
UNCRC	United Nations Convention on the Rights of the Child
UNESCO	United Nations Educational, Scientific and Cultural Organization
YPI	Youth and Philanthropy Initiative

A note on 'Citizenship' and 'citizenship'

Where citizenship is used with a lower case 'c' I am referring to the general concept, rather than the school subject. Similarly citizenship education, as a general area, appears consistently in lower case. Citizenship appears with a capital 'C' only where it refers to the national curriculum subject (and of course at the start of a sentence).

Introduction

In 1997 the Labour Party returned to power in the UK after eighteen years of Conservative government. This was to become the longest period in office in the party's history, and Tony Blair became the longest serving Labour Prime Minister. One of the government's first acts was to establish an Advisory Group to start the process of introducing Citizenship into the national curriculum in England. The subject was finally introduced into secondary schools in 2002 and this book looks back over the first ten years of statutory citizenship education in England to provide a case study of curriculum reform. In essence the book aims to answer two questions. First, what kind of citizenship education did New Labour create, and how did it fit in with a broader reform and modernization agenda? And second, what happened to the vision in reality, in other words, what kind of citizenship education happened as a consequence of the policy?

England's model of citizenship education has received attention from educators all over the world, and England has moved rapidly from being one of the only countries not to have formal citizenship education, to being one of the frontrunners. This is at least in part because Citizenship in England has attempted to steer clear of a traditional civics model, in which knowledge is fore-grounded, and has embraced a more holistic model in which young people learn through participation. However, there is a danger in comparing models of citizenship education around the world – one may be tempted to develop perfect curriculum designs in theory, without paying sufficient regard to the political cultures that give rise to curriculum reform. Therefore this book aims to explore the connection between the model that developed in England and the political context from which it emerged.

The need for this more contextualized approach is underlined by two existing accounts of the Advisory Group, which was chaired by Bernard Crick. First, Kiwan's (2008) study included interviews with members of the Advisory Group and tends to focus on the dynamics of the group and their eventual recommendations as being the most important factors in explaining why citizenship education was introduced. Kiwan includes a rather cursory discussion of the context, focusing only on the narrow political perspective of identifying the 'window of opportunity', which almost entirely follows Crick's own 'insider account' of how the policy process worked. The second study analyses the Advisory Group's work from a Foucauldian perspective, focusing on the concept of governmentality (Pykett, 2007). Pykett places her analysis of citizenship education within the broader policy discussions of civil renewal and immigration, but fails to explore in any great detail precisely what kind of citizen is envisaged within these broad discourses. In a later article Pykett (Pykett et al., 2010) also makes a strong case for the need to understand citizenship education policy in its context – locating it in a time and place. She rejects the tendency in much of the citizenship education literature towards universalizing normative approaches and also criticises the evaluative literature for being too narrowly focused on educational impact without acknowledging the relevant political contextual factors which shape citizenship education. Whilst I share Pykett's commitment that, 'sensitivity to context is central [and] this includes sensitivity to the fate of good citizen discourse in different times', (Pykett et al., 2010: 525) her focus on the educational context alone prevents her from achieving a clear understanding of how England's citizenship education policy has developed under New Labour.

There have also been attempts to analyse citizenship education within the broader political context of New Labour (Gamarnikow and Green, 2000; Kisby, 2009), which specifically focus on the contribution of this policy to the broader programme of creating social capital. I argue that the focus on social capital is itself too narrow, but I intend to build on this kind of approach, which is to say I aim to develop an analysis of citizenship education policy which is firmly embedded in an account of the broader political context in which it developed. Dunn and Burton have outlined the case for such an analysis in their discussion of the relationship between New Labour's communitarian foundations and the development of citizenship education policy, but they argue that there is a need for a study which connects the broad analysis of political principles to the actions of teachers (Dunn and Burton, 2011). This book responds to that call, although in doing so it broadens the discussion from Dunn and Barton's concern with communitarianism to consider other influences that informed New Labour.

Locating this book in the wider debates about citizenship education

There are a growing number of books on citizenship education pedagogy, ranging from theory to classroom tips, but this book does not aim to make a contribution to the 'how to' literature. Rather it belongs to a wider tradition which aims to examine citizenship education in the broader context, and in seeking to do this, the book draws on several types of literature.

First, there is a *justificatory* literature which focuses on making a strong theoretical case for citizenship education within broader models of democracy. Here the primary concern may be with the model of democracy to be promoted, and education is discussed because of its perceived supportive role. Examples of this approach are provided by Kymlicka (1995) who refers to the role of education in promoting his preferred model of multicultural citizenship, and Barber (2003) who discusses education as one strategy for embedding strong, participatory politics in society. Sometimes the focus is more directly on providing a persuasive case for citizenship as a concern for educators, for example Callan (1997) explores in some detail the type of education that will support liberal democracy. Brighouse (2006) provides a more discursive example of this literature and guides the reader through the problems with making citizenship education compulsory, before concluding with cautious support.

Second, there is a *definitional* literature which is predominantly concerned with seeking to construct or explore definitions of ideal forms of citizenship education. There is a clear link to the justificatory literature mentioned above, and there may well be overlap; for example, Wringe (1984) includes a broad discussion of the nature of democracy and a fairly detailed discussion of the educational implications, along with examples of educational practices that might be appropriate. Some of this literature focuses more narrowly on the nature of citizenship education, and therefore appears to be more accessible by, and targeted to, a teaching audience. An example is provided by Cogan and Derricott (1998) who promote a cross-cultural multidimensional model of citizenship education. Some of this literature also develops models of citizenship informed by specific political commitments, for example Alderson (1999, 2000a, 2000b, 2008) discusses human rights; as do Osler and Starkey, albeit within a broader model of cosmopolitan citizenship (2003, 2005a); whilst Annette focuses more on active citizenship (2000, 2003), and Davies has written about the connections between global and citizenship education (Davies et al., 2005a).

Third there is a *comparative* literature which is helpful in developing a broader understanding of the possibilities for the construction and implementation of citizenship education. In this category one might include comparative work such as Osler and Starkey's survey for UNESCO (Osler and Starkey, 2005b) and Hahn's discussion based on five countries (1998); as well as work from particular regions, such as the European programme for promoting Education for Democratic Citizenship (Audigier, 2000, Bîrzéa, 2000, Dürr, 2004, Liégeois, 2005); and individual country case studies such as those included in the 'Sage Handbook of Education for Citizenship and Democracy' (Arthur et al., 2008) as well as those published separately (for example, Ai, 1998 on Singapore; Ekholm, 2004 on Finland; McCowan, 2009 on Brazil).

Fourth, *historical* material is also useful for similar reasons to the comparative literature. For example, accounts of US projects from the 1950s (Meier et al., 1952) and of English projects from the inter-war period (Happold et al., 1937) are useful as a source of ideas against which to measure and understand contemporary developments. They are also valuable because of the light they shed on the connections between the specific type of citizenship education envisaged and the context in which such schemes arose. In considering how citizenship education developed prior to New Labour, Derek Heater has documented the history very thoroughly (Heater, 2001, 2004), and the development of Bernard Crick's ideas can be traced in his earlier work for Hansard (Crick, 1978). If one returns to Crick's formative work on political literacy, it is also useful to be aware of the context in which these ideas were formed, for example Brennan (1981) provides a useful reminder of how conflict models of politics rendered citizenship education radical and controversial during the 1970s. Brennan himself called for transformative student democracy and dismissed anything short of that as a 'sham'; he quoted White (1973b) calling for students to be taught how to alter or remove institutions and described one peer's attack on the Politics Association as a 'socialist conspiracy' (Brennan, 1981: 12).

Finally, some publications are essentially *evaluative*, exploring the impact of specific projects and programmes, or simply measuring levels of knowledge and understanding. Examples include the International Association for the Evaluation of Educational Achievement (IEA) Civics Study (Torney-Purta and Klandl-Richardson, 2002; Torney-Purta et al., 2001), and Niemi and Junn's (1998) analysis of the impact of civics classes. In relation to the introduction of citizenship education in England, the National Foundation for Educational Research (NFER) conducted a longitudinal survey (see for example Benton et al., 2008), which is discussed in some detail in later chapters. Other small scale evaluations discuss specific dimensions of the Citizenship curriculum, such as participation (Davies et al., 2009), debate and discussion (Jerome and Algarra, 2005) or political understanding (Rowe, 2005).

Clearly any research in citizenship education must draw on several of these categories of existing literature, and the influence of these publications will be evident in the chapters that follow. However, the essential point I have drawn from them all reinforces the issue I want to explore in this book, namely that any policy can only be properly understood within the political context in which it arose.

The structure of this book

The first chapter sets the scene for the reader who is relatively new to the field of citizenship and citizenship education. I outline why citizenship is such an important and useful concept and discuss the liberal tradition which dominates thinking about citizenship. The citizenship education literature mentioned above is of course important but ultimately draws on more foundational work in political philosophy which shapes the way we think about the purposes of teachers and schools. Therefore this opening chapter considers these underlying traditions through explaining some of the key issues within liberalism, and some of the responses to them, including communitarianism, civic republicanism and deliberative democracy.

Chapter 2 establishes a broad methodological approach to understanding citizenship education policy in the wider political context. It draws on a range of ideas from the literature on policy analysis and establishes a 'toolkit' to develop the analysis in subsequent chapters.

Chapter 3 considers New Labour's period in office to establish the overall policy context in which citizenship education developed. This chapter applies some of the ideas from Chapter 1 to consider three inter-related discourses, which together form the trope of the 'new citizen', who inhabits a powerful role in the construction and validation of a broad range of policy initiatives, especially relating to welfare reform. I argue that the 'new citizen' is constituted through discourses relating to (i) responsibilities as well as rights, (ii) active participation and (iii) the relationship between the individual and their community.

Chapter 4 applies these three discourses to the evolution of citizenship education policy through a more detailed analysis of two key policy documents – the Crick Report and the Ajegbo Review. This discussion tracks these discourses within the two reports and considers ways in which the discourses change, both in their own terms and in their relationship to one another. This chapter establishes some of the changes and continuities in official ideals of citizenship, and clarifies some of the unresolved tensions in statements of policy.

Chapter 5 starts the next section of the book, which turns more explicitly to the implementation of citizenship education policy and outlines some of the practical and ideological issues which emerged as the abstract concept was translated into a curriculum subject. This chapter considers the broad issues of staffing, status and the nature of school subjects by describing some of the difficulties experienced in creating Citizenship as a curriculum entitlement.

The next five chapters draw on a range of data from large national research projects conducted by the NFER to two school case studies, which were constructed to shed some light on how the subject was experienced and perceived by individuals. Chapters 6 and 7 start to explore the process of policy implementation from the teacher perspective and then the student perspective. The next three chapters consider the evidence in relation to the three discourses established in the first section of the book: rights and responsibilities (Chapter 8), community and diversity (Chapter 9), and active citizenship (Chapter 10).

Finally, Chapter 11 draws together these various arguments and sources of data to consider the overarching question which drives the book: to what extent does the citizenship education taking place in schools reflect the government's aims for the subject? The conclusion draws together reflections on two themes running through the work. The first theme is concerned with the overall political context in which citizenship education evolved and here I address the overall question directly and consider the extent to which the political intentions were realised. The second theme considers the factors that have influenced the implementation of citizenship education, and considering these enables me to make some recommendations about the next steps for citizenship education in England.

Part One

Thinking About Citizenship Policy

Thinking About Citizenship

Citizenship and contemporary politics

All modern governments face a bewildering array of decisions about so many aspects of our lives that it is often difficult to keep track of policy and legislation. To take some of the most significant aspects of the modern state, governments frequently change their positions on the way to organize benefits: who is eligible? What rates of income are adequate? What kinds of housing should people have access to? And do some people deserve more help than others? Governments also make decisions on the judicial system: under what conditions can people access legal aid? When should people be tried by a jury? When is community service better than imprisonment? They also make decisions every day about the borders of the country: who can enter the country? How long can they stay? Under what circumstances will they be sent home? And of course government also makes decisions about how much money to take in taxation, what to spend it on and where to make savings. These kinds of decisions are a feature of every modern government and although they have a technical dimension they are also issues of life and death, affecting as they do the life experience and life chances of millions of people. But these enduring issues are also supplemented by an equally bewildering array of other decisions relating to unforeseen events. In recent years in England notable examples have included what to do about apparently spontaneous riots and looting in a number of cities around the country (2011); how to respond to outbreaks of foot and mouth disease (2007) and threatened pandemics of avian flu (2009); what to do about overweening and corrupt media empires (2011) or arrogant and corrupt MPs (2009); how to respond to acts of terrorism (Glasgow airport, 2007; the London bombings, 2005); and what to do about the murder of vulnerable children (Baby Peter, 2007; Victoria Climbie 2000).

In every case we expect the government to take a view and to take action, and in the decisions they make, the government draws and re-draws the boundaries between itself and the individual – confiscating or destroying private property, intruding into people's family lives, monitoring our movements more closely, attempting to influence our beliefs and values, restricting or allowing business practices. Day in day out, state representatives intervene in people's lives to restrict some freedoms and enhance others and the interplay between these decisions is the business of citizenship. Citizenship is about many things, but at its core is the relationship between the individual and the government.

Foucault's concept of governmentality incorporates this relationship, and he described the detailed ways in which the state has developed an increasing regulatory focus on its own population (Foucault, 1991). Oestreich perceived the relationship between governance and urbanization in terms of new forms of citizenship:

> Greater social complexity brought a greater deployment of authority. People had to be 'coached', as it were, for the tasks created by the more populous society and the claims which it made on its citizens… a start was made on educating people to a discipline of work and frugality and on changing the spiritual, moral and psychological make-up of political, military and economic man (Oestreich 1983 cited in Gordon, 1991: 13).

Citizenship is not a natural state. It is created in specific contexts and has to be sustained through a variety of social processes. Foucault's discussion of the broad historical trend towards a new form of mutually constituted relationship between the state and individuals identifies two strands of activity – police and pastoral work. The state became concerned for the well-being of citizens and devised mechanisms for controlling them. This latter control does not need to be of the Orwellian type, a constant state of threat, it can also be seen in the provision of entertainments to enhance well-being and satisfaction (Foucault, 1991). Foucault explained the power of this approach which aimed 'to develop those elements constitutive of individuals' lives in such a way that their development also fosters the strength of the state' (Foucault, 1988, McNay, 1994: 121).

In a democracy citizens also exercise some control, or at least some measure of scrutiny, over government; and in its turn, the government helps to define and defend the citizen. There is nothing absolute about being a citizen – the freedoms of a citizen will ebb and flow over time depending on the decisions taken by governments day by day. Somehow all those decisions – the everyday processes of government and the interactions between citizens and other citizens and representatives of the state – all add up to create contemporary citizenship (Lemke, 2007: 7). As Bernard Crick noted, 'there are no final answers in the name of democracy... there is only a continual process of compromise... politics itself' (Crick, 2002a: 109).

And precisely because it is so difficult to keep track of all those policies and decisions, and because it all boils down to what we can and cannot do and the kinds of opportunities available to us, politicians often talk about citizens as a short hand for communicating ideas about the kind of society they are trying to promote. Every rhetorical dystopia is peopled by dysfunctional deviants and every imagined political panacea is populated by idealized individuals. In America's New Deal in the 1930s, even while the state was assuming greater power it promoted active, local citizens' engagement and in his inaugural speech Roosevelt spoke about duty and a common discipline to tackle national challenges. In his inaugural speech as South African President in 1994 Mandela set about mending a truly broken and divided society with a new vision of a 'rainbow nation at peace with itself' and thus began to promote a new identity for South African citizens. And at the time of writing this book, the British Prime Minister David Cameron's vision of a Broken Britain identified too many Britons failing to take their responsibilities seriously, and choosing to live isolated, ignorant, individualistic lives as the root of the problem. These broad brush political sketches are often dismissed as hot air, but actually they serve an important role in communicating a vision, or a sense of purpose. Politicians want to promote an overview of what they stand for, and imagining new futures serves to help us develop a sense of an overall purpose.

These broad images are easy to draw, and thinking back over several decades of British governments one can recall Wilson's 'white heat of technology', Heath's 'Selsdon Man', Thatcher's 'property owning democracy', John Major's much maligned 'Citizen's Charter' and 'Back to Basics' campaign, and Blair's 'Cool Britannia' project and the 'Third Way'. Importantly, each of these visions also entails an equally vivid characterization of the people – the citizens. As these politicians imagined a bright new future and encouraged voters to share in that vision, they simultaneously re-imagined them, both as the subjects of policy and as the agents of change. Wilson imagined the British shrugging off conformity and finding a new meritocratic order. Heath (initially at least) wanted people to become more entrepreneurial, more independent of government – a Conservative theme Thatcher returned to more vehemently, and in order for her vision to make sense she also had to have faith that people would want a mortgage and be willing to abandon landlord councils. Similarly, Major needed people to pick up the phone to alert the traffic cone hot-line about unnecessary obstacles on the roads. Each of these messages can be dismissed as a bit of political gimmickry, and surely some were more serious than others, but each also captures some important sense of what the government was about, and what its overall direction of travel would be.

Perhaps the extent to which some of those characterizations ring true now is a reflection of how successfully each leader was able to impose some overall sense of direction on their period of government. Clearly Thatcher's vision did emerge through the myriad of individual choices she had to make, and Britain did see a shift in the balance between private and public housing; not to say a shift between public to private provision in a range of other walks of life. Perhaps Wilson's vision of white heat was somehow cooled by the industrial strife he had to deal with; and perhaps also John Major will be best remembered for his hypocrisy and naivety in requiring MPs to stand up for basic family values only to be pilloried in the press as some of them were revealed as perjurers and adulterers. But the important point is that these messages give us a handle on the political vision – whether or not it is successfully implemented – and a shorthand way to discuss the politicians who would change the country and the people along with it.

David Cameron's Big Society, and Tony Blair's Third Way might be different in some important regards, but at root they serve similar purposes, and suffer from similar drawbacks. On the one hand both big ideas serve to provide some kind of overarching theme or narrative to a range of disparate reforms. New Labour invoked the Third Way to connect a raft of policies from Anti-Social Behavioural Orders (ASBOs) to parenting orders, and education reforms to National Health Service (NHS) reorganizations; whilst the Big Society has been used to justify localism, a voluntary national service for young people and housing benefit reform. They also do similar rhetorical work: the Third Way solution always seems more attractive because it is not the First Way (unfettered free market, neo-liberalism) nor the Second Way (stifling big government) (Fairclough, 2000); whilst the Big Society solution is deemed to be attractive for similar reasons – it is not Big Business nor is it Big Government. Of course very few politicians or political parties in England have ever favoured one of these old alternatives exclusively, but the ability to position themselves away from clearly imagined extremes underlines these leaders' own credentials as politicians of the middle ground: un-ideological, pragmatic, but radically so. In a speech in 2009 David Cameron used this rhetorical trick to position himself between two extremes when he pointed out, 'just because big government has helped atomize our society, it doesn't follow that smaller government would automatically bring us together again' (Cameron, 2009). And Tony Blair's memoirs demonstrated similar rhetorical work when he described the Third Way project he shared with Bill Clinton as a 'way of moving beyond the small-state… ideology of the Republicans; and the big-state… ideology of much of the traditional Democratic base' (Blair, 2010: 231–2). For each big vision, as we have noted above, there is a concomitant citizen – for Cameron, the Big Society needs citizens who will embrace a new philanthropy, cooperate with others to create new social enterprises to replace direct state provision, and engage in a form of national service to serve and learn; for Blair the Third Way made demands of local community leaders, newly professionalized public sector workers and empowered consumers of state services.

Very little of this is new, although the way the ideas are brought together and translated into specific policies may often be innovative. The remainder of this book is concerned with the distinctive ways in which citizenship was imagined and created in the period of New Labour. Before returning to the specifics of this case study though, in the remainder of this chapter I turn to some of the important traditions of citizenship and the debates that have preoc-cupied political thinkers over the generations. These provide the basic store of concepts and models I use later in the book to characterize what was happening in England in relation to citizenship more generally and citizenship education policy in particular.

Traditions in citizenship

Because citizenship relates to so many aspects of our individual and collective lives, and because it is so bound up with the nature of politics, it is a complex area to grasp. Broadly though, we might approach it from one of two directions – normative and empirical approaches (Frazier, 2008). Normative approaches are generally the domain of philosophers, and are concerned with thinking through possible models of citizenship, and deriving some coherent sense of what expectations might connect the individual to a particular political world-view. Empirical studies on the other hand are more likely to be conducted by sociologists, historians or political scientists, keen to explore the actual models of citizenship that have developed in practice. Clearly the tradition from which one approaches citizenship makes a profound difference to the precise types of question one seeks to answer. For example those with a background in psychology might be more interested in how individuals actually come to make decisions about how to behave in groups, and how social norms affect them;

whilst sociologists might focus on the ways in which various social groups experience citizenship differently. Clearly work on citizenship needs to connect with the ways in which citizens and would-be citizens actually live their lives and relate to one another and the state, and I will draw on much of this literature in the subsequent chapters of this book. However, the normative literature will be more helpful as an introduction to thinking about citizenship and so we shall turn to that as a source of ideas to map out the terrain.

Following Crick (2002a), Bellamy (2008) and Faulks (2000), we start with the contrasting traditions found in Ancient Greece and Rome. Whilst there were some important similarities in the way both societies developed forms of democracy, there were also important differences, which have influenced philosophers thinking about the nature of legitimate government. Perhaps the biggest difference relates to the connection between citizenship status and citizenship participation (Bellamy, 2008). The Athenian model of democracy was premised on the small scale city state, which provided a small enough community for the practice of direct democracy, although as Crick points out it is important to remember that this citizen involvement only formed one element of the ideal form of politics described by Aristotle (Crick, 2002a). In such a system the few wealthy Greek men who enjoyed the status of citizen were directly involved in the governance of their society, or polis. Participation was the most important characteristic of citizenship and citizens had to be prepared to participate in the decision-making Assembly; to serve in juries; to take responsibility for the administration of government by holding office as a magistrate; to contribute to local government; and to engage in military service (Bellamy, 2008). Manville argued that 'citizenship and the polis were one and the same' (quoted in Faulks, 2000: 16) and it is this which has been seen as the most influential aspect of the Greek system – the extent to which a civic ideology came to dominate politics and society, so that the 'polis was considered as prior to, and constitutive of, the individual' (ibid). As Thucydides expressed it in his Periclean Oration, 'we do not say that a man who takes no interest in politics minds his own business, we say that he has no business here at all' (Crick, 2002a: 19).

By contrast, although the Romans maintained some of the democratic elements of the Greek system, they had to adapt a form of citizenship which would serve a different function in an expanding empire, rather than in a city state. Thus Roman citizenship became divorced from ethnicity and participation and became a 'tool of social control and pacification' (Faulks, 2000: 19). Conferring a form of citizenship status to conquered populations in the empire helped to: establish systems of government; embed new territory in the empire;

Table 1.1 Thick and Thin Citizenship

	Thin citizenship	*Thick citizenship*
Rights and responsibilities	Rights are privileged Citizenship as legal status	Rights and responsibilities are mutually supportive Citizenship as moral duty
Participation	Passive Opportunity to participate	Active Obligation to participate
Community	State seen as a necessary evil Citizenship as public status Independence Freedom through choice	Political community as positive Pervades public and private Interdependence Freedom through civic virtue

Adapted from Faulks, 2000: 11

and signify inclusion through the extension of the rule of Roman law. It was not feasible, nor was it practically required, to maintain the expectation of citizen participation, and so as Faulks comments, the rise of the Roman Empire was accompanied by a weakening of citizenship as it became an 'increasingly thin and legalistic concept' (ibid).

This distinction enables us to think about different forms of citizenship. On the one hand we have the rather demanding Athenian model, which places great emphasis on the collective life of the polis, and the individual's role within it, which is defined by the *practices* and *obligations* of citizenship. On the other hand we have the more minimalist concept of the late Roman Empire, which makes fewer demands on the individual, and which is more concerned with citizenship as a *status* and the citizen as a bearer of *rights*. This initial distinction has been elaborated by citizenship theorists and may be simplified into two traditions of citizenship, which Faulks characterizes as 'thick' and 'thin' (Table 1.1).

Liberalism and citizenship

In many ways the dominant ideology of western democracy has been premised on a rather thin account of citizenship, and consequently many theories about the relationship between the state and the citizen tend towards protecting the individual against the state. In a nutshell, this is the liberal tradition, and its main strength and enduring appeal lie precisely in its unswerving support for the liberty of the individual, as is evident in the following statement from John Stuart Mill's essay 'On Liberty':

> If all mankind minus one were of one opinion and only one person were of the contrary opinion, mankind would be no more justified in silencing that one person, than he, if he had the power, would be justified in silencing mankind (Mill, 1859/1990: 1115).

If we take the individual as the main focus of a theory of citizenship, we may end up, as did Locke, advocating a rather minimalist expectation of government which is limited to the 'preservation of [individuals'] lives, liberties and estates' (quoted in Barber, 2003: 4).

Some modern philosophers have extended the tradition of the minimal state. For example, Nozick argues that the state's role is to protect individuals' rights to their own property, regardless of the fact that this will lead to inequality (Kymlicka, 2002; Nozick, 1974). On this libertarian view, which is often referred to as neo-liberalism, almost all situations in which the state intervenes in some way to take resources from one person in order to provide services to others is seen as unjust. Clearly this extremely thin concept of citizenship leaves almost no room for notions of obligation, focused as it is on the protection of individuals' rights, and their property rights above all.

Other forms of liberalism tend to have a rather expanded notion of the concept of rights, so that a recognition of rights includes some measure of the chances of someone actually being able to enjoy that right. A classic example of this is the right to life. A libertarian might accept this as a reasonable right, but interpret it narrowly as the freedom *from* another's deliberate murderous actions. Achieving this merely requires other people to leave us alone. But most liberals would acknowledge that in order to achieve this there must be some resources to ensure the right is more meaningful; for example we need a police force to enforce the law against murder, a criminal justice system to ensure this law is administered fairly, and a prison system to hold people who have infringed the law. Even on this fairly minimal interpretation, there is a justification for the state to find resources, which it might efficiently secure through taxation, which requires us to give up some of our wealth to fund this collective good. This is already further than Nozick thinks is justifiable, but once we have come this far, why not invest also in street lighting to enhance our safety, and hospitals to ensure we have access to emergency care if we come to harm? And once we have committed to that collective expenditure, why not fund the hospitals to help us prolong our lives, devise public health campaigns to encourage us to adopt healthy lifestyles, and hire life coaches to support those trying to quit drugs? Clearly once one acknowledges that the realistic achievement of basic rights requires some measure of redistribution, the point at which we think it is reasonable to stop collecting taxes and funding worthwhile health schemes is a nuanced judgement, not a matter of principle (Plant, 1990). Many liberals choose to place strict limits on the government by insisting that taxes must be designed to fund services for all, rather than merely redistribute income for the sake of 'fairness'; others might be more relaxed about this, although the general point adopted within liberalism in this regard is to ensure the state does not *unjustly* intervene in the individual's property rights and thus does not disrupt the efficient working of the market and the distribution of resources that flows from that (Gray, 1986). The notion of what constitutes a *just* intervention is one that concerns many liberal theorists.

Whilst liberalism often discusses rights in abstract terms, and in particular may be concerned with the notion of civil rights, Faulks argues that these foundational ideas might be more accurately seen as relating to 'market rights' (Faulks, 2000: 78). Korten argues that this represents a distortion which allows the 'moral philosophers of market liberalism' to equate 'the freedom and rights of individuals with market freedom and property rights'. The end result of this logic is that:

> The freedom of the market is the freedom of money, and when rights are a function of property rather than personhood, only those with property have rights (Korten, 1995: 83).

This aspect of liberalism means that is has often been used to justify a particular way of governing society which on one level achieves a level of formal civil equality, but in reality creates and sustains profoundly unequal outcomes, both within individual societies and between societies in the global system (Wallerstein, 1995).

As Barber points out in his book *Strong Democracy*, 'from this precarious foundation, no firm theory of citizenship, participation, public goods or civic virtue can be expected to arise' (Barber, 2003: 4). Indeed, as Gray points out, liberalism, with its commitment to limited government does not even advocate particularly for democracy as a form of government, remaining primarily concerned with how to protect individuals' freedom to make their own decisions about their own lives (Gray, 1986). So, despite its intrinsic appeal, liberal traditions of citizenship have been supplemented with other theoretical perspectives, which in essence seek to 'thicken up' the model of citizenship, without succumbing entirely to a 'tyranny of the majority' and thus sacrificing the individual to the collective. As we consider some of these additional perspectives it is useful to recap some of the limitations of liberalism and the outstanding questions that need an answer (see Table 1.2).

Table 1.2 Limitations of Liberalism

	Criticisms of liberalism	Questions
Rights and responsibilities	– Focus on rights at the expense of responsibilities – Paying into the system through taxation needs careful justification – Rights are often seen as non-negotiable rather than contingent on context	– What is the correct balance between rights and responsibilities? – What are the proper limits of individual rights? – Where do our rights actually come from? – To what extent do our rights enable us to make claims against others?
Participation	– No obligation to participate just the opportunity – Politics often based on participation in the public sphere in order to further one's individual interests	– To what extent should people be compelled to participate in democratic culture? – What level of participation is required to maintain a healthy democracy? – What should be done about free-riders, who benefit from democratic culture but do not sustain it through participation?
Community	– Excessive focus on individualism does not reflect the reality of community influence on our lives – No theory of what we, as society, should value and strive for beyond individual autonomy and property – Toleration of significant inequalities which reduce people's life chances – Market inequality means formal equality masks practical inequality	– What is the relationship between the individual and their community(ies) and how should this be reflected in citizenship? – To what extent should people be encouraged to feel a shared sense of civic identity? – What claim does the community have over the individual and what restrictions can be placed on people in the name of the common good? – To what extent can the community limit the market?

Responses to liberalism

In thinking about how we might answer these questions, it is useful to remember the distinction between thick and thin citizenship. The advocates of thin citizenship will answer them in ways which privilege the individual and play down the role of the community, whilst those who support thick citizenship will tend to focus more of the need to sustain healthy communities which are seen as fundamental in underpinning the good life for the individual. Obviously there are many ways in which each question can be answered, and there are many more ways in which the various answers can be woven together into overarching theories. Below we will mention three broad types of responses, which attempt to retain some of the most useful elements of liberalism, but which also attempt to accommodate a greater role for the community. These approaches are called communitarianism, civic republicanism and deliberative democracy and they have been chosen because they all have a role to play in the analysis in the subsequent chapters of citizenship under New Labour in England.

Talisse envisages these terms as rather confusingly merged together, arguing that communitarianism and civic republicanism represent two intertwined responses to the outstanding challenges within liberalism, and that liberals, communitarians and civic republicans all draw on deliberative ideas to extend their own approaches (Talisse, 2005). This blending of ideas is illustrated by influential writers such as Sandel who has consistently criticized liberalism, but adopted the label of both communitarian and civic republican at various stages (Aronovitch, 2000). Talisse discusses communitarianism as a policy-focused response, which is frequently espoused by politicians and sociologists seeking to address the problematic political consequences of liberalism's excessive individualism. By contrast, he perceives civic republicanism as a predominantly theoretical enterprise, in which political philosophers seek to resolve some of the theoretical weaknesses of liberalism and, as a consequence, this is a tradition which often struggles to identify clear implications for everyday politics. Adopting a rather different approach, Kymlicka argues that communitarianism evolved as a counter-balancing reaction to liberal theory, and that civic republicanism and deliberative democracy emerged as attempts to move beyond the communitarian-liberal debate and towards a new form of citizenship (Kymlicka, 2002). Because these three approaches revolve around the need to find democratic alternatives to traditional liberalism, they do have much in common, and to some extent it seems the precise way in which one draws the boundaries between these terms depends on which authors one focuses on and which aspects of their work. For us, some broad definitions will have to suffice, although we will have to remember that because of their vagueness they will be contentious.

First then, communitarianism starts with the perceived weakness of liberalism, and recognizes that in reality individuals are formed within communities, and their lives only have meaning within the resources (physical, ethical, cultural etc.) of those communities. Walzer points out that 'empowerment is more often a familial, class or communal achievement than an individual one', (Walzer, 1997: 100–1) and therefore starting with the individual as one's unit of analysis distorts the system of government and tends to leave to chance the continuing health of the communities which are required for a good life. In short communitarians are concerned that liberalism might just about work as a theory of governance if one can safely assume a degree of order and homogeneity underpinning society, but they point to the mounting evidence that populations in modern societies are increasingly diverse and increasingly focused on personal well-being rather than the well-being of the community as a whole. This is evident in the declining levels of trust in politicians, declining turnout in elections, rising levels of ignorance about politics, declining support for the institutions of the welfare state, and the supposed decline in collective identity, which is threatened by a tendency towards supranational government and identity (e.g. European Union) and sub-national and regional identity (e.g. Scottish nationalism, Cornish nationalism) (Putnam, 2000; Talisse, 2005; Taylor-Gooby, 2009; Walzer, 1997).

Communitarians then are responding to a theoretical weakness in liberalism and a practical series of democratic crises, which means we now need to address the well-being of the community, rather than focus on the rights of the individual. Once one has adopted this stance, one can see community influence over individuals as the recognition of 'authoritative horizons' in our lives, rather than 'arbitrary limits' (Kymlicka, 2002: 222). Communitarians argue that we need to understand individual rights in balance with community interests; indeed they are more likely to understand rights as emerging from the community itself, rather than as standing outside of it as some sort of protection for the individual. Thus they are open to the criticism that communitarianism has no real answer to the problem of the 'tyranny of the majority'. If a community decides that an activity is not conducive to its well-being, then it has the moral authority to seek to stop that activity. Thus communitarianism often includes elements of social conservatism, as proponents fear that we have gone too far down the road of a 'permissive society', which of course sets off alarm bells for many people in those groups who have benefitted from these changes – women, ethnic minorities, lesbian and gay citizens to name some of the most obvious ones. But communitarians do not exclusively pursue this nostalgic route, they also look forward to re-creating a sense of shared identity, and such proposals might include forms of national service to bring people together in the common interest (Kymlicka, 2002: 272) – not unlike, in fact, the Conservative Party's policy for a National Citizen Service.

Civic republicans believe that granting authority to the community to determine what is appropriate for individuals is an unnecessarily restrictive step to take. Rather than risk undermining the power of the individual in his or her relationship with the community, they seek to re-discover an older approach which enables individuals to largely pursue their own ends, but which also asserts political participation in the community as a valuable element in any good life. To this end Bernard Crick's influential work, *In Defence of Politics,* asserts that politics is, like sex, a fundamental and natural activity arising from people's mutual engagement in communities (Crick, 1982). Civic republicans often complement this view by analysing why, if participation is such a self-evident good, there has been a tendency towards increasingly privatized lives. Consumerism is therefore a target as it is essentially seen as acting as a distraction from the genuine pursuit of the good life (Barber, 2003); as Bauman starkly expressed it, 'the consumer is an enemy of the citizen' (Bauman, 2008:190).

Civic republicans therefore abandon the usual neutrality of the state associated with liberalism and adopt a more proactive agenda to promote a range of civic virtues, as constituent factors in the good life. Individuals remain free to pursue their own ends, but they are encouraged to espouse certain shared values, which support the practice of public democratic engagement. Governments might legislate for compulsory participation, for example Australia requires all citizens to vote, but most proponents of civic republicanism tend to favour policies which promote these virtues indirectly rather than mandating them. In doing so they identify a range of suggestions and schools emerge as one obvious place where governments can seek to create the 'seedbeds of democratic virtue' (Kymlicka, 2002: 301–12). Crick was optimistic about this when he wrote that he felt there was a growing recognition by governments that whilst they might want an education system that promotes conformism and 'good' citizens, they also recognise the need to create critical 'active' citizens, who would be less predictable but more genuinely democratic (Crick, 2002a: 115). Barber is more sceptical about the role of formal education and explores other ways for the state to provide education in communities as and when it is required to inform political decisions and deliberations (Barber, 2003: 234).

Finally in this brief summary we turn to deliberative democracy. Habermas is very closely identified with this tradition, which simply asserts the democratic imperative for citizens to talk through issues of public policy with one another (Habermas, 1999; Morrow and Torres, 2002). Deliberative democratic theorists explore the conditions under which such exchanges can be facilitated, the rules which would best regulate them and their potentially transformative impact. Here the commitment to public deliberation requires that participants enter the discussion prepared to listen and learn, rather than merely to talk (Couldry, 2010), and through doing so, minority groups, who would tend to be marginalized in simple aggregative voting, are offered genuine recognition (Phelan, 2001). Clearly there is an agenda here linked to the promotion of civic virtues, associated with civic republicanism, as individuals have to be prepared for the acts of public deliberation through education and by having carefully constructed opportunities made available to them (Barber, 2003; Talisse, 2005). There is a strong tradition in education which promotes the appropriate skills and aptitudes to engage in deliberative debate (Harris, 2002; Jerome and Algarra, 2005), although such skills are valuable in all models of democratic citizenship.

Looking forward

This is essentially the backdrop for the rest of this book. The debates about which form of citizenship are most appropriate continue through the formal political process, and the models of citizenship discussed here inform the decisions politicians make. But whilst these ideas may have an influence on politicians, no one political party has a 'pure' philosophy, which can simply be described as liberal or communitarian etc. Rather, these theoretical models give us a language to describe the developments. They help us compare the alternatives on offer and to foresee what problems might arise when certain positions are promoted, and to think about what further ameliorative policies might be helpful in addressing them.

In brief, the rest of this book aims to do two things. First it explores New Labour's ideas about citizenship, and in doing so it seeks to use some of the ideas in this chapter to describe the model(s) of citizenship being promoted and some of the tensions and difficulties embodied in its approaches. The analysis focuses on education policy and seeks to clarify what kind of citizenship was being promoted – how was it influenced by the broader developments in government, and how can we characterize it in terms of the various models of citizenship available in contemporary theory? The second aim is to explore the ways in which the policy was implemented – what did teachers do and what impact has it had on young people? In dealing with this second dimension I am ultimately interested in exploring the ways in which education can actually be used to promote better forms of citizenship, and thus to test out some of the practical conclusions drawn by democratic theorists. As Kymlicka argues, these suggestions are often rather tentative and weak, and do not appear to offer robust responses to the prevailing powerful social conditions that affect how citizens actually behave. In England, in the years between the launch of Citizenship in schools and the publication of this book, we have had a decade long experiment in citizenship education and the data collected during this experiment sheds some light on the practical business of changing citizenship.

Studying Education Policy

This book is concerned with understanding the nature of citizenship education policy in England and as such I set out, in this section, some of the ideas that underpin my approach to education policy analysis. This discussion is intended to clarify the approach taken in terms of how to define and analyse policy and to identify some specific starting points for the detailed analysis of citizenship policy that follows.

Trowler draws attention to the multifaceted process that influences the creation of education policy (Trowler, 2003). He argues that, in order to fully understand the evolution of a policy, we need to think about a range of factors. First, we need to consider the nature of the evidence available about the issue. Second, we should consider the nature and content of educational research and expertise related to the issue. Third, we should think about the range of stakeholder interests; for example, the implications for parents, pupils, teachers, local government, but also crucially for the minister and civil servants. Fourth, we must be aware of the political considerations; for example, the popularity of the policy or of the government at the time, the relative political positioning of ministers within the broader political context, and the viability of getting a policy successfully adopted in the contemporary context. Finally, and linked to the tactical political considerations above, we should be aware of the deeper ideological commitments of the government, what might be called the more strategic political dimension, or, to use a phrase popularized by Estelle Morris, the 'direction of travel' of government (BBC, 2006a).

Such an approach to policy can be applied to policy conceived as an *object*, what Ball (1994) describes as:

> a specification of principles and actions, related to educational issues, which are followed or which should be followed and which are designed to bring about certain goals.

But it is also important to apply the analysis to policy conceived more broadly as a *process* in which conflict between policy makers and between them and policy implementers is negotiated (Ozga, 2000: 2). On this view, the researcher who sets out to analyse policy must also be alert to the ways in which professionals interpret policy according to their own personal and professional commitments and in their own context. It is also important to remember that whilst there may well be a myriad of relevant actors' intentions which influence policy production and implementation, there is also an element of conflict, compromise and 'muddling through' (Trowler, 2003). Policy analysts should therefore be wary of overly neat and conceptually pure answers, as the reality is likely to be fragmented and often contradictory (Power et al., 2004: 457).

A starting point

Pulling together these starting points one might represent the process in diagrammatic form (Figure 2.1). Codd (1988) identifies this particular diagram as representing a 'technical-empiricist' model of policy analysis which embodies the 'intentional fallacy' (a term borrowed from literary theory) by assuming that policy documents express 'intentions'. However, for the purposes of this investigation I contend that the diagram does include some useful key phases and focal points, which might form the basis of a policy analysis; after all, policy documents are not quite the same as objects of literary criticism, and should not be simply subjected to the same types of analysis. Codd quotes from Barthes, 'a text is not a line of words releasing a single "theological" meaning... but a multidimensional space in which a variety of writings, none of them original, blend and clash', (quoted in Codd, 1988: 239) in order to justify his own approach, which is to focus less on 'intentions' and more on 'the differing effects that documents have in the production of meaning by readers' (Codd, 1988: 239). This focus on drawing attention to the interpretation and meanings ascribed to policies seems an appropriate *additional* perspective to incorporate in policy analysis, but it is difficult to see how this can be justified as an alternative to a consideration of intention, even admitting that this is difficult to be certain about and may often incorporate multiple and contradictory intentions.[1]

In this version of the model the final column notes some of the issues to which the researcher should be particularly attuned, in order to avoid imposing a simplistic narrative on a complex series of phenomena. That said, the diagram

---

[1] This is a discussion I return to towards the end of this chapter, when justifying the 'toolkit' of approaches I have developed.

Figure 2.1 Simple 'technical-empiricist' representation of policy

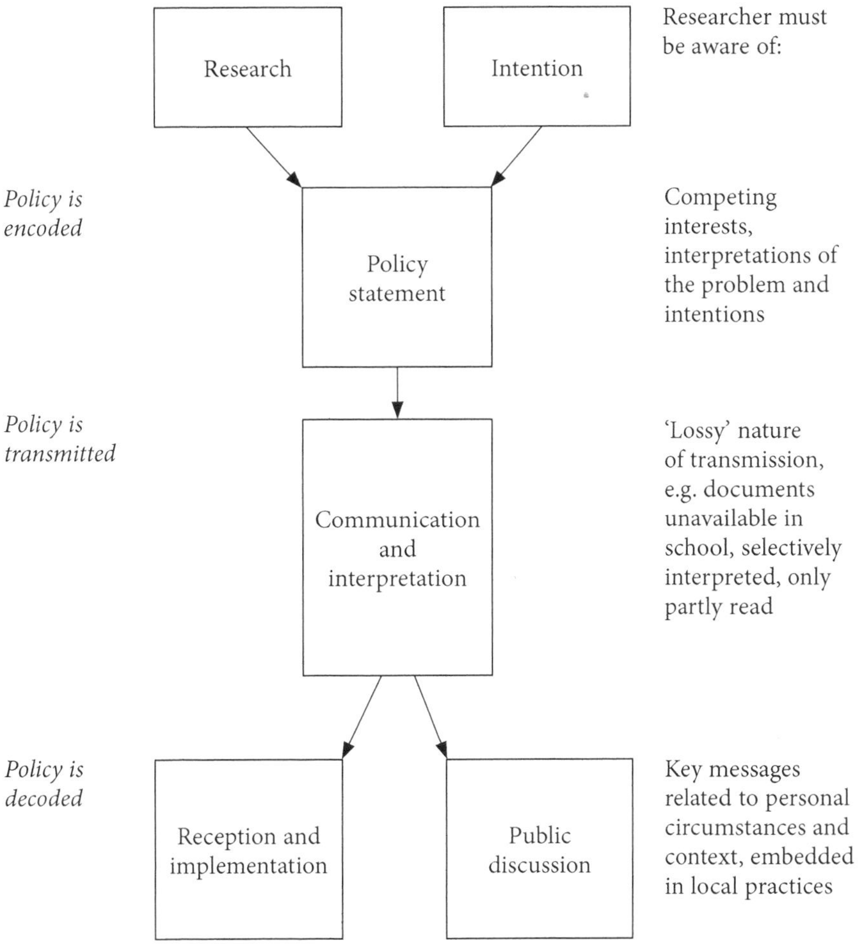

	Research	Intention	Researcher must be aware of:
Policy is encoded		Policy statement	Competing interests, interpretations of the problem and intentions
Policy is transmitted		Communication and interpretation	'Lossy' nature of transmission, e.g. documents unavailable in school, selectively interpreted, only partly read
Policy is decoded	Reception and implementation	Public discussion	Key messages related to personal circumstances and context, embedded in local practices

Adapted from Olssen, Codd et al. 2004: 61, and Trowler 2003

does represent a top-down perspective on policy, and it is important to bear in mind that this represents a rather simplistic approach to the flow of policy initiatives, which are seen as being shaped outside of schools initially and then actively responded to within schools. Despite the direction of the arrows in the diagram therefore, one has also to actively embrace a 'bottom up' perspective on policy, which recognizes that policies are interpreted and re-interpreted at local level (Ball, 1994). This bottom-up perspective also enables the researcher to recognize that schools are themselves complex institutions in which one is unlikely to encounter a single set of values, or responses to a policy (for an example of research relating to diverse interpretations of citizenship in schools see Leighton, 2004). Clearly it is impossible to provide a full account of the meaning and impact of a given policy if one fails to recognize the impact of these different responses.

Moving from the idea to the real

McCowan has developed a model for policy analysis which bears some similarity to this overview, but which focuses on the 'leaps' which are required to move between stages (McCowan, 2008). He argues that these leaps are of particular interest because they represent transitions between ends and means, and between models of the ideal to reality. This model retains the directional flow that was noted in Figure 2.1 in so far as policy analysis starts with the formulation of the policy vision in government and ends with the reality on the ground in schools, but it is an improvement in that it focuses more explicitly on the key transition points as policy moves from one context to another.

McCowan developed this model to analyse the development of a citizenship education programme in Brazil. The first leap concerns the transition between ends and means as the ideal vision of the 'citizen' is translated into ideal curriculum structures and guidance. McCowan argued that democratic citizenship and participation are learned through the exercise of the same processes and noted that in his case study there was a 'separation' rather than 'harmony' because most of the teaching and learning activities were fairly traditional and didactic, as opposed to the interactive pedagogy proposed in the curriculum framework. Focusing on this leap allows one to assess the extent to which the guidance offered to schools achieves coherence and is congruent with the initial aims espoused by the policy initiators.

The second leap represents the transition from ideal to real curriculum, as teachers interpret the general curriculum guidance to develop their classroom practice (or not). In his case study, McCowan argued that this was particularly problematic in Brazil because of teacher disengagement and wider political constraints, which are related to a political climate in which teachers felt they were taking risks if they moved away from deliberate neutrality. This reinforces Ball's argument for recognizing teacher agency (Ball, 1994), and echoes Walkington and Wilkins findings that:

Citizenship education is highly dependent on the particular teachers involved, and the compatibility or dissonance between their worldviews and that of the initiative (quoted in McCowan, 2008: 162; Walkington and Wilkins, 2000).

This leap therefore encourages a focus on teachers' understandings of citizenship education, and their own accounts of what they are trying to achieve in their teaching.

The third leap is concerned with the relationships between the curriculum as it is taught by teachers on the one hand and as it is learned by young people on the other hand. This stage of his analysis is thus concerned with assessing the extent to which the teaching activities actually impact upon the learners. McCowan argued that in Brazil superficial teaching, which focused on knowledge about democratic systems and processes such as voting, led to superficial learning. He described how a tendency to focus on the transmission of knowledge meant learners were more likely to have adopted the discourse of the project, without internalizing the new values with any depth (McCowan, 2008: 166). In interviews, some learners commented on the traditional forms of teaching, which were at odds with the values being promoted (i.e. lecturing about democracy). There was also some evidence that the learners engaged with the programme as active agents and questioned the purposes and forms of education being promoted. Some of the young people felt the official messages in the programme did not fit with their own political perspective and were therefore sceptical. In exploring this leap one must focus on the 'received' messages about citizenship education and I will do this through interviews and discussions with young people to understand their experiences.

McCowan's model seems to be particularly useful therefore for drawing attention to the processes through which policy is implemented and to the active role of curriculum constructors, teachers and learners in interpreting the policy. It is especially useful, in an investigation such as this one, to remember the agency of teachers and students in shaping, interpreting, selecting, and even ignoring aspects of policy according to their abilities, interests, experiences and beliefs.

The role of ideology

By contrast, Ozga focuses on the fifth element of Trowler's list of explanatory factors (above) and argues that we need to be much more explicit in our recognition of the ideological context in which contemporary education policy is being developed. She writes about the need to locate policy analysis in the contemporary context of the 'economizing' of education, through which 'education becomes the acquisition of the appropriate mix of skills, and a technical consensus is built around concepts such as efficiency, quality and accountability... deprived of tension or debate' (Ozga, 2000: 56). This approach is echoed to some extent by Olssen et al. (2004: 1–17) in their assertion that policy analysis should concern itself with the neo-liberal policy framework generally adopted by western states as part of their response to globalization. Like Ozga, they focus rather more than Trowler does on the centrality of this ideological context. It follows from this position that one key task of policy analysis is to 'illuminate how discursive practices and assumptions which operate supranationally come to effect specific national policy developments'. (Olssen et al., 2004: 4). They take some care, however, not to overstate the actual erosion of state control, which accompanies some analyses of globalization. Instead they argue that education becomes an increasingly significant policy arena through which the nation state seeks to protect its economic strength in the global economy. Therefore it is not so much globalization per se, which shapes education policy, but rather the neo-liberal policies adopted by governments to deal with globalization (Olssen et al., 2004: 13).

Given the importance of globalization and the national political responses to this, Olssen et al. extend the framework of analysis in Figure 2.1 by seeking to explore the ways in which specific policies articulate with wider discourses. For them:

> Reading neo-liberal educational policy... requires an understanding of the various elements of the social structure and their intersections in the context of history. Policy documents are discursive embodiments of the balance of these dynamics as they underlie social relations at particular points in time... The meanings of policy texts... do not reside unproblematically in the text itself as something to be 'discovered' or rendered 'visible', but in the relationship between the text and the social structure (Olssen et al., 2004: 2–3).

They base their approach on Foucault's own characterization of critique as a method of enquiry:

> A critique is not a matter of saying that things are not right as they are. It is a matter of pointing out on what kinds of assumptions, what kinds of familiar, unchallenged, unconsidered modes of thought, the practices that we accept rest (Foucault, 1988: 154 cited in Olssen et al: 40).

But they are also critical of Foucault's tendency to focus on the analysis of broad discourse, at the expense of textual analysis. Here they turn to the work of Fairclough (1989: 26 cited in Olssen et al: 68), who argues that:

> In seeing language as discourse and as a social practice, one is committing oneself not just to analysing texts, not just to analysing processes of production and interpretation, but to analysing the relationship between texts, processes, and their social conditions, both the immediate conditions of the situational context and the more remote conditions of institutional and social structures.

This understanding of discourse leads Fairclough (1989) to identify three dimensions to discourse (i) texts, (ii) processes of production and interpretation, and (iii) the social conditions of production and interpretation. There are three corresponding levels of critical discourse analysis (i) formal description of the text, (ii) interpretation of the text and the ways in which others interact with it and vice versa, and (iii) explanation of the relationship between these interactions and the social context. This third level (social practice) represents an additional level of analysis to the process outlined in Figure 2.1. The analysis of the text, therefore, must be embedded in an analysis of wider discursive practices (Ball, 2006/1993), and in turn these must be related to particular economic, political and institutional settings, within which discourse is generated (Fairclough, 1992: 71 cited in Olssen et al: 69).

In his analysis of New Labour's political language, Fairclough argued that the 'Third Way' was an important starting point for understanding New Labour and that it was ongoingly constituted and reconstituted as a discourse in the documents, speeches, interviews, etc. of New Labour politicians (Fairclough, 2000: 9). This led him to focus on extracts from speeches and policy documents to analyse the ways in which the Third Way project was being constructed, which exemplifies the focus on 'text'. Secondly, he treated the Third Way as 'a creation in language, something that is constructed in discourse' (Fairclough, 2000: 9), which exemplifies the analysis of discursive practices. And thirdly, he acknowledged that any analysis of the language of politics and government must also be combined with a broader analysis of government action, which exemplifies the analysis of social practices in relation to the development of discourse (Fairclough, 2000: 11). In the chapters that follow I engage with these three levels: first I explore the Third Way and the development of citizenship discourses across government, second I consider the ways in which these discourses relate to specific examples of citizenship education policy documents, and third I consider aspects of implementation.

Ozga lists a series of questions which she has used in policy research and these complement the structure advocated by Olssen et al. In relation to the analysis of policy texts, I have adapted Ozga's specific questions (Ozga, 2000: 99) to arrive at the following generic questions to stimulate thinking about policy:

- What ideas and categories are presented regarding the policy area? Are they new? What is absent/silent in the account?
- Construction of narrative – what story is being presented here? What kind of story is it, what images are presented and are any of them new?
- What is the logic/discursive construction of the argument in the text?
- How does the text construct its subjects? How are teachers and learners constructed – individually and relationally?
- What does the text imply about the relationship between its subjects, community, society and the state? (p. 99)

Ozga (2000: 95) also argues that the analysis of policy texts should shed light on the following aspects of policy:

- What are the sources of the policy? Whose interests does it serve; what is its relationship to global, national and local imperatives?
- What is the scope of the policy? What is it assumed it is able to do? How does it frame the issues and what are the policy relationships embedded in it?
- What are the patterns of the policy? What does it build on or alter, in terms of relationships? What organizational and institutional changes or developments does it require?

A 'toolkit' for analysing citizenship education policy

Whilst my discussion of citizenship education policy draws on the ideas presented here I do not set out to adopt an explicitly Foucauldian perspective in my analysis (following Olssen et al.), nor a critical theory perspective (following Ozga). Instead I take my lead from Ball who argues for a conceptual toolbox and a rather more eclectic approach to policy analysis (Ball, 2006/ 1993, 2007). In the following chapters I will first follow Fairclough's example by setting the scene for citizenship education by exploring the significance of citizenship for New Labour more generally. Then I consider the texts of two key policy documents to analyse change and continuity in government intentions for citizenship education. Finally I turn to consider the process of policy 'decoding' and 'reception' in more detail. Through these various approaches I aim to incorporate the valuable insights of each of the models described in this chapter into my analysis of citizenship education policy as text and discourse; aspiration and reality; object and process.

I have summarized these elements in the diagram below (Figure 2.2), which is intended to synthesize the discussion above into a toolkit for analysing Citizenship in secondary schools in England. Following McCowan, I aim to interrogate the notion of the 'ideal citizen' as envisaged by the initiators of policy through an analysis of how the idea has been developed by politicians, and how it has been encoded in policy documents. As Pykett and her colleagues

Figure 2.2 Toolkit for analysing citizenship education policy in England

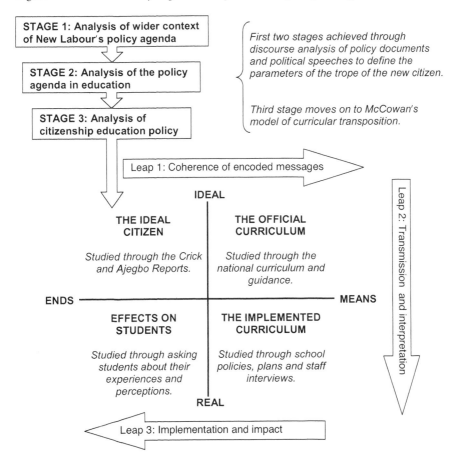

have pointed out, 'a theory of the good citizen cannot… help but be contextual', (Pykett et al., 2010: 535) and the aim of this first phase is to explore both the ways in which the good citizen has been characterized and the connections between these attributes and broader New Labour discourses.

Leap 1 – Encoding the vision in policy documents

The first phase of the research is concerned with identifying the nature of the ideal citizen envisaged in New Labour discourse and encoded in policy. In order to clarify the stance adopted in this phase I want to return to an earlier observation about Codd's work (1988) in order to clarify the role of discourse analysis in this toolkit. Codd imports the notion of 'intentional fallacy' from literary criticism to suggest that it is fallacious to assume one can explore the intention behind a policy, rather one should consider the interpretations reached by the various audiences and actors who negotiate the policy. In this approach the analysis of policy documents may be reduced to little more than textual analysis and this represents a danger in pursuing post-structuralist insights too far. It seems to me that, whilst one may legitimately argue about whether art needs any more justification than its creation *as art* (i.e. does the author's/creator's intention outside of merely creating art matter?), it is naive to transpose this thinking to policy and politics.

   Having said that, one must recognize that policy analysis is enriched by borrowing from these approaches but it cannot settle for analysis at this superficial level only. The first point to make then is that policy certainly does serve a rhetorical purpose in the positioning and public performance of politics, and that aspects of literary analysis are helpful in shedding light on this aspect of policy. Secondly, policy also benefits from discourse analysis because policy itself is constituted by and through available discourses which are themselves constituted more broadly than in the realm of 'formal politics' through a range of social interactions. However, policy must also be understood as more than a particular articulation of positions within such intersecting discourses. The third point then is to recognize that policy also seeks to settle and assert a position, or at least accommodate in some way a range of positions, within a set of discourses with a view to promoting certain solutions and actions. This echoes Crick's (1982) views of politics as an eternal wrangling and the (temporary) settlement of legitimate differences. Policy is simply one way in which these *political solutions* are encoded and bring about *change*. Fundamentally this third point represents a challenge to the analytical perspectives inspired by a

Foucauldian theorization of power and returns to a different conceptualization of power, which incorporates simpler notions of power residing within one's ability to secure action in others (Lukes, 2005).

It is important to recognize the process through which such policy is encoded, transmitted, decoded and implemented (which is open to misinterpretation and active reinterpretation). To recognize this process enables us to fall between the two extremes; on the one hand we avoid the accusation of pursuing a naive linear model of top-down implementation; whilst on the other hand, we reject the equally naive notion that political will and intention have no significance, a view which ultimately renders politics as mere cultural, symbolic activity. Instead this blend of bottom-up and top-down analysis recognizes that in this process of mutual constitution policy does have profound effects on individuals, and individuals have similarly profound effects on policy. However, this process is not one in which the power of policy makers and policy implementers should be mistaken as being equal (Hatcher and Troyna, 1994). In relation to citizenship, Smith has noted that:

> Citizenship laws... are among the most fundamental of political creations... They distribute power, assign status and define political purposes (Smith, 1997).

In relation to education it is important to note that the New Labour government set out to reconstruct the policy process so as to maximize the chances that the government's intentions would be implemented more thoroughly.

Barber, who took responsibility for 'delivery', describes this as 'deliverology':

> Supposing a minister promises, as David Blunkett did, to improve standards of reading and writing among eleven-year-olds. Implicit in this commitment is that, in one way or another, the minister can influence what happens inside the head of an eleven-year-old in, for example, Widnes. The delivery chain makes that connection explicit (Barber quoted in Gunter and Chapman, 2009: 4).

Whilst this does not, indeed it cannot, break out of the basic relationship of mutual constitution of policy and people, it does seek to re-balance the relationship by reducing the room for manoeuvre of other actors. One returns, as one so often does, to Marx's basic observation that individuals make their own history (exercize agency) but not in circumstances of their own choosing (within structural constraints). New Labour's approach to 'deliverology' sought to constrain the extent to which agents could exercize their autonomy in interpreting and implementing policy. It did so partly through influencing the discourses relating to professionalism, in which certain possible actions seemed more or less desirable; and also through the implementation of direct control mechanisms.

Leap 2 – Transmission to and interpretation by teachers

Leap 2 is concerned with the coding and subsequent de-coding and re-coding that takes place between government agencies defining the curriculum and teachers making decisions about what to actually teach. One key issue during this transition is the way the broader vision for citizenship – essentially an idealized form envisaged through a variety of philosophical lenses and conjured into being through politicians' rhetoric – becomes translated into a more prosaic school subject. Whitty et al. (1994) undertook extensive research into the ways in which schools were approaching cross-curricular themes in the 1990s in England, and as this was the most recent attempt to introduce citizenship education into schools in England, their observations are helpful in identifying an agenda for analysing this translation from vision to reality.[2] Applying a conceptual framework based on Bernstein's (1971a) sociological analysis of curricula they suggested that the reasons for the failure of the cross-curricular themes was related to the principles which informed the construction and maintenance of the curriculum.

Most schools' curricula in the early 1990s, (as remained true during the early 2000s) were dominated by highly defined subjects with clearly articulated programmes of study. In Bernstein's terms the subjects were strongly classified and framed. Although schools were free to construct alternative approaches, few did. For pupils the distinction between subjects was further enhanced by different teaching methods, which established a unique set of recognition and realization rules for each subject area. Through the rooms that are used, the equipment needed and the sort of discourse permitted and so on, pupils gain a very clear idea of what subject they are experiencing and the sort of knowledge and skills involved.

The work of Whitty et al. shows that there is much more to being a school subject than simply having a series of learning outcomes. Building on this theoretical framework to analyse the introduction of Citizenship as a subject, Adams and Calvert (2005) argued that Bernstein's ideas help explain why Citizenship can be described as a 'square peg in a round hole'. In one sense, by adopting some of the traditional characteristics of a curriculum subject,

---

[2] The following section summarises arguments explored in greater depth in Chapter 5.

Citizenship sought to mould itself to the requirements of England's collection code curriculum, with a strong vertical organization within schools, which they argued is as much due to a lack of shared discourse between subjects as it is to the assertion of a distinctive identity within subjects. On the other hand, many of the proponents of Citizenship (and some official curriculum guidance) continued to assert its potential to influence how young people see themselves as active agents in society and in the school community, which was represented in Crick's call for cross-curricular partnership with other subjects. Adams and Calvert point out that this amounted to a simultaneous embracing of the strong collection code and a desire for a more integrated approach, with horizontal links between subjects.

These structural tensions meant individual teachers became particularly important because they defined and re-defined citizenship education in relation to their own understanding, their own decisions about what should count as a priority, and their own beliefs and experiences of Citizenship. They have to negotiate routes through established curriculum structures, and as the data will illustrate, there is much scope for individual agency to have a significant impact. Thus, Chapter 6 will focus on teachers' views about their role and their understanding of Citizenship education.

Leap 3 – Implementation and impact on students

In this investigation I explore the perspective of young people through two forms of data. First, I consider some of the large scale surveys undertaken into young people's experiences of and attitudes towards Citizenship. Second, I discuss data drawn directly from research undertaken with young people in two schools. In this research I have chosen to work collaboratively with young people as co-researchers, rather than treating them merely as the objects of a research programme.

The idea that research in schools can benefit from working with students as co-researchers or as researchers in their own right has gained credibility in recent years. This acknowledgement sits comfortably within the broader development of what has been loosely termed student voice – a term which has been used to describe a range of strategies for promoting children's participation in decision-making in schools (Fielding, 2004a, Fielding, 2004b). Indeed, the Ajegbo Review recommended the development of student voice as one of the strategies schools should adopt to embed citizenship education in the life of the school (Ajegbo, 2007: 9). Rudduck has championed the development of student participation in school development (Flutter and Rudduck, 2004, Rudduck et al., 1996) and Hannam conducted research, funded by the DfES under Blunkett (Hannam, 2001), which concluded that pupil participation was at least compatible with (and possibly supportive of) high standards of academic achievement. Mary Kellett has trained primary school pupils as researchers and helped them to identify their own agendas for research in their schools. The publications arising from these collaborations illustrate how young people's involvement allows issues to emerge which adult researchers may miss (Carlini and Barry, undated; Kellett et al., 2004). And during the course of the research reported in this book, the Department for Children, Schools and Families (DCSF) also issued guidance to schools, which promoted a range of strategies for developing pupil participation, including students as researchers (DCSF, 2008).

In relation to investigating the implementation of citizenship education in particular there are several benefits to be derived from recruiting young people as co-researchers. First, there is likely to be significant value in involving young people as active partners in the research process at the earliest possible stage, so that the research benefits from the young people's perspectives and understandings of citizenship education and the research strategies and instruments can be shaped by them. This is likely to be especially useful in relation to citizenship education where much terminology is school specific. For example, some schools might deliver Citizenship through PSHE or vice versa, and others have created their own integrated programmes, such as 'personal development', which provide a vehicle for the Citizenship programme. Such an approach allows the research design to benefit from the kinds of in-depth understanding usually available only to ethnographic researchers who are able to embed themselves in the research context for a significant length of time (Stark and Torrance, 2005). Kellett argues that whilst working with young people as researchers requires some training in research techniques, it does bring the benefit of their 'expertise' in childhood and the school context (Kellett, 2005a; Kellett, 2005b). By recruiting co-researchers from Years 9 and 10 these student researchers are likely to have several years experience of the school to inform their conceptualization of citizenship education.

Second, the active involvement of students in constructing research instruments is likely to ensure that questions are phrased in ways which will be understood by their peers. This is akin in some ways to conducting an ongoing and immediate process of piloting in which questions are phrased and rephrased according to young people's own understanding, which is likely to make the questions more accessible and therefore more valid. This helps to ensure that a questionnaire measures what it is supposed to measure (construct validity) as well as being easily understood and unambiguous (de Leeuw, 2008).

Third, the young people have access to other students in school and can collect data, for example through peer interviews, which would be time consuming for one researcher to collect alone, and which may benefit from a less formal peer-to-peer conversation, rather than a formal interview with an adult researcher unknown to students. The issues associated with establishing good relationships and eliciting relatively honest responses in such formal situations have been discussed at length in the literature (see for example Fontana and Frey, 2005; Lincoln and Guba, 1985: 268–73) and although enlisting students as peer researchers does not solve all the problems associated with influencing respondents, it does seem to solve some of the problems associated with the formality of interviews and the issues of power imbalances (Dunne et al., 2005: 35).

Fourth, the interpretation of data is likely to benefit from the student researchers' knowledge of the context. For example, they will be aware of the significance of teacher reputation and of other relevant issues, which may fall outside of the Citizenship focused data collection strategies adopted. In addition, it seems a potentially useful process for the researcher to check their tentative interpretations with a group of student co-researchers, to gain feedback on the degree to which such interpretations or explanations appear to be valid or plausible from the perspective of the very people with whom the research is concerned. This has the potential to yield some of the benefits of checking for accuracy with respondents, or providing full feedback to all respondents for their comment (Denscombe, 2007: 201), but does not assume all respondents will be uniformly interested in such additional engagement.

Fifth, working with young people to encourage them to think critically about the collection and analysis of data has the potential to empower them as individuals in terms of their own critical citizenship skills, and potentially for further involvement in the life of the school. This is significant in relation to the ethical dimension of the research as the participants gain some educational benefit from their participation (Kellett, 2005a) and the school at least has the potential to tap into a group of informed student researchers.

Finally, such an approach honours the spirit of Article 12 of the UN Convention on the Rights of the Child (UNCRC), which promotes the involvement of young people in decisions that affect them (Alderson, 2008). This has led to some sensitive investigations of the ethical imperative to include children more actively in research and the need to address the power inequalities within research relationships (David et al., 2005, MacNaughton and Smith, 2005). Although this last point relates specifically to children's rights, it does reflect a broader debate in research ethics about the role of respondents in research. Some authors resist conceptualizing people as 'subjects' of research and strive to view them as 'participants' in research (Fontana and Frey, 2003) and this has given rise to approaches to interviews, for example, which 'play' with the boundary between interviewer and interviewee (Dunne et al., 2005: 35). Given that this research project is concerned in part with young people's experiences and interpretations of citizenship education, it seems particularly significant that some young people should be actively involved in formulating and conducting the research to ensure that they are genuine participants.

Next steps

There are perhaps two main issues that emerge from this discussion and which form the basis of the rest of this book. The first is concerned with what the 'vision' was for citizenship in the New Labour government and what function it served (allowing for the fact that this will not yield a single answer but reveal a contested site for various competing political concerns). The second broad issue relates to what happened in schools. The first issue is dealt with in the next two chapters, and the second is dealt with in Chapters 5–10.

3

Imagining the New Citizen

This chapter applies some of the ideas from Chapter 1 to the specific context of the New Labour governments. The central ideas of the Third Way are discussed in order to shed some light on the models of citizenship which underpinned a raft of policy reforms. Having discussed these general ideas in the first part, the chapter ends with a series of examples which illustrate the ways in which they can be used to read education policy. In the next chapter, the framework developed here is used to inform a more detailed discussion of citizenship education policy.

New Labour, New Citizens

Through the theoretical foundations of the Third Way, and through the raft of reforms introduced by New Labour, it is possible to discern the construction of a trope of the *new citizen* – a citizen who is capable of entering into productive relationships with other citizens and the state, and thus who enables the government to construct new solutions to various policy challenges. Significantly, this vision of the *new citizen* is normative rather descriptive, and so represents a political project in itself.

The term trope has been used variously within literary theory, anthropology and history (McClintock, 1995; Townsley, 2001; White, 1973). Writing from an anthropological perspective Rapport and Overing argue that:

> The codification of experience as trope can be understood as a kind of hypothesis which is being brought to bear on an inchoate subject out of a need for more concrete identity and understanding (Rapport and Overing, 2000: 49–50).

The use of the term trope in this chapter is based on this tradition and below I argue that the trope of the *new citizen* serves as an organizing idea which helps to explain many New Labour reforms, and which is constituted through the interplay of three related discourses. One of these discourses concerns the links between the individual and the state and is constructed in terms of the connection between *rights and responsibilities*. A second discourse, which might be seen in some ways as a sub-section of the first, is concerned with the relationship between citizens and other citizens, as well as citizens and the state, and explores the demands of *active citizenship and participation*. A third discourse relates primarily to relationships between citizens, and is concerned with the nature of *community and diversity* and has been increasingly associated with the term community cohesion. These discourses are discussed below and related to the emerging trope of the *new citizen*.

Whilst the balance between these discourses changed over the period of New Labour's period in office, and the focus within each discourse also adapted to context and audience, these broad discourses remained central to the way in which New Labour presented itself and framed many of its policies.

New Labour and the Third Way

During their first two years in government, New Labour famously prioritized economic prudence but this was accompanied by a radical agenda of consti- tutional reform (Driver and Martell, 2006), which included a raft of measures that would profoundly affect the nature of citizenship in the UK, including: devolution to Scotland and Wales (and eventually to Northern Ireland); the establishment of regional development agencies, as a possible precursor to some measure of regional devolution; a strategic authority and elected mayor for London; reform of the House of Lords; the Freedom of Information Act; and the incorporation of the European Convention on Human Rights into domestic law (Hennessy, 2000: 508–9).

Kennedy argues that the reform process was really only symbolically attractive as a means to signal 'modernization'. On this reading Prime Minister Blair distanced himself from the Human Rights Act as soon as it became law, through fear of being linked by the media to the spurious cases the media expected to emerge once the legislation was enacted (Kennedy, 2004: 303). But Blair was less reticent about promoting big ideas such as the Third Way, which enabled him to present the New Labour government as distinctive and fresh, breaking free from old dogmatic traditions and free to forge new solutions to the problems facing the UK. On the simplest reading of the Third Way it represents a non-ideological, practical orientation to government; as Blair said, 'a large measure of pragmatism is essential. As I say continually, what matters is what works to give effect to our values' (Blair quoted in Driver and Martell, 2006: 50). But the Third Way also provided a means for clarifying and presenting the values that would underpin government action.

The Third Way was given a more substantive definition by academics such as Giddens (1998), for whom the Third Way thesis responded to two significant developments. First, during Margaret Thatcher's leadership, the mantle of 'radicalism' in British politics had shifted from Labour to the Conservatives. Secondly, the traditional 'emancipatory' politics, which was concerned with the redistribution of rights and resources, was being replaced by a type of 'life politics', in which identity and quality of life became key issues. This challenged old notions of the Left/Right political divide and made a Third Way essential if the Labour Party was to find a new radical politics. The substance of the Third Way therefore represented an alternative to the 'Old Left' model of classical social democracy, with cradle-to-grave welfare provision, a mixed economy, egalitarianism and a sense of collectivism on the one hand, and the Thatcherite or neoliberal model on the other hand, with its focus on the welfare state as safety net, free market principles, acceptance of inequality and autonomous civil society. For Giddens, the Third Way represented a new response to the social challenges of globalization which moved beyond the New Right free market solutions to establish the legitimacy of a radical (interventionist) centre in a market economy (Driver and Martell, 2006: 47–8). On one reading, this agenda amounts to the recognition that the state is relatively powerless to control the increasingly globalized economy and therefore shifts its focus to changing society (Gamarnikow and Green, 2000: 95), in order to 'secure insertion into a changing global division of labour... through the constitution of the welfare subject' (Morris, 2007: 39). This is significant for the analysis that follows because I argue that Morris' *welfare subject* is re-imagined as a *new citizen*. In this I adopt a similar position to that discussed by Taylor-Gooby in his book 'Reframing Social Citizenship' in which he explores the connections between welfare reform and political conceptions of citizenship (Taylor-Gooby, 2009)[1].

The Third Way embraced a new balance between the state, civil society and welfare. Fairclough (2000) demonstrates how the discourse of the Third Way shifted depending on time, speaker and purpose, but one might identify the

---

[1] Taylor-Gooby's use of the term 'social citizenship' echoes Marshall's earlier analysis of citizenship. Marshall (1964) argued citizenship was constructed through three sets of rights – civil, political and social. The social rights achieved in the post-war welfare state represented a concern with ensuring citizens had access to the means to live in addition to formal equality in relation to the state.

following features as fairly constant: a radical centre of government, positive welfare, a new mixed economy, equality as inclusion and active civil society (Driver and Martell, 2006; Giddens, 1998). Early 'positive welfare' policies included welfare to work schemes as well as targeted tax credits to tackle the twin problems of welfare dependency and poverty. Even in his critical appraisal of the government's record on income inequality, Giddens reiterated this essentially Third Way approach to such issues by declaring the new egalitarianism as being driven by the urgency to 'invest in human and cognitive capacities that promote individual opportunity, rather than... reparation after the event' (Diamond and Giddens, 2005: 105). For Taylor-Gooby, these reforms formed one half of the overall programme, on the one hand government sought to shape the behaviours of welfare claimants, whilst on the other welfare institutions were compelled to adopt managerial models which reflected practices in the private sector. Together, these reforms represented a thorough-going reconceptualization of the welfare state, and of social citizenship (Taylor-Gooby, 2009).

For Mouffe (2005: 56–60), the key problem with the Third Way project is that it rested on a conception of politics which was essentially consensual and post-political. The promotion of a form of politics capable of transcending the old adversarial politics rested on the theoretical eradication of the Left/Right (i.e. class) divide. Mouffe argued that this division was clearly not resolved and contended that the danger of the Third Way lay in its theoretical blindness to the systemic antagonisms which continue to have profound impacts on national economies, social groups and individual life chances.

> By redefining the structural inequalities systematically produced by the market in terms of 'exclusion', one can dispense with the structural analysis of their causes, thereby avoiding the fundamental question of which changes in power relations are needed to tackle them (Mouffe, 2005: 62).

What was left then was simply a 'social democratic variant of neo-liberalism' (Hall, 2003) in which the state sought primarily to empower individuals to take responsibility for their own lives within free-market conditions, albeit one in which the worst excesses of the market should be curbed by symbiotic state interactions with civil society and business partnerships (Kivisto and Faist, 2007: 96–101).

Despite these criticisms, the supporters of the Third Way felt it offered a route to new solutions, as is illustrated by John Gray (1997), who had shifted from being a supporter of neoliberalism, to an increasingly barbed critic (Klein, 1999), and who argued that the new substantive philosophy which would supersede the old Left/Right politics would not be a mere meeting in the middle of these two traditions:

> Our position is not a compromise between two discredited ideologies. It is a stand on a new common ground...

Significantly though, policy solutions *were* often presented as occupying the middle ground, and the Third Way thus fulfilled an important presentational or rhetorical function, not least related to its power to apparently reconcile two separate Left/Right ideas. In an example of this Third Way rhetoric Tony Blair (quoted in Newman, 2001: 45) espoused:

> 'Patriotism *and* internationalism; rights *and* responsibilities; the promotion of enterprise *and* the attack on poverty and discrimination'.

This deliberate pairing of concepts to minimize the tensions and stress the prospects of reconciliation was dismissed by Lionel Jospin, then Prime Minister of France, as the 'politics of in-betweenism' (quoted in Newman, 2001: 46).

This rhetorical use of the Third Way was exemplified by the use of the formula of presenting two discredited extreme policy proposals, against which a Third Way policy was favourably contrasted. This served to make the Third Way option appear reasonable and less stridently ideological. The following example is drawn from a 1998 policy document on welfare reform (Newman, 2001: 44–5):

Option 1: Privatization of the welfare state safety net (New Right)
Option 2: Status quo with rising costs (Old Left)
Option 3: Opportunity instead of dependence, new partnerships (New Labour)

In this example one can also see some of the terms often used in New Labour policy rhetoric – opportunity (instead of equality) and partnerships (instead of state provision).

Rights and responsibilities

New Labour approaches to rights and responsibilities drew on Third Way principles relating to an implied contract between the individual and the state, but they also connected to an important ethical tradition of Christian Socialism as well as elements of civic republicanism and communitarianism.

The Christian Socialist tradition combined a commitment to equality (or at least equal worth) with a belief in individual responsibility, and as Deacon (2000) pointed out it was no coincidence that Tony Blair, Frank Field (as Minister for Welfare Reform 1997–8) and Jack Straw (as Home Secretary 1997–2001), all committed Christians, were in the forefront of the debate to establish a new moral basis for the welfare state. Deacon argues that this does not explain the reform agenda entirely, rather that it helps to set the scene for the transference of ideas that had been developed by the US Democrats, and which Deacon referred to as 'Anglicanised communitarianism' (Deacon, 2000: 11).

This had been a recurrent theme throughout Blair's leadership (Deacon, 2000: 11), for example in a 1995 speech, entitled, 'The rights we enjoy reflect the duties we owe', he spoke of the need to eliminate the 'social evil of welfare dependency amongst able bodied people'. A year later in a speech in South Africa he declared:

> 'At the heart of everything New Labour stands for is the theme of rights and responsibilities. For every right we enjoy, we owe responsibilities... You can take but you give too. That basic value informs New Labour policy' (Deacon, 2000: 11).

We can see how this played out in housing through tenancy agreements specifying good behaviour as a condition of being housed (see Illustration 3.1), and in the welfare to work reforms:

> 'Our welfare system must provide help for those who need it but the deal that we are trying to create in Britain today is something for something. If we provide job opportunities we expect people to take them' (Blair quoted in Fairclough, 2000: 39).

In this rhetoric of a new contract between the state and citizens (a 'New Deal'), and of a renewed social order, based on shared commitments and accepted duties, Deacon argues we can see clear echoes of Etzioni's communitarianism (Etzioni, 1993). The communitarian tradition has been criticised for inevitably leading to majoritarian and coercive moral communities (Dunn and Burton, 2011) and Morris argues that in the transition from philosophy to practice, notions of voluntarism and mutuality were replaced by contract (and one established by the state at that) as the main route to establish cohesive communities (Morris, 2007: 40).

Illustration 3.1 shows how the narrow rights and responsibilities of tenants were established alongside the broader expectation that tenants would participate in the management of provision through a compact, association, panels, liaison groups and a management organization. In this small example one can see the application of discourses about the citizen's responsible use of welfare resources and their broader responsibilities in relation to the management of such resources. Such an area of policy illustrates how the discourse relating to rights and responsibilities can be applied to clarify the 'contract' between the individual (envisaged both as a service user and as a citizen) and the state, in this case mediated through local government provision.

Illustration 3.1 Rights and responsibilities in the public housing sector

Being a good neighbour

- Control the volume of sound from radios, stereos and TVs, at all times of the day. Do not put these systems against shared walls. Place them on a rubber mat or carpet.
- Make sure you do housework or DIY at reasonable times of the day.
- Keep noise, in or near your home, right down from 9 pm to 8 am.
- If you have a dog, do not leave it barking constantly in the home, on a balcony, or out in the garden, and clear up any mess it makes.
- Warn neighbours when you are going to do something particularly noisy: drilling, hammering or having a party.
- Make sure your children think about how their playing habits might affect neighbours.
- Be quiet when you return home late at night. Don't slam car doors, hoot car horns, or shout to your friends.

Can I be made to leave my home?
Yes, but only if your tenancy has come to an end or if you do not keep to the terms of your tenancy agreement by, for example, not paying your rent or causing nuisance to neighbours.

Tenant participation
This is where tenants are brought in to join managers from Hackney Homes to discuss proposals for change and improvement to the housing service provided to tenants. We are actively working to build more ways for tenants in all areas of Hackney to have their opinions represented on a permanent basis… The Tenant Participation Team provides support, advice and training to resident groups. Each Neighbourhood has its own Tenant Participation Officer.

What is the Tenant Compact?
The Council and representatives from Tenant and Resident Associations have made a formal agreement about how tenants will be involved at the heart of decision-making about the housing services.

How tenants get involved

- Tenants' and Residents' Associations (TRAs).
- Neighbourhood Panels.
- Resident Liaison Group.
- Tenant Management Organizations (TMOs).

Source: www.hackneyhomes.org.uk/hhs-tenants-handbook.htm

For David Blunkett (who was responsible for introducing citizenship education into the national curriculum as Secretary of State for Education, 1997–2001), the same theme was central to his personal political beliefs, but he set it in the context of a civic republican philosophy in which:

> 'Citizens owe duties to one another as members of a world held in common, and *must* play a responsible part in public life… In performing these roles, citizens display civic virtue – actions and dispositions that express their loyalty to the community and their willingness to share in the responsibilities that flow from membership' (Blunkett, 2001: 18–19).

On this view, the commitment to shared responsibilities and mutual obligations was even wider than that envisaged by Blair in the quotations above, as Blunkett's position also emphasized the duty to participate responsibly in the public realm, not merely the requirement to take individual responsibility.

Active citizenship

One of the ways in which these broader concerns influenced policy can be seen in the promotion of active citizenship (Clarke, 2005) and there were numerous programmes designed to explore and promote effective active citizenship in communities throughout the New Labour period of government. Some of these projects were produced through the Home Office (especially the Civil Renewal Unit) and then the Office of the Deputy Prime Minister, for example:

- *Together We Can*[2], a web-based resource for active citizens who wanted to affect change in their local communities.
- *Take Part* (www.takepart.org), an adult education resource to encourage active citizenship education.
- *Active Learning for Active Citizenship* (Mayo and Annette, 2010; Woodward, 2004), a project which included a report on how the government could better coordinate the learning that occurs through informal and voluntary participation, and a range of initiatives in the Department of Communities and Local Government to promote active citizenship and participation in local government and regeneration.

The following illustration (3.2) demonstrates the breadth of government activity relating to the provision of opportunities for active involvement in the public realm and the related provision of education and training to enable people to take up those opportunities. It demonstrates how pervasive the idea had become, that government needed citizens who were capable of assuming responsibility within their communities and acting to bring about positive change, and also that the government should organize educational programmes to create this capacity.

These projects illustrate the range of approaches developed to create the empowered and sufficiently competent active citizens required to bear the burden placed on them by New Labour's policy prescriptions. Linking to the example of housing in Illustration 3.1, McCormack has analysed how policy went beyond merely creating opportunities for tenants to participate in the management of their housing, but actually sought to educate them so that they could assume the responsibilities created, and take on active roles in making decisions about new forms of ownership and management (McCormack, 2011). This illustrates Pykett's thesis that the government assumed the role of the 'pedagogic state' to try to mould citizens (Pykett, 2010). Whilst some degree of welfare reform can be achieved by providing financial incentives and penalties, there is also a wider need to educate people, especially to encourage them to assume personal responsibility, at least in partnership with the state.

---

[2] This website has since been closed down

Illustration 3.2 Government initiatives to promote active citizenship

Department	Active citizenship	Strengthened communities	Partnership in meeting public needs
Home Office	Active citizens active learning regional hubs Civic pioneers Year of the volunteer Citizenship day	Adventure Capital fund Community Cohesion Pathfinders Connection Communities scheme	Change Up Future builders
Office of the Deputy Prime Minister		National Community Forum Neighbourhood Renewal Fund Single Community programme (Community Chest, Community Learning Chest, Community Empowerment Fund) New Deal for Communities programme Safer and Stronger Communities Fund	Beacon Council Scheme Neighbourhood Management Pathfinders Local Development Framework (statement of community involvement) Local Area Agreements Local Strategic Partnerships

Department	Active citizenship	Strengthened communities	Partnership in meeting public needs
Department for Education and Skills	Citizenship curriculum Millennium Volunteers Young Volunteers Challenge Active Citizens in School (pilot programme) Higher Education Active Community Fund Go Givers Foundation and Trust schools	Community Champions Pathfinder Young Community Champions Local Network Fund Community Cohesion	On Track programme Y Speak Consultation Fund

(Adapted from Jochum et al., 2005)

Duties and expectations of citizens

There was some tension between a commitment to promoting a culture of human rights as a universal values framework and a narrower definition of rights as privileges (McGhee, 2008). New Labour's preoccupation with moral and contractual discourses around rights and responsibilities (Fairclough, 2000) led to a situation in which 'rights' represent a privilege which has to be earned and as such [they] offer governments a valuable tool in the management of population and society' (Morris, 2007: 54). This was declared in the starkest terms by Gordon Brown in an article on 'earned citizenship' on the Downing Street website:

> 'For people coming to Britain, and wanting to become British, citizenship should depend upon actively entering into a contract through which, by virtue of responsibilities accepted, the right of citizenship is earned' (Brown, 2008).

This particular example comes from the third New Labour term in office and demonstrates a position within the rights/responsibilities discourse that has been present for the whole New Labour project. The demand that citizenship be earned as a valuable status in itself, as proof of one's membership of the community, sits comfortably within the tradition of communitarianism.[3] This logic was extended with the introduction of the concept of 'probationary citizenship' for some immigrants in the Borders, Citizenship and Immigration Bill (Home Office, 2009; Lord Goldsmith, 2008).

McGhee (2008) has argued that there was a tension throughout the New Labour period between the position that a commitment to human rights could provide a foundation for inclusive citizenship, and a narrower position on rights being seen as earned, and therefore not simply universally applicable. He argued that the latter position emerged more strongly as a result of increased security concerns and that the focus on security, anti-terror and anti-extremism marginalized people who appear to opt out of 'mainstream' British society or values (especially Muslims) and that this in turn led to a reigning in of 'rights' so they are defined within parameters derived from security concerns rather than in their own terms, or in relation to international rights documents.

The contractual discourse (Fairclough, 2000) was also extended more widely than defining the rights and responsibilities of immigrants seeking citizenship. While rejecting any accusations of continuity between Conservative and New Labour policy in this area, David Blunkett (2001: 88) illustrated how this enhanced sense of personal responsibility impacted on discussions of the welfare state:

> 'Active welfare means two things. It challenges failed welfare policies by insisting that the individual should be actively involved in shaping his or her own solutions. This is partly a question of moral principle but also one of beliefs in human potential. Second, it requires government and communities increasingly to mobilise resources beyond the state to help individuals to take managed risks to improve their life chances. This implies a new interface between individuals and the benefits or labour support system'.

Here then one can see the implications of the discourses relating to rights/responsibilities and of active citizenship. Citizens were required to be much more active, both in terms of making demands for high quality services, but also in negotiating solutions for themselves.

---

[3] What remained difficult for New Labour to explain, given the thrust of these discourses (which hold out the promise of recognition, membership, identity and fulfilment) was why some immigrants chose not to apply for citizenship status. This was recognised by Lord Goldsmith (2008) in his review of citizenship, which encouraged the government to reduce the application fee, so that it would be cheaper to apply for citizenship soon after arrival in the country.

Andrews identifies another unacknowledged and unresolved tension here between the individualistic consumer-citizen, making demands of public services for him or herself and their family, and the public-minded citizen, who shares an interest in promoting good services for all (in the communitarian tradition) (Andrews, 2004: 7–9). Jordan argues a similar point, insisting that the focus on 'choice' as a means by which to improve standards creates unintended effects which deny equal access (as patterns in access to public services tend to reproduce the existing patterns of social inequality) and create new social divisions (Jordan, 2005). Taylor-Gooby examines opinion poll evidence which suggests that over the long term, the individualistic focus of consumer-driven models of welfare is eroding the foundational values of reciprocity and inclusion which are required to maintain the legitimacy of the whole welfare system (Taylor-Gooby, 2009). Later models of public service reform (PMSU, 2006) attempted to balance this 'choice' with mechanisms for increasing 'voice', i.e. greater direct participation in local services and consultation, coupled with greater responsiveness on the part of the services, although it was unclear how these more fundamental tensions could be resolved as individuals use both choice and voice to engage with public services (Coffield et al., 2007). Butler and Robson's study of the gentrification of parts of the East End of London illustrates the problem; they showed that whilst some families attempted to invest time and effort in their local school, others simply 'played the game' to negotiate access to desirable schools, without necessarily producing any wider benefits in local provision (Butler and Robson, 2003).

Community and Diversity

As we have already seen, notions of the 'community' feature heavily, both in the politician's rhetorical landscape and in the commentator's analytical toolkit. Perhaps the most significant element of the discourse around community relates to the debates that emerged concerning race relations, multiculturalism and identity – what came to be referred to as community cohesion. Although more obviously a concern during the second term of New Labour, in the aftermath of the Oldham, Burnley and Bradford riots and in the post 9/11 era, there were some significant developments in the first term of government (Toynbee and Walker, 2005). In 1998 the Home Office established a Race Relations Forum to advise the Home Secretary (Home Office, 1998) and also introduced the Crime and Disorder Act, which established the concept of 'racially aggravated crimes'

(McGhee, 2005: 95). The enquiry into the police investigation of the murder of Stephen Lawrence also made a significant impact on how racism was discussed and on subsequent legislation. The formal response included a welter of conferences and training to tackle institutional racism (McGhee, 2005: 16–18), and the new public duty 'to promote equality of opportunity and good relations between persons of different racial groups' outlined in the Race Relations (Amendment) Act, 2000.

McGhee has analysed policy regarding racism, homophobia, Islamophobia and other examples of hate crimes and argues that New Labour's position could be characterized as an 'intolerance of intolerance' within a diverse society (McGhee, 2005: 11). But as with the other examples of 'New Deals' discussed above, McGhee also argues that there is a two-sided expectation at work here within a project of *cosmopolitanization*. On the one hand the rights and interests of minorities were being protected more vigorously, through what might be described as 'protective inclusionism' (McGhee, 2005: 3). On the other hand, there was an expectation that communities thus protected would have less recourse to the defensive mechanisms of withdrawal into their own communities:

> It is not the effect of prejudice, discrimination and intolerance that is the target of cosmopolitan citizenship alone, rather it is the recourse to defensive monolithic cultures, traditions, identities and community formations that are the targets of this model of citizenship, which is dedicated to the promotion of dialogue between groups and across boundaries (McGhee, 2005: 164).

The problem as McGhee perceived it was that this process had been too firmly focused on the minority groups themselves, and not sufficiently balanced by action to address prejudice in the majority community.

Whilst some commentators accepted that the government's policies in relation to minority rights and anti-discrimination laws were largely positive, this was often contrasted with the approach towards refugees, asylum seekers and immigrants more generally. Lister, for example, wrote towards the end of the first term that,

> 'exclusionary policies on asylum… serve to undermine a generally more progressive stance on 'race', as exemplified by the Stephen Lawrence inquiry and the strengthening of race relations legislation' (Lister, 2001: 429).

Whilst asylum policies such as dispersal, detention centres and the withdrawal of benefits were criticized, both outside and within government (Burnett and Whyte, 2004, Spencer, 2007), policy seemed to evolve so quickly and to attempt to strike so many different chords that it is also possible to discern positive advances, for example in the official recognition that immigration brought benefits to society and the economy (Spencer, 2007). The fundamental tension here was exemplified by Giddens (2002), who described the policy as one which sought to be 'tough on immigration, but tough on the causes of hostility to immigrants' (quoted in Gilroy, 2004: 112). The problem for Gilroy was simply that the hostility toward immigrants often seemed to be coming from ministers and MPs.

This tension (if not downright contradiction) can be partly explained within McGhee's analysis of cosmopolitanization, which required that the numbers of immigrants be more firmly managed in order to make room for a more reasonable debate and the nurturing of better community relations:

> The heat of... emotions associated with immigration and asylum are being systematically cooled to allow the nation, in all its current diversity, to become more comfortable with its irrevocable diversity, through the tougher management of inward migration. This process is thus a... strategy dedicated to avoiding further disorder (dis-ease) in the social body through attempting to pacify 'Middle England' at the same time as attempting to draw established minority groups into the wider political community (McGhee, 2005: 181).

The problem with this strategy has been exacerbated by the practical difficulties successive Home Secretaries had in managing and reforming the asylum and immigration system (Toynbee and Walker, 2005), and the inherent problems with attempting to conduct a debate about immigration in terms of numbers, which Spencer argues is almost certainly bound to fail (Spencer, 2007).

Whilst the debate continues about the overall intention and impact of the government's asylum and immigration policies, it is clear that these issues have provided a significant arena for the development of New Labour's ideas about citizenship. Through the debates about multiculturalism, diversity and social segregation it is possible to discern a broad discourse around the notion of community cohesion.[4] This was fundamentally concerned with how people in Britain should perceive themselves as a political community and how they should maintain the boundaries between their newly defined selves and the 'others' who inevitably emerged from this process. As Blunkett (2001: 126–7) summed it up, 'acceptance by residence, as well as nationality of citizenship, therefore must entail recognition and adherence to fundamental rights and

---

[4] The promotion of community cohesion eventually became a specific duty for schools, but here one can see the broader context in which the idea developed.

duties'. In other words, if immigrants wanted to stay in the UK, let alone become citizens, they would have to accept the logic of that other New Labour discourse, which described the links between rights and responsibilities. Similarly, the other key discourse discussed above, active citizenship, also had a role to play in this discussion:

> 'The UK has had a relatively weak sense of what political citizenship should entail. Our values of individual freedom, the protection of liberty and respect for difference, have not been accompanied by a strong, shared understanding of the civic realm. This has to change' (Blunkett quoted in McGhee, 2005: 165).

In this context it seems unsurprising that, having produced his report on citizenship education (Advisory Group on Citizenship, 1998), Bernard Crick moved with David Blunkett to the Home Office to apply his analysis of citizenship to immigration through his chairmanship of the Advisory Board on Naturalization and Integration. Here the commitment to active citizenship and full participation in the public realm became part of the new core of citizenship – a new identity. This clarified the meaning behind Blair's earlier call for 'a new spirit in the nation based on working together, unity, solidarity, partnership. One Britain. That is the patriotism of the future' (1995, quoted in McGhee, 2005: 163).

But this third discourse around community cohesion did not simply represent a blend of the rights/responsibility and active citizenship discourses. It also incorporated a more substantial search for mechanisms through which a positive sense of belonging could be promoted. One function of talking about community cohesion is that language can become de-racialized, or at least rendered non group-specific, so that general assertions about communities, identity and belonging replace specific analyses or prescriptions in some policy documents (Worley, 2005). Worley illustrates her argument by reference to Asian communities, and especially Muslims, who, after the 2001 mill town disturbances, became the focus of 'community cohesion' programmes. She notes the slippage here between 'cohesion' and 'integration' in some policy documents, with overtones of assimilation, so that:

> British Muslim communities… are expected to show 'which side they are on', through an allegiance to a 'phoney' (Kundnani, 2005) construction of Britishness (Worley, 2005).

In a speech about just this aspect of New Labour discourse, entitled 'Towards a Civil Society', Blunkett (2003: 15) indicated that this was not just a slippage of vocabulary between policy makers but rather a deliberate running together of a variety of concepts:

'This increased diversity requires a new focus on civic integration… This is not an argument for assimilation. It is an argument for integration with diversity: neither a monoculture, nor segregation and endless difference'.

Note here the classic Third Way construction of alternatives – 'integration with diversity' both reconciled positions hitherto seen as incompatible and was offered as a more palatable alternative to 'monoculturalism' or 'segregation'.

As for the 'phoney' construction of Britishness, Blunkett also spent some time outlining what Britishness might entail. It should be defined through:

'Our shared values, our history of tolerance, of openness and internationalism, our commitment to democracy and liberty, to civic duty and the public space. These values, embodied in our great institutions – such as the NHS, the BBC, the Open University – tell a national story that is open to all British citizens. This vision of Britishness both embraces the diversity of our multi-national, diverse state, *and* unites us through our values, history, culture and institutions. It provides a shared framework for national and local identities' (Blunkett, 2005: 4).

Whilst Blunkett aimed to create an inclusive vision of national identity he ended up falling back on a rather predictable list of personal elements of Englishness, which could be celebrated on St George's Day, including a love of landscapes, poetry, traditional music, democracy, radicalism and English humour (Blunkett, 2005: 8–9). Whilst these may well form part of English history, they seem rather nostalgic and focused on a particular interpretation of culture, which is nearer to Gilroy's discussion of post-imperial melancholia (Gilroy, 2004) than to a vision of patriotism that might unite the diverse nation.

As one can see from the above discussion, the discourse around community and diversity included several themes. They were united by the search for a core identity, which was supposed to provide the social glue to bind active citizens to one another and to the state. This search for community cohesion entailed a desire for a process of social change, through which all citizens and their traditional communities could evolve to embrace a new unified sense of citizenship. It therefore focused in part on the processes through which such cohesion might be built and also frequently strayed into the difficult territory of defining the substance of this new sense of identity. In part at least, this latter element represented an attempt to end the far right's monopoly over discussions of nationality and patriotism and to form a new civic nationalism (Jerome and

Clemitshaw, 2012), but the desire to create an alternative political definition of patriotism did not eradicate the tendency towards nostalgic and even melancholic accounts of identity, more often associated with more conservative or even reactionary traditions.

A flexible and fluid approach

Through the range of examples considered above one can discern the *new citizen* at the heart of New Labour's political project. Within the broader context of re-imagining Britain and the role of the state, politicians were constantly imagining and re-imagining the ideal citizen who would take his or her productive role within the New Labour policy landscape, and make welfare reform work. This new citizen positively identified as a British citizen and accepted greater responsibility for their own welfare and the welfare of others in their community and beyond (Andrews, 2004). The new citizen was both assumed, as the rational user of welfare services, and also created, through the detailed prescription of policy reforms. However, the trope of the new citizen can only describe the broad parameters of this imaginative process; it cannot provide a definitive account of the model citizen. It is, though, useful as an analytical construct for two reasons.

First, focusing on the trope enables one to identify areas that might be most fruitful in further exploration of New Labour's policies, for example the tension between rights and responsibilities and between this discourse and others, such as the security agenda, which is incorporated within what I have referred to as the community and diversity discourse. McGhee's (2008) exploration of these tensions has highlighted the ways in which rights are re-interpreted, with a subtle shift from the possibility of a rights-based culture of given entitlements, towards one which views rights more as earned privileges, the boundaries of which are expediently established by the current needs of the community (of which security is deemed to be paramount). Whilst rights are always negotiated to some extent, and few can be absolute, this change of emphasis and increasing 'conditionality' (Deacon, 1994) demonstrates the tensions inherent in the communitarian roots of much of New Labour's thinking, where universal rights are difficult to combine with the primacy of the community (Talisse, 2005). So the trope provides a useful guide for exploring the main points of contention within the New Labour project.

Second, the trope is useful as a starting point when one is attempting to read any particular policy, or period of reforms. The particular type of citizen imagined within policy helps us to locate that instance of policy formulation within the broader imaginative project of New Labour. The rest of this chapter considers the trope of the new citizen in relation to education policy, and then in the following chapter it is the starting point for a discussion of the (changing) formulation of citizenship education policy over New Labour's period in office.

Education as a context for citizenship policy

As has been noted above, the ideal citizen becomes implicated in public service reforms, both as an agent of change and as the object of changes. Partly because of the symbolic significance of education in the 1997 manifesto this particular service emerged as a key area to symbolise the drive to 'modernisation' (Ball, 2007).

Example 1: Educating the New Citizens

Given the economic arguments employed to underpin welfare reform it should be no surprise that, when one turns to New Labour's overarching vision of the purpose of education, one can also see a significant response to the demands of the global economy as education is seen as a core element of economic policy (Stedward, 2000). Blunkett expressed this succinctly in a speech to the Institute for Economic Affairs in 2001 when he said, 'the work of the DfEE fits with a new economic imperative of supply-side investment for national prosperity' (Jones, 2003: 144).The responses from the Department for Education to this 'economic imperative' ranged from extending provision in the early years, to increasing access to higher education. Most education policies can be seen as fitting within a narrative of a 'new age – the age of information and of global competition… in which the key to success will be the continuous education and development of the human mind and imagination' (extract from the 1998 Green Paper 'The Learning Age' in Edwards et al., 2004: 131). In the subsequent White Paper, we can see how this basic economic imperative connected with New Labour's broader policy discourses around citizenship:

> 'Lifelong learning can enable people to play a full part in developing their talent, the potential of their family, and the capacity of the community in which they live and work…It also contributes to sustaining a civilized and cohesive society, in which people develop as active citizens and in which generational

disadvantage can be overcome' (Blunkett in the foreword of the White Paper 'Learning to Succeed' DfEE, 1999: 3)

Here we can clearly see the construction of the new citizen, taking responsibility for improving his or her own life chances through education, and, through their action, improving their community.

Example 2: Citizens exercising choice and voice to improve schools

Levin has described the ubiquity of market-led reforms of public services as a 'policy epidemic' (quoted in Ball, 2008: 39), which Ball argues is driven in part by international organizations such as the Organization for Economic Cooperation and Development (OECD), the World Bank, the International Monetary Fund (IMF) and the World Trade Organization (WTO), through their emphasis on open markets in goods and services (Ball, 1999, 2008). In relation to the education system, Ball's analysis identifies three 'policy technologies' – the market, managerialism and performativity (Ball, 2008). As Jones notes, such policies represented a direct link to the Conservative reforms from 1987 onwards (Jones, 2003: 143–6) and it is in this period that the basic architecture of the system was established with the introduction of an element of parent choice, local management of school budgets, and increasing school autonomy from local authority control.

Within this framework, the central market-style element was choice, and therefore diversity of provision was pursued as a matter of principle. Within schools, this manifested itself in the promotion of selection, streaming and setting (Jones, 2003: 158), whilst between schools it was reflected in the proliferation of different types of school, including the promotion of faith schools (Gardner et al., 2005), academies (Beckett, 2007), and specialist schools (Ball, 2008). By 2007, 90 per cent of eligible state funded schools had become a specialist school, academy or City Technology College (SSAT, 2007).

By providing parents with sufficient information to make informed decisions about the school they want their children to attend, and by forcing headteachers to respond to this demand (by attaching funding to pupil numbers), a quasi-market was maintained. This market based model was envisaged as providing a virtuous cycle for ensuring all public services are locked into a cycle of continuous improvement (PMSU, 2006). On this analysis, as Ball points out, education policy is 'almost entirely subsumed within an overall strategy of public service reform' (Ball, 2008: 101).

The role of responsible parents in this cycle of improvement was noted in DCSF evidence to a Parliamentary committee in 2008:

'We want them [national tests] to enable parents to make reliable and informative judgments about the quality of schools and colleges' (David Bell's evidence to the Children Schools and Families Committee (House of Commons), 2008a: 14).

When asked about this by members of the committee, Jim Knight, the Minister of State for Schools and Learning, said:

'We explicitly want to move to a position in which parents choose schools, rather than schools choose parents' (Children Schools and Families Committee (House of Commons), 2008b: Q336).

And when pressed about the extent to which the system privileged some parents over others, he argued that all parents should consult league tables, read Office for Standards in Education, Children's Services and Skills (OfSTED) reports, speak to their neighbours about local schools and arrange to visit prospective schools.

'However articulate parents are, and however much technology they have at home, those are the sorts of things that we expect them to do when choosing schools for their children' (Children Schools and Families Committee (House of Commons), 2008b: Q338).

Thus the responsible parent should not only make the right decisions for their own child, but by doing so would also play a crucial role in driving education reform and improvement.

Example 3: Educating citizens for their responsibilities

This universal expectation of parents was broader than merely exercising sufficiently informed choice in identifying an appropriate school; it also extended into a more general appeal to parents to support their children's education. David Blunkett included the following appeal in his Conference Speech in 2000:

'I appeal to parents to take their responsibilities seriously and think what is best for their child – what will help them best begin the process of learning and play, and how important it is for them to arrive at primary school with the confidence and social skills needed to make a good start. Education is a partnership in which parents have a critical role. We want them to engage much more in the education of their children than in the past' (Blunkett, 2000).

Where individuals failed to take their responsibilities seriously the government sought to take action to enforce the implied 'contract' between parents and state. For example, in the 2006 Education and Inspections Act the government extended parents' responsibilities to ensure their children attend school and behave appropriately. This built on previous legislation which had already led to over 5,000 parents a year being taken to court for their children's behaviour, including truancy (Ball, 2008: 176).

Some local initiatives, such as the Education Action Zones, placed new relationships between schools, parents and local businesses at the heart of reforms. The following strategic aim from Newham's bid for EAZ status reflects how seriously these parenting deficits were taken:

> To turn parents and local communities into good consumers of education services, with positive attitudes towards schools and education, and to engage them actively in children's and community learning (Gamarnikow and Green, 1999: 3).

The key word here seems to be 'turn', thus education policy was seen as having parents as one of the targets, rather than children or teachers. In his memoirs, Tony Blair reflected on some of the families who failed to live up these basic expectations and argued that the minority of families which seem incapable of assuming such responsibilities require 'gripping and seizing'. He continued:

> 'To do that effectively their 'rights' need to be put into suspense, including the right to be a parent' (Blair, 2010: 645).

This demonstrates how far he had gone down the path of seeing rights as conditional on an appropriate fulfilment of responsibilities.

Of course, Blair put his case more strongly in his memoirs, partly because he was reflecting on an area of policy that he no longer controlled, and which had not been entirely successful. Whilst in government though, Ministers did pursue several strategies to tackle these problems – providing support as well as penalties. To support parents who failed to meet the government's expectations, there was a range of additional measures including civil parenting orders, support through Sure Start schemes, Parentline and parenting classes (Ball, 2008: 177). As Blunkett expressed it:

> 'We need parents who are prepared to take responsibility for supporting their child's education and we need a culture which values education and demands the best' (Blunkett 1999 in Gewirtz, 2001: 365).

Gewirtz locates these aspects of policy in an historic tradition including the extension of health visitors to working class mothers and the Conservatives' Parents' Charter (Gewirtz, 2001: 366). She argues that the ideal parents from the New Labour perspective had the following attributes:

1 They were active consumers in the education market place.
2 They monitored and closely policed what schools provided, intervening when necessary to rectify any shortcomings.
3 They possessed and transmitted appropriate forms of cultural capital to their children.
4 They possessed social capital – i.e. the social contacts, networks and self-confidence that enabled them to exploit the education system to their children's best advantage.

According to Gewirtz, middle-class parents embodied these attributes more than working class parents. Whilst one response might therefore be to dismantle the system which privileges such differences, she claims New Labour's response was to attempt to universalize these attributes (Gewirtz, 2001: 367). Echoing Mouffe's criticism (above) of the Third Way, Gewirtz claims that such a project was flawed because it ignored the socio-economic divisions underlying different patterns of engagement.

However, read within the broader project of the construction of the new citizen, who could assume new roles and relationships in society, these changes held out the promise of ending the old social barriers and patterns of inequality. As Secretary of State for Education, Blunkett believed that such citizens, when taking advantage of services which were managed effectively, would end the 'excuses' for underachievement and breakdown social inequalities. In a speech in 2000 to the National Union of Teachers, he argued:

> 'There are cynics out there who say that school performance is all about socio-economics and the areas that these schools are located in. No child is preordained by their class, gender, ethnic group or home life to fail' (Carvell, 2000).

This optimistic description of an education system which dismantles the obstacles to personal fulfilment serves to illustrate both how important education policy was to create the new citizen of tomorrow, and how crucial it was to devise compensatory policies to overcome the barriers that prevented this potential from being realized. Hence education policy also sought to tackle perceived parenting deficits through the 'responsibilization of parents' (Williams, 2004: 419), as well as challenging low aspirations and the toleration of low achievement within the system. The practical effects of this raft of reforms is much debated within the literature, but what is unquestionable is the centrality of education as the route to a responsive, reflexive society in which new citizens could take on a central role in creating and sustaining change.

Example 4: Schools strengthening communities and strong communities supporting schools

Within this broader project of re-building citizenship, there is one other aspect of education policy that is particularly relevant to the discourse on community and diversity, and that relates to the reinvigoration of faith schools under New Labour. On the one hand such a development has been justified as a belated extension of the established voluntary-aided system to all religious groups (Gamarnikow and Green, 2005). On this reading, even some sceptics have argued that it is better for the state to have some involvement with such schools, rather than to force religious groups to operate schools outside of the state system (Brighouse, 2005). Others though, have developed a stronger case for such schools. For example, Whitty's reading of research in the United States into Catholic schools indicates that, whilst much of the apparent higher outcomes is due to selection procedures, there is a residual effect, which he puts down to community, or social capital (Whitty, 2002: 119). This reading is echoed by Gamarnikow and Green (2005) who also point out how faith schools illustrate a more general commitment of the government to promote schools with a distinctive ethos, which may or may not be religious:

> At the heart of our vision for transforming secondary education is the ambition for every school to create or develop its distinct mission and ethos... Schools with a distinct identity perform best. (quoted from DfES (2001) 'Schools: Achieving Success' in Gamarnikow and Green, 2005: 95)

Given the earlier discussion about the communitarian roots of much of New Labour's thinking, Annette's description of faith schools as embodying 'religious communitarianism' (Annette, 2005) is a useful way to think about the role of such schools.

Whilst justifications in the early phase of New Labour's period in government for extending faith schools might be couched within the language of 'rights' and 'standards', the disturbances in Bradford and other mill towns and the continued debate about Islamic extremism, meant that the policy inevitably reflected some of the tensions within this discourse. Some commentators have argued that, contrary to some appeals to 'common sense', religious schools have not actually exacerbated the problems of segregation in society. By promoting the development of a secure identity, enhancing the life chances of children in deprived communities, and educating children in moral reasoning, it is possible to argue that faith schools serve multicultural societies well (Halstead and McLaughlin, 2005). Certainly Barker and Anderson (2005) argue that Christian education in Bradford has done more to ameliorate the social divisions there than contribute to them, and again point to the importance of broader social divisions and deprivation, which are often reflected in schools, rather than created by them. But Alan Johnson, as Education Secretary, became entangled in these tensions, when he attempted to force through legislation that would compel faith schools to enrol a proportion of students who were from others faiths and none. Whilst this has been common practice in many Christian schools, this attempt at compulsion attracted a strong response from many religious communities and eventually the policy was changed. The compromise solution led to a new duty for all schools to promote community cohesion (BBC, 2006b).

Summary

Whilst there is evidence that the three discourses which constitute the trope of the *new citizen* have had some resonances within education, I have not claimed that these discourses have driven education policy. Rather I have sought to illustrate some of the ways in which aspects of education policy have reflected these specific discourses. Table 3.1 summarizes some of these connections between the three discourses, domestic policy in general and education policy in particular. In drawing attention to these connections I have sought to illustrate how these discourses played a part in shaping solutions – education was seen as the route to creating *responsible citizens*; parents were re-imagined as *active agents* in their children's education and where necessary subjected to a process of *responsibilization*; schools were seen as sites of value and identity formation and given responsibility for contributing to community cohesion.

By turning next to consider citizenship education policy in some detail it will be evident how this aspect of policy reflects these three discourses much more thoroughly and how the development of policy over several years reflected the ways in which these discourses have developed. In citizenship education one can discern the most explicit example of the state's attempt to imagine and then bring into being the new citizen at the heart of welfare reform.

Table 3.1 Examples of New Labour's new citizenship programme

	Key events and issues	Policy developments	Education policy developments
Rights and responsibilities	– Anti-social behaviour – Modernizing the constitution – Rising number of immigrants with social welfare rights – Third Way approach to welfare reform	– Anti-Social Behaviour Orders (1998) – Human Rights Act (1998) – Immigration and Asylum Act (1999) included new restrictions on welfare entitlements e.g. dispersal, vouchers – New Deals focused on groups of welfare users (1998) – 'Respect Agenda' launched at start of third term (2005)	– Rights and responsibilities in Cit Ed curriculum (from 2002) – Support for Student Voice projects, including student associate governors (2003), school councils (2008) – Parental responsibilities reflecting 'choice' and 'voice' public service reforms – Government sponsored guidance e.g. 'Right Here, Right Now' (2009)
Participation	– Concern over falling turnout – Regeneration projects in deprived communities	– Electoral Commission (2000) – Range of initiatives to promote adult participation (see illustration 2)	– Responsible action in Cit Ed curriculum (from 2002) – Local authority youth consultations – Support for Community Service Volunteers (CSV) and other NGOs

| Community and Diversity | – Concerns about underclass
– McPherson Report and 'intolerance of intolerance'
– Terrorism, riots and security fears
– Islamophobia
– Integration of immigrants | – Social Exclusion Unit (1997)
– Acknowledgement of 'racially aggravated' crimes (1998), Race Relations Amendment Act (2000), range of equality legislation aimed at specific groups e.g. equal age of consent (2000), civil partnerships (2005), prohibition of LGBT discrimination in goods and services, culminating in the Single Equality Act (2010)
– Community Cohesion (2002) and 'bridge building' project funding
– Terrorism, Crime and Security Act (2001); Britishness debate in 'Governance of Britain' Green Paper (2007)
– Nationality, Immigration and Asylum Act (2002) introduced citizenship tests and ceremonies | – Diversity and identity in Cit Ed curriculum (from 2008)
– Community Cohesion duty (2006)
– Duty to promote good race relations strengthened (2000) and expanded under single equality duty to include gender, sexuality, disability and religion (2010)
– 'Prevent Strategy' anti-extremism guidance for schools (2007)
– Aiming High projects (2003) targeted underachievement for specific groups
– Expansion of faith schools (1998) |

4

The New Citizen in Education Policy

Citizenship Education Policy – Crick and Beyond

This chapter begins the detailed investigation of citizenship education policy with an analysis of two core texts, the Crick Report (Advisory Group on Citizenship, 1998) and the Ajegbo Review (Ajegbo, 2007). The analysis considers each text's key arguments and ideas in relation to the three discourses discussed in Chapter 3. In doing so it explores the vision of the *new citizen* as it developed over New Labour's period in office. The chapter addresses McCowan's first 'leap' in the policy implementation cycle and traces the transition from ends to means as policy visions were translated into curriculum structures (McCowan, 2008).

There were relatively few key players in the official formulation of citizenship education policy, which makes this particular policy slightly easier to read than other more nebulous policies which were influenced by diverse groups with slightly different policy agendas (see for example the discussion of Education Action Zones in Power et al., 2004). The main two agents were Sir Bernard Crick and David Blunkett. Bernard Crick was a political philosopher with a long-standing interest in promoting a greater understanding of politics, which was evident in his teaching, academic publications, journalism and in his support for the Hansard Society's political literacy project in the 1970s and the Politics Association. He taught David Blunkett in Sheffield University, and when Blunkett became Secretary of State for Education in 1997, he invited Crick to chair an Advisory Group to recommend how best to introduce citizenship education into the national curriculum. The partnership between Crick and Blunkett led to a series of reforms relating to citizenship, including a national programme for post-compulsory citizenship education and subsequent changes to immigration policy when Blunkett moved to the Home Office. In terms of secondary school education policy, the main document to consider is the Advisory Group's Final Report 'Education for Citizenship and the Teaching of Democracy in Schools' (Advisory Group on Citizenship, 1998), which was completed under the chairmanship of Crick and which will be subsequently referred to as the Crick Report. This in turn gave rise to the amended national curriculum (QCA, 2000) and guidance from the Qualifications and Curriculum Authority[1]. As I trace the evolution of policy I will also consider subsequent guidance from OfSTED, and the Ajegbo Review 'Diversity and Citizenship' (Ajegbo, 2007), which informed the production of new programmes of study for Citizenship (QCA, 2007).

There are several published accounts of the development of the Crick Report. Bernard Crick has written about the work of the Advisory Group and his intentions in 'steering' their work (Crick, 2000a, 2000b, 2003). David Kerr, who was seconded to the QCA as Professional Officer to the Advisory Group, has produced several articles which detail the work of the group and which offer commentary on the main recommendations and implementation challenges (Kerr, 1999, 2003; Kerr et al., 2008). David Blunkett discussed his intentions when introducing citizenship education in a book he wrote as he made the transition from the Department for Education to the Home Office (Blunkett, 2001). And more recently, Jessica Pykett and Dina Kiwan have separately conducted research with members of the Advisory Group, and used their data to discuss the various aims and interests reflected in the group (Kiwan, 2008; Pykett, 2007). From these accounts, and from the Crick Report itself, it is possible to identify a range of factors, which set the scene for the introduction of citizenship education:

- England was in a very small minority of democratic countries which did not have any formal citizenship education, so to some extent this was seen as an opportunity to correct an historical omission.
- A political opportunity was presented by Blunkett's appointment as Secretary of State for Education – he was known to have some sympathy for citizenship education.
- Some describe a sense of crisis, against which citizenship education might be seen as part of the solution. Echoing the sentiments in much of the discussion of the 'Third Way' (see Chapter 3), Kerr described the context in which citizenship education was introduced in the following terms:

'This period of unprecedented and seemingly relentless change has succeeded in shifting and straining the traditional, stable boundaries of citizenship in many societies'. (Kerr, 2003: 2)

---

[1] The QCA published schemes of work, which were intended to provide teachers with models of how to interpret the curriculum, and several booklets of advice in the years following the publication of the National Curriculum Programmes of Study.

- Concern about perceived political apathy, reflected in low turnout at elections.
- A more general disengagement from politics, especially among young people.
- A duty under human rights legislation to educate young people about their rights.
- Growing discussion of issues around citizenship, especially in relation to immigration and asylum.

Kiwan identifies three types of explanation which were offered by her inter-viewees. First, some respondents simply suggested there was a timely 'cocktail' of factors that precipitated the development. Second, some claim there was a 'trigger', akin to a media induced moral panic, which decisively shifted public perceptions to accept that schools should do something to address young people's anti-social behaviour – suggestions for such a shift included references to the Jamie Bulger case[2]. Third, some suggested that the fact that citizenship education was taken seriously at this time was as much to do with 'luck' as anything else, given that it is always difficult to predict when an issue would come to the fore (Kiwan, 2008: 26–8). Of course, it is impossible to construct a definitive statement to explain why citizenship education was introduced, but all of the factors listed reflect the issues discussed above in Chapter 3, in relation to New Labour's wider policy agenda. The sense of society moving towards a new settlement in which the role of the state, and the relationship between the state and citizens, would change are at the heart of the discussion of the Third Way and are reflected clearly in the statements of members of the Advisory Group on Citizenship. As the quotation from Kerr (above) indicates, this change to a new settlement is also often seen as being bound up with a collapse, or at least erosion, of the status quo, what McLaughlin refers to as a 'civic deficit' (McLaughlin, 2000).

Once the introduction of citizenship education had been agreed by government, it attracted to it a whole range of other justifications, reflecting the wide range of factors that were also seen as challenges for the new citizen. In Hansard, there are a range of references to citizenship education which claim

---

[2]   The murder of toddler James Bulger by two ten-year-old boys took place in 1993 and attracted huge media attention and considerable public debate. Although the boys had been found guilty in November 1993, this respondent's mention of the case in relation to the Crick committee's work four years later illustrates to what extent the case was seen as totemic in representing a general problem of 'out of control' youth.

it as the government's response to a variety of problems. For example, Charles Clarke, then a junior minister in the Department for Education, claimed it was about environmental education:

> 'Those ideas – the relationship between the individual, the environment and society – are at the core of our ideas for PSHE and citizenship' (Clarke, 20 July 1999).

Similarly, when asked about plans to implement the McPherson Report's recommendations on tackling institutional racism, the then Home Secretary Jack Straw answered:

> 'My right hon. Friend the Secretary of State for Education and Employment is taking a number of steps aimed at promoting cultural diversity and preventing racism in our schools. Citizenship education, which will foster an understanding of cultural diversity in Britain, has a prominent place in the revised national curriculum' (Straw, 29 March 1999).

One can see that Citizenship has the potential to be used as a repository for many political issues. In the following discussion I focus on the three discourses which formed the basis of the analysis in Chapter 3 and consider what the statements of policy had to say in relation to rights and responsibilities; active citizenship; and diversity and community cohesion. The Crick Report starts by quoting the terms of reference set for it by the DfEE:

> To provide advice on effective education for citizenship in schools – to include the nature and practices of *participation* in democracy; the *duties, responsibilities and rights* of individuals as citizens; and the value to individuals and society of *community activity* (my italics Advisory Group on Citizenship, 1998: 4).

This explains to a large extent why the text of the report has more to say about the first two discourses than it does the third. However, as I trace the development of the curriculum over the decade following the publication of the Crick Report, the shift between these discourses becomes apparent.

Rights and Responsibilities in the Crick Report and beyond

For each of the themes I started my analysis of the documents by conducting a simple search for terms relating to each discourse. In this case I used the terms 'rights', 'responsibilities', 'duties' and 'obligations'. A majority (88 per cent) of the occurrences included the term 'rights', which left only 12 per cent of all occurrences referring to 'responsibilities', 'duties' or 'obligations' alone. Half of occurrences including the term 'rights' paired it with 'responsibilities'. The Lord Chancellor's statement, which ended the main section of the report summed up the tenor of many of these connections:

> Citizenship education must give people confidence to claim their rights and challenge the status quo while, at the same time, make plain that with rights come obligations (Advisory Group on Citizenship, 1998: 61).

This sentiment echoes the report's early discussion of models of citizenship in which the duties of participation were stressed:

> In the political tradition stemming from the Greek city states and the Roman republic, citizenship has meant involvement in public affairs by those who had the rights of citizens: to take part in public debate and... in shaping the laws and decisions of a state... We now have the opportunity for a highly educated 'citizen democracy' (Advisory Group on Citizenship, 1998: 9).

And in turn, this is clearly reflected in the statement of aims for the new curriculum for Citizenship, which the report phrased in the following terms:

> The purpose of citizenship education... is to... enhance the awareness of rights and duties, and the sense of responsibilities, needed for the development of pupils into active citizens (Advisory Group on Citizenship, 1998: 40).

The links between rights and responsibilities are evident in Table 4.1 which summarizes the report's recommendations for the curriculum.

It is notable that pupils are required to 'know', 'understand' and 'be aware of' aspects of rights and responsibilities. In relation to this dimension, the focus is clearly on knowledge. It is important though not to misrepresent the intentions of the report and in the sections on skills and aptitudes there are relevant references to a range of processes which are clearly related to rights and responsibilities. Most of these are more concerned with the kinds of skills one needs in order to assume the general duty of participation, which reflects Crick's commitment that 'children learn responsibility best and gain a sense of moral values by discussing with good guidance from the earliest age real and controversial issues and by having opportunities to participate and take responsibility' (Crick, 2000a: 128–9) (this will be considered below when we turn to the report's treatment of active citizenship). But one could also read the recommendation that children in all Key Stages 'use imagination when considering the experience of others' (Advisory Group on Citizenship, 1998: 46–51) as being

Table 4.1 Rights and Responsibilities in the Crick Report

Key Stage 1 *expectations*	know about differences and similarities between people in terms of... rights, responsibilities...
Key Stage 2 *expectations*	understand that there are various sources of authority in their duties understand the meaning of terms such as rights and responsibilities understand the meaning of terms such as... human rights
Key Stage 3 *expectations*	understand... the legal rights and responsibilities of young people... ...with particular reference to the UN Convention on the Rights of the Child understand the general nature of legal aspects and responsibilities of other citizens understand the rights and responsibilities underpinning democratic society... ...with particular reference to the European Convention on Human Rights be aware of issues surrounding rights such as freedom of speech know about the Universal Declaration of Rights and why it was developed understand the meaning of terms such as... human rights
Key Stage 4 *expectations*	understand the meaning of terms such as... civil rights

(Source: Advisory Group on Citizenship, 1998: 46–52)

linked to an appreciation of the skills required to really understand individual responsibility to one another.

There has been some criticism that the Crick Report tended to see citizenship as an outcome of a trajectory or preparation, rather than a current status for young people (Alderson, 2000, Biesta and Lawy, 2006). Looking at the text of the Report there is clearly some tension between these two views as there is mention made both of young people's status as current citizens and as future citizens. The report included a lengthy quotation from a submission by the British Youth Council (BYC):

> [The curriculum] should look at children and young people's rights and responsibilities as citizens... [The curriculum] should also look at the law and the justice system and how it relates to their rights and responsibilities... We believe that the most important issue facing young people as citizens is their lack of knowledge about... their actual rights and responsibilities as citizens. (Advisory Group on Citizenship, 1998: 19–20)

Whilst the wording itself is from the BYC, the quotation is endorsed by the Advisory Group as essentially summarizing their intentions. It is significant therefore that these references explicitly acknowledge the existence of children's rights and responsibilities as they presently affect them, rather than merely as preparation for future citizenship. Alderson points out the significance here, of the fact that the BYC extract was the only evidence cited from a youth organization (Alderson, 2000).

In contrast to the implications of the BYC quotation, there were several references to rights, which focused on them as something to be developed for adulthood. One of these was a direct quotation from legislation; one was part of an argument for post-16 citizenship education. The other two were slightly ambiguously worded but seemed to imply that pupils would become citizens, as distinct from becoming better at exercising their current citizenship status. One example appeared in the recommendations section:

> there should be a DfEE Order setting up the entitlement and this shall... include the knowledge, skills and values relevant to... the duties, responsibilities, rights and development of pupils into citizens (Advisory Group on Citizenship, 1998: 22).

Another example is taken from the section on aims:

> The purpose of citizenship education... is to... enhance the awareness of rights and duties, and the sense of responsibilities, needed for the development of pupils into active citizens (Advisory Group on Citizenship, 1998: 40).

These latter references certainly lend some weight to Alderson's assertion that the Crick Report 'tends to see democracy as a set of mainly abstract ideas and adults' systems instead of activities in schools which can raise strong feelings about how to share responsibilities, resources and power fairly' (Alderson, 1999: 195).

Crick has subsequently explained the importance of rights within a citizenship education programme, but also stressed that rights alone could not provide (in his opinion) a sufficient underpinning for such a project. He pointed out that the report dealt with this complex debate by 'always linking rights with duties, or rights with responsibilities' (Crick, 2000a: 127). This clearly resonates with broader developments under New Labour, where rights have frequently been seen as conditional, and where there has been a sustained effort to encourage citizens to assume the responsibilities established by government as part of a wider reform of welfare policy.

For Crick, the rejection of rights as providing the foundations for citizenship education was rooted in an historical appreciation that 'free citizenship preceded any clear idea of human rights' (Crick, 2000a: 127). This reflects the argument developed in his early and influential book, *'In Defence of Politics'*, in which he saw politics as a process, which was a fundamental part of human nature, and which should be embraced in its own right and defended against other ideologies that seek to encompass it (Crick, 1982). One of Kiwan's respondents felt that they and others had moved Crick to some extent on the issue and that rights became more prominent in the final report than the interim one, but this interviewee recognized that whilst rights had a higher profile in the final report they were certainly not fundamental to the conception of Citizenship it presented (Kiwan, 2008: 66).

Whilst Crick's published arguments go some way to explain why the tension is unresolved within the Crick Report (i.e. between children as having and realizing rights now, and simply learning about them), it does leave the problem for later interpretation, and also misses the opportunity to focus on school organization as a key way in which rights and responsibilities can be explored through real experience (Alderson, 1999, 2000; Osler and Starkey, 2005b). The Ajegbo Review represents a slight shift in this aspect of the debate in that it explicitly recommends that schools should do more to ensure that 'pupil voice is heard and acted upon' (Ajegbo, 2007: 9). It is interesting to note though that the Review makes fewer references to rights (in its 126 pages) than the Crick Report (in its 88 pages).[3] To some extent this reflects the differences in the brief of the two reports (Ajegbo was asked to review diversity and identity specifically) but it also reflects a change in style between the two reports. Whereas the Crick Report reads like a summary of judiciously selected evidence from a wide range of interested parties, which makes a case for citizenship education and then rather technically defines the shape for such a policy, the Ajegbo Review bears the imprint of being led by a head teacher who was more engaged with the legal and practical aspects of managing the curriculum and broader school systems to achieve certain ends.

In the only substantial discussion of rights in the Ajegbo Review, the authors criticize some of the ways in which rights have been conceptualized in the QCA schemes of work.

---

[3] Because the Ajegbo Review includes fairly detailed schemes of work in the appendices I have omitted these from the searches, as this would distort the findings and may give the impression that these terms were more widely spread throughout the Review.

Unit 3 on Human Rights, for instance, proposes that by the end of the Unit, most pupils will 'know that the Human Rights Act is underpinned by common values'. Whilst it is important that human rights are recognized as essential to understanding citizenship, it does not explore whether these are universal common values, or whether these are common values for the UK. So what is not clarified is the distinction between an *individual* with human rights – underpinned by common values for all human beings; and being a *citizen* – with rights based on being a member of a nation state. It is not clear how these common values are distinctive to citizenship in the UK context, in contrast to other nation-state settings. There must be a clear and explicit rationale of how human rights relate to citizenship (Ajegbo, 2007: 94).

Here then we see an exploration of some rather technical definitional dimensions to rights becoming significant precisely because the focus of the Ajegbo review is on identity and belonging. These issues will become more relevant when we come to consider the third discourse (below), but here it is useful to note how this change of emphasis changes the official perception of the job that needs to be done, when teaching rights. Under Crick there is knowledge to be learned about the rights people have; under Ajegbo it becomes more significant that young people understand the source of those rights – especially where the source can serve the purpose of providing some sense of unity, that is, where rights spring from the very fact of our belonging within the British state.

The authors of the Ajegbo Review conclude this discussion by arguing that, "the motivation for citizens to participate in society is logically predicated on a sense of belonging, or 'identification' with, the context where they are participating" (Ajegbo, 2007: 95). Ajegbo thus assumes that, if young people understand how the rights they enjoy spring from their membership of British society, they will be more motivated to become involved in their society. This is questionable and it seems at least arguable that, whilst a sense of belonging is part of citizenship (Osler and Starkey, 2005b), that sense might emerge from interacting with others in the public realm, rather than preceding such participation. Klein has argued, in another context,[4] that hearts and minds are easier to win over through action and behavioural change, rather than seeking to change attitudes first (Klein, 1993: 129). The assumption that we need to make the teaching of values and attitudes a priority does however fit comfortably into the broader political discourse promoted by Gordon Brown who argued in 2006:

---

[4]   Klein's discussion is about how to affect change in teacher attitudes and practice in relation to tackling racism.

'When we take time to stand back and reflect, it becomes clear that to address almost every one of the major challenges facing our country… you must have a clear view of what being British means, what you value about being British and what gives us purpose as a nation' (Brown, 2006).

Brown's contention was that one needs to identify core values before one can determine policy on the NHS, the EU or any other significant area of government. It seems Ajegbo's stance is comparable in that he contends young people have to develop a sense of identity that connects them to fellow-citizens before they can act together.

Despite the fact that the Ajegbo Review had relatively little to say in relation to the discourse on rights and responsibilities, the Qualifications and Curriculum Authority (QCA) review of the programmes of study for Citizenship did make some significant changes. Structural changes in the Key Stage 3 curriculum meant that every subject had to be defined in terms of processes and concepts first, and therefore the specific knowledge for each subject was relatively less important. Whereas rights and responsibilities were mentioned in the first programmes of study, this was elevated (from September 2008) to one of three core concepts underpinning the whole of the programme of study for Citizenship.[5]

Active Citizenship in the Crick Report and beyond

The initial report of the Crick Advisory Group characterized citizenship education as being based on three strands – political literacy, social and moral responsibility and community involvement (Advisory Group on Citizenship, 1998: 63). The central place of community involvement in the final report should therefore cause little surprise, although the argument for this strand in relation to the suggested curriculum is weaker than may have been expected. A majority of the references to 'action' and 'participation' linked the terms with 'community'. This tendency to link active citizenship with community clearly resonates with the civic republican beliefs of Crick, and seems particularly appropriate to the earlier discussion of communitarian influences on New Labour's approach to citizenship. In its exploration of the type of community

---

[5]   The others are 'Democracy and Justice' and 'Identity and Diversity'. These core concepts and the processes are intended to provide a clear framework through which teachers should interpret the knowledge they include in lessons.

action that should be promoted, the report argues in favour of volunteering and community service, although it also acknowledges that 'voluntary and community activity cannot be the full meaning of active citizenship' (Advisory Group on Citizenship, 1998: 11).

References to community participation and active citizenship also reflected the tension noted above with regard to whether citizenship education concerned young people as citizens, or young people being prepared for citizenship. The BYC submission placed more stress on young people's role as active citizens by calling for a curriculum which covered 'practical skills that enable young people to participate effectively in public life', although the statement also acknowledged that roles do also evolve as children become adults and argued that part of the task of the citizenship curriculum would also be to 'prepare them to be full citizens' (Advisory Group on Citizenship, 1998: 19).

Perhaps one of the best known and certainly one of the most widely used quotations from the Crick Report makes the point about the centrality of active citizenship very clear:

> We aim at no less than a change in the political culture of this country both nationally and locally: for people to think of themselves as active citizens, willing, able and equipped to have an influence in public life and with the critical capacities to weigh evidence before speaking and acting; to build on and to extend radically to young people the best in existing traditions of community involvement and public service, and to make them individually confident in finding new forms of involvement and action among themselves (Advisory Group on Citizenship, 1998: 7).

This central theme was reiterated by the Lord Chancellor, who provided the 'last word', in which he emphasized the civic republican belief that, 'the path to greatest personal fulfilment lies through active involvement in strengthening... society' (Advisory Group on Citizenship, 1998: 61).

Such a call to action responded to a construction of some sort of crisis. In relation to this discourse the Crick Report referred to evidence submitted by 'Citizenship 2000', a group of citizenship and education organizations, which argued that:

> Citizenship education is urgently needed to address this historic deficit if we are to avoid a further decline in the quality of our public life and if we are to prepare all young people for informed participation... This will not happen unless there is a firm political and professional commitment to citizenship education (Advisory Group on Citizenship, 1998: 14).

The report discussed a range of evidence about the lack of engagement of young people in politics and their general lack of knowledge about, or interest in, politics. However, even within the report the evidence of such a crisis is not unequivocal and brief reference is made to a 1997 study by the Trust for the Study of Adolescence, which found that a majority of their sample of young people had been involved in political or community action in the previous year (Advisory Group on Citizenship, 1998: 15). Weller discusses other survey data which focuses on young people's 'non traditional' participation, and stresses that one needs to acknowledge what young people do (petitions, campaigns), that is of a political nature, as well as what they do not do (join political parties, vote in elections) in order to gain a full appreciation of young people's citizenship engagement (Weller, 2007: 34). This echoes Annette's earlier discussion of research into young people's participation, which led him to conclude that 'young people, while having an antipathy to politicians and formal politics, do see civic participation as a meaningful political activity' (Annette, 2000: 80). Indeed a later inquiry, funded by the Joseph Rowntree Foundation, found evidence to suggest that this pattern was becoming a more general characteristic across society (Power Inquiry, 2006).

There is a debate about whether the perceived problem reflects a general decline over time, or simply represents a feature of the political life cycle of citizens, who 'grow into' traditional politics (Watts, 2006, Weller, 2007). The Crick Report acknowledged this debate but concluded that whilst 'things may not be getting dramatically worse, they are inexcusably and damagingly bad, and could and should be remedied' (Advisory Group on Citizenship, 1998: 16). What is apparent is that (i) the Report's authors were responding to what they perceived as a serious deficit among young people; (ii) that their solution was premised on a civic republican commitment, in which active participation in the public realm is central; and (iii) that the text included many references to active citizenship, participative democracy and community participation. The Committee's consultation also indicated that 'there was a widespread feeling that learning about citizenship should be active and participatory and should involve participation from members of the wider community' (Advisory Group on Citizenship, 1998: 76).

Given the centrality of this dimension in the Report, the recommendations were surprisingly ambivalent in this regard:

'We also discussed whether service learning or community involvement... should be part of a new statutory Order for Citizenship education... However, we have concluded not to ask for their inclusion in a statutory Order at this time, mainly for fear of overburdening school and teachers' (Advisory Group on Citizenship, 1998: 25).

This is reflected in the recommendations, which tended to focus on the values, knowledge and attitudes to support active citizenship, rather than on the direct experiences of active participation. Crick explained this in a later commentary on the work of the group:

'The Report strongly recommended pupil participation both in school and in the local community as good practice, but not to be part of the statutory order – 'value added' if you like. We thought we were being politically prudent... and the classroom curriculum was enough, we thought, for starters... But the Secretary of State sent word to the working party who were drafting the consultative order (civil servants, QCA, teachers, advisers) that actual participation could be mandatory, if we cared so to recommend... Without the experiential, participative side of citizenship learning, some schools could turn... the brave new subject into safe and dead, dead-safe, old rote-learning civics' (Crick, 2000a: 119).

This reflected Blunkett's commitment to civic republicanism, as explored above in relation to New Labour's more general policy discourses, in which 'citizens owe duties to one another... and *must* play a responsible part in public life [and...] engage actively in the life of the political community' (Blunkett, 2001: 18, my emphasis). This position also fitted comfortably within somewhat older guidance from the Council of Europe's Committee of Ministers' recommendation that 'democracy is best learned in a democratic setting where participation is encouraged' (Council of Europe, 1985 in Osler and Starkey, 1996: 181–3). This intervention by Blunkett certainly reinforces the impression that citizenship education was introduced in large part because of his tenure in the Department for Education and Employment. Without this compulsory element, as Crick says himself, the subject would have likely been turned into a 'safe and dead' area of the curriculum.

Despite what we might call a 'wobble in confidence' in the Report over the extent to which teachers would be able to assume responsibility for providing active citizenship experiences, Crick subsequently wrote about the nature of experiential learning he considered most useful and relevant. In one example of how this call to action could be misunderstood, he described a school which claimed to be doing an active citizenship project by enabling a group of pupils to plan a party for old people in a residential home near to the school.

The young people negotiated with the staff, bought provisions and organized entertainment. On the face of it this seems to demonstrate participation, but this is not, according to Crick, what active citizenship is about (Crick, 2002b). In considering what could have transformed the project into active citizenship he suggests:

- A prior investigation into the complex policy area of health care, and provision for the elderly.
- An investigation into why some of the residents were being cared for in a state funded institution, and whether the level of funding was adequate.
- Representations to the relevant public authorities.

In essence, what would be needed is some knowledge base, in order that the situation is understood. Indeed it is the notion of young people being 'informed' which marks Hart's distinction between genuine participation and non-partici-pation, which can see good intentions result in tokenism or manipulation (Hart, 1992). It may be a harsh reality for some schools, but, according to Crick, the fun party at the 'old folks home' might be valuable for all sorts of reasons, but it is not valuable as part of the citizenship education programme in the school.

This distinction is especially important in the light of debates about the erosion of social capital in some modern societies (Putnam, 2000). One might want to encourage young people to participate in the project outlined above because (a) they will get to know groups within the community; (b) they will build relationships with people from another generation; (c) they may feel the satisfaction of a job well done and enjoy helping out; and (d) it may also serve to boost their sense of self esteem and their appreciation of others. Through these outcomes the project may build 'bridging social capital' (Putnam, 2000) and therefore it may play a part in the school's overall vision for developing citizens. Annette (2008) outlines at least four different ways in which the term 'community' is conceptualized in citizenship education; and in his terms such projects may be useful for their connection to the community as a place or neighbourhood, and even to some extent with the communitarian inspired notion of community as a normative ideal, in which relationships of duty and respect connect us. It may also draw on community as a source of cultural identity, but it does not demonstrate participation in the community as a political ideal, at least not in the civic republican tradition espoused by Crick.

In this example one can discern a potential area of confusion, one which seems to be built into the whole project of creating Citizenship as a national curriculum subject. On one view there is a broad sense in which good schools promote good citizenship, through providing opportunities for young people to gain experience of working with others in respectful and productive ways. Kisby (2006) has attempted to analyse citizenship education primarily as an attempt to recreate or strengthen social capital. Similarly, Gamarnikow and Green (2000) draw attention to the similarities between a model of citizenship for promoting social capital and that proposed in the Crick Report. Even Crick acknowledged the value of everyday associations in his major work, *In Defence of Politics*, where he argued that politics is an essential element of what it is to be human:

> 'The more one is involved in relationships with others, the more conflicts of interest, or of character and circumstance will arise. These conflicts, when personal, create the activity we call 'ethics'... and such conflicts, when public, create political activity' (Crick, 1982).

From this perspective such 'public interactions' could be seen as the bedrock of political education, and there is no obvious reason why the joint effort required to negotiate and organize the party for elderly people discussed above would not fulfil these criteria.

Crick was first and foremost a political philosopher and, as we have seen, declared himself a civic republican, one of the hallmarks of which is the Aristotelian commitment that fulfilment comes through political participation (Crick, 2002a). In his guidance to clarify for teachers what counts as active citizenship, there is a tendency to focus on overtly 'political' issues, often those linked to policy or party political debates, rather than adopting an approach which sees all public interactions as examples of everyday politics. This more expansive definition seems to be more compatible with his general account of politics (Crick, 1982) and there are other reasons provided by contemporary political philosophers for returning to this broader definition. Perczynski (1999) has written about *associative democracy*, as a form of democratic theory linked to civic republicanism, in which democracy is seen as being embedded within the interplay of different associations, which are formed by citizens interacting according to a range of interests. In turn this connects to Habermas' conception of the ways in which people participate in the public sphere (Habermas, 1999: Ch.9), and of the significance of participation in 'New Social Movements' (Habermas discussed in Morrow and Torres, 2002: 137–40). For Habermas, the nature of the interactions between citizens in the public sphere seems more important than the purpose of those interactions. The mere fact of coming together, of engaging in deliberative acts, of perceiving ourselves in relation to others, is a key element in sustaining democracy. Similarly, Iris Marion Young's discussion of democracy seeks to give 'prominence to processes of discussion and citizen involvement in the associations of civil society' (Young, 2000: 40). This strong theme in thinking about democracy, often described as *the deliberative turn* (Dryzek, 2000), indicates that there may be some merit in promoting the skills and attributes for democracy through experiences of interacting with others in the public sphere, which could include the school.

These arguments about social capital and the different theoretical perspectives on the value of association indicate that the activities and ends themselves may not have to be overtly *political* to promote citizenship, at least not in the way Crick implies; indeed this may also be perfectly compatible with a broad commitment to civic republicanism (Cunningham, 2002). If we expand our notion of relevant experiences to recognize that democracy is lived in the acts of coming together to discuss, resolve and take action we derive a significantly different agenda for school based citizenship education. This agenda is actually closer to Dewey's understanding of the purposes of education and the link to experiential learning, as he put it:

> Is it not the reason for our preference [for democracy] that we believe that mutual consultation and convictions reached through persuasion, make possible a better quality of experience than can otherwise be provided on any wide scale?… Personally I do not see how we can justify our preference for democracy and humanity on any other ground (Dewey, 1997/1938: 34–5).

This strengthens the argument that the foundations of education for democracy might best be established by focusing on the experience of getting along together, and by engaging in meaningful deliberation rather than by a premature induction into public policy debates.

To some extent, the Crick Report acknowledges the value of such activities, but as we have already seen, he also demands more of experiential learning activities that are to count as 'citizenship education'. Crick's stance in relation to this definitional problem strengthens the interpretation that citizenship education policy aims primarily towards the creation of the ideal new citizen, rather than simply as an attempt to build social capital. This reflects Crick's linking of citizenship education to the broader policy context in which the government was attempting a shift from state responsibility for welfare, towards community and individual responsibility (Advisory Group on Citizenship, 1998: 10). Significantly for schools, this move to a narrower definition of active citizenship as requiring a connection to issues which are somehow defined as more political than others rules out many of the opportunities for participation that can be readily identified in schools. This tension, unresolved in Crick's own writing, manifested itself in subsequent advice from government agencies responsible for interpreting and clarifying the curriculum.

Wood has explored the ways in which such agencies subsequently issued slightly different advice concerning what would be acceptable as active citizenship. The QCA, which was responsible for writing and providing the framework for assessing the Citizenship curriculum, provided advice and guidance which Wood (2006: 31) argues, focused on the 'helpful' citizen, more than the political and critical citizen. This requirement to define 'minimal' responses was also evident in the guidance of OfSTED, the government inspection service, which helped to set the benchmark for what was acceptable in practice. Whilst it upheld the focus on participating students being 'informed', the recognition of letter writing or publishing conclusions on a school website as active citizenship, was seen as setting a workable minimal entitlement for all students (Wood, 2006: 33). Whilst these efforts were in part aimed at making the new curriculum manageable for teachers, who had to work within the confines of the classroom, they did appear to move away from the initial intentions for active citizenship. Indeed in one extract from an OfSTED report, the judgement seemed to directly contradict Crick's efforts to explore the links between political literacy and real action by apparently accepting a fairly minimal example of pupil engagement in the classroom as an example of active citizenship:

> The third strand of citizenship, the skills of participation and responsible action, has been developed well in some schools through the use of discussion and other methods, including role play and collaborative working in the context of citizenship knowledge and understanding (Ofsted, 2004a: 3).

This shifting emphasis illustrated a continuing lack of clarity in this crucial aspect of citizenship education.

Turning to the Ajegbo Review, there is again a stark difference to the way such issues were discussed in the Crick Report. Whereas Crick included 45 references to community and a variety of terms directly linked to participation or activity, the Ajegbo Review included only three such phrases. As in the earlier discussion of rights, Ajegbo addressed himself more than Crick, to the school leaders and implementers of citizenship education policy. Despite these apparent differences, the Ajegbo Review does indicate there was a substantially shared vision with the Crick Report, in relation to active citizenship. This was most obviously evident in the vision statement Ajegbo establishes at the beginning of his report:

In five years, for all schools to be actively engaged in nurturing in pupils the skills to participate in an active and inclusive democracy, appreciating and understanding difference (Ajegbo, 2007: 1).

The Review also shared some of Crick's assumptions that active citizenship must be grounded in knowledge development:

In many schools teachers do not sufficiently anchor and integrate work on developing pupils' skills to knowledge and content; and there is evidence that some 'active citizenship' projects are insufficiently grounded in relevant knowledge and understanding. Currently in Citizenship, issues of identity and diversity do not tend to be linked explicitly enough to political understanding (of legal and political systems) and active participation (Ajegbo, 2007: 8).

To a substantial extent therefore, Ajegbo reinforced the original conceptualization of active citizenship, with the attendant problems discussed above. This continuity was also reflected in the key processes in the new national curriculum programmes of study, which still included 'taking informed and responsible action' as one of the three key processes,[6] much as the original Citizenship programmes of study included 'participation and responsible action' as one of the prescribed skills.

Community and Diversity in the Crick Report and beyond

This third broad area of policy discourse was not a main focus of the Crick Report, partly because it was not included explicitly in the terms of reference and partly because it had not emerged as being particularly significant at the very beginning of New Labour's period in office. When thinking about how the discourse emerged over the early years of the first term it is important to remember (as discussed in the previous chapter) that, although the inquiry into the murder of Stephen Lawrence became a defining moment in thinking about the government's responsibility for tackling racism, the inquiry report (MacPherson, 1999) was not published until the year after the Crick Report. Therefore, although citizenship education later came to be discussed in relation to the government's response to Macpherson's discussion of institutional racism (see for example Straw, 29 March 1999), it did not feature in the Crick Report itself. Similarly, the disturbances in Oldham, Burnley and Bradford, which came

---

[6]   The other two are 'critical thinking and enquiry' and 'advocacy and representation'.

to be seen as key events requiring some form of government response, did not take place until 2001. The 9/11 attack on the World Trade Centre, which had a huge impact on the way government conducted debates about community relations and sparked a wave of Islamophobia in much media coverage, similarly happened in 2001 and so it is significant to recall the somewhat more innocent age in which the Crick Committee met to discuss the nature of citizenship and citizenship education.

Despite the early years of New Labour being characterized by a less urgent need to confront issues of cultural diversity, racism and community relations it would be naïve to think these issues were not already established as part of the New Labour agenda. In the introduction to his review of New Labour's sustained attack on 'intolerance', McGhee argued:

> The Third Way ideals of increased equal opportunities and personal respon-
> sibilities through the facilitation of active citizens in active communities are
> implicated in wider strategies of attempting to achieve commonality, of moving
> to and finding 'common ground' in relation to the shared values and standards
> of an emergent citizenship for a multi-ethnic, multi-lingual and multi-faith
> Britain (McGhee, 2005: 12).

This argument clearly incorporates the three related discourses, which have formed the basis for this analysis, into the broader project of creating new citizens for new times ahead.

It is also essential to remember that as well as reconceptualizing the ways in which existing British residents saw themselves, their relationship to the state, and to each to other, the government was also involved in a series of significant policy discussions relating to immigration and asylum. These were concerned with the most basic elements of citizenship – residency rights and status. Thus, whilst aspects of New Labour's policy discussions related to forging a new and positive perception of citizenship in Britain, other aspects related to policing borders, keeping some people out and eventually treating them in very different ways than we had witnessed in the UK before. The concerns with 'bogus asylum seekers' and 'benefit fraudsters' had already entered public discourse by 1998, and the White Paper of that year led to legislation which introduced compulsory 'dispersal' around the country, which had the twin effect of denying asylum seekers access to community resources already established by earlier migrants, and introducing immigrants to many communities around Britain which had little or no experience of dealing with new arrivals. This inevitably had an impact on public discussions relating to race and diversity (Spencer, 2007).

These factors are useful reminders of the context in which the Crick Report was published and of the discourses within which it was produced. In beginning to analyse the report itself I searched the document for references to several related terms: 'cohesion', 'community', 'ethnicity', 'diversity', 'minority', and 'identity' (and terms derived from these). Taken together, there are 79 references to these terms. Interestingly, given how the term 'community cohesion' came to be commonly used in subsequent years, this phrase was not used once in the report, although the Citizenship 2000 group's evidence referred to a decline in 'civic cohesion', which citizenship education should address (Advisory Group on Citizenship, 1998: 14).

Of 59 references to community, ten were concerned with improving links between schools and their communities. The same number was also related to an explicit discussion of the place of communities within a broader model of politics, which might loosely be described as 'communitarian', and which clearly resonates with the earlier discussion of the Third Way philosophy. These references included clear attempts to lay out the theoretical stance adopted within the report in relation to the role of communities:

> Government is attempting a shift of emphasis between, on the one hand, state welfare provision and responsibility, and on the other, community and individual responsibility (Advisory Group on Citizenship, 1998: 10).

Such references also included examples of evidence submitted to the Advisory Group, which spelled out the ways in which citizenship education should take account of communities and equip young people with attributes (and knowledge) to participate effectively. The following quotation is taken from a submission by the Hansard Society:

> Young people... should be encouraged to take pride in themselves and the communities to which they belong (Advisory Group on Citizenship, 1998: 20).

Such sentiment echoes discussion in the literature about the nature of democratic virtues which citizenship education should seek to inculcate (Kymlicka, 2002).

Several of the references to community also drew links to discussions about diversity and the reality of living together in a multicultural society. For example, the section on Key Stage 1 expectations set out the expectation that 5 to 8 year olds should:

> Know where they live, in relation to their local and national community, [and] understand that there are different types and groups of people living in their local community (Advisory Group on Citizenship, 1998: 47).

More significantly, in relation to the subsequent debates about multiculturalism, the need to create a common sense of citizenship was a recurrent theme in the Report. The Citizenship Foundation's evidence expressed the concern that "the greater cultural diversity and the apparent loss of a value consensus" means that, "'Cultural diversity' raises the issue of national identity" (Advisory Group on Citizenship, 1998: 17). The Report's response was to affirm that:

A main aim for the whole community should be to find or restore a sense of common citizenship, including a national identity that is secure enough to find a place for the plurality of nations, cultures, ethnic identities and religions long found in the United Kingdom. Citizenship education creates common ground between different ethnic and religious identities (Advisory Group on Citizenship, 1998: 17).

The report began to explore the implications of a concern with identity for the curriculum and in the following extract suggested some specific content that could usefully be studied to provide young people with the required information to understand their own identities:

Matters of national identity in a pluralist society are complex... we all need to learn more about each other. This should entail learning... about the European, Commonwealth and global dimensions of citizenship, with due regard being given to the homelands of our minority communities and to the main countries of British emigration (Advisory Group on Citizenship, 1998: 18).

This final phrase has been identified as particularly problematic by some critics, who argue it betrays a set of assumptions mired in a mindset which views multicultural Britain as essentially them and us; that is, indigenous Britons and immigrants. This interpretation was further reinforced by the following extract, which sat uneasily within mainstream discourses about Britain as a multicultural society.

"Majorities must respect, understand and tolerate minorities and minorities must learn and respect the laws, codes and convention as much as the majority – not merely because it is useful to do so, but because this process helps foster common citizenship" (Advisory Group on Citizenship, 1998: 17).

As Osler and Starkey pointed out it was difficult to reconcile these quotations with conceptions of multiple and hybrid identities, and one is left with a vague impression that the report conceived all minorities as being similar, and that one dimension of this similarity was that their values somehow appeared to be at odds with the law-abiding values of the 'majority' (Osler and Starkey, 2000).

Osler and Starkey criticized the Crick Report as having a 'somewhat colonial flavour' and being 'somewhat patronising' in its terminology (Osler and Starkey, 2000: 7). Referring to the absence of explicit references to racism, Osler concluded that:

> The writers of the report either consider the subject too controversial to include in the school curriculum, or… they themselves are victims of a culture in which institutional racism is so powerful, and so ingrained, that it is invisible to those who do not experience it directly (Osler, 2000b: 31).

In a similar vein to the criticisms levelled at Crick by Osler and Starkey, Olssen argued that the Crick Report, 'tends to ignore racism, multiculturalism, and any sophisticated understanding of how the politics of difference might inform citizenship education' (Olssen, 2004: 188) and 'largely fits within an assimilationist political framework' (Olssen, 2004: 185).

These criticisms included a range of issues from the language and tone of the Crick report, to the more substantial omission of a discussion of racism and diversity, which in turn led to the absence of such issues from the recommendations. Whilst to some extent this might appear to damn the report, both Osler and Olssen recognized that the model itself was robust enough to provide a vehicle for developing anti-racist, multicultural and inclusive citizenship education. Olssen concluded that whilst the report may well have ignored racism 'it need not do so, at least on the grounds of theoretical coherence' (Olssen, 2004: 188). Olssen's solution was to enrich the Crick text with the more nuanced understanding of diversity embodied in the Parekh Report (Runneymede Trust, 2000), and Osler and Starkey argued that one could develop an anti-racist citizenship within the existing Crick model. They argued that, whilst 'the concept of racism is absent from the Crick Report… with its emphasis on political literacy, the report does provide a key tool by which citizenship education programmes might be transformed to enable young people to confront and challenge racism' (Osler and Starkey, 2000: 15), which was also the essence of Crick's own defence of his position.

References to racism within the report tended to be concerned, as we noted with rights, with ensuring that young people should acquire an understanding of the phenomenon, which Crick took to mean an understanding of the terminology and the nature of ethnic diversity. Whilst this fell short of the expectations of his critics (Osler, 2000a), Crick defended his model of citizenship as robust enough to provide a vehicle for inclusive citizenship education. In essence he argued that effective citizenship education would result from a balance of the three strands in the report (social and moral responsibility, political literacy and community participation), and he was overtly sceptical about the prospects of 'full frontal' assaults on racism, which he felt were likely to be 'inflammatory – just what the racist white lads will look forward to in classroom discussion' (Crick, 2000a: 134). Instead he argued that, 'the need for citizenship arises from far broader considerations than anti-racialism, and true citizenship has no place for racism and provides a secure framework against its recurrence' (Crick, 2000a: 132). For Crick, looking at citizenship and citizenship education in the round, the challenge was, 'to cure the disease as a denial of free and equal citizenship, not constantly to battle with the symptoms' of racism (Crick, 2000a: 132).

Crick maintained that his model of common citizenship could accommodate multiculturalism, and went on to refute some of the criticisms levelled against him:

> To demand full acceptance rather than toleration is to demand assimilation rather than integration, a single common culture rather than, what we have long had, a pluralist society. The practices of a common citizenship hold together real differences of national, religious and ethnic identities to the mutual advantage of minorities and majorities alike (Crick, 2000a: 135–6).

As we have seen, four years later Olssen still accused Crick of being essentially 'assimilationist', but this seems rather harder to maintain in the light of this more sophisticated argument. Indeed, Osler and Starkey largely conceded the same point when they wrote, 'there may be elements of a national identity which all might share, but this core identity might be supplemented so that individuals might identify with the nation in a variety of ways' (2000: 12). It seems that the debate on this point simply revolved around the nature and extent of this 'core' identity. This is an issue that goes to the heart of contemporary political philosophy and citizenship theory. For example, Michael Walzer explores the limits to the individual construction of identity (Walzer, 1997), Will Kymlicka discusses the extent to which states can make demands from minority groups with distinctive values that are in tension with the majority (Kymlicka, 1995), and even Rawls' justification for establishing a minimum common mutual commitment can be seen as significant for this debate, insofar as it establishes bonds between people simply on the grounds of shared status as members of a polity (Rawls, 1971). Given Crick's avowedly civic republican stance, we should not be surprised that his vision of citizenship was one which relied on a strong shared civic identity, although as such it faced the same challenges as

New Labour's later policy statements about identity and belonging (discussed in Chapter 3).

A final criticism I shall consider in this section concerns Crick's preference for promoting a rather abstract model of citizenship, from which citizenship education is derived. Crick's three strands share some similarities with Marshall's classic conceptualization of citizenship rights, which he described under three headings – civil, political and social (Marshall, 1964). One criticism levelled at Marshall was that he did not pay sufficient attention to the role of agency – the political processes that led to changes in rights (Kivisto and Faist, 2007: 51–6). Similarly, some commentators have argued that the discussion of citizenship in the Crick Report seems remarkably disengaged from the real experiences of citizens in Britain. The seeds of this criticism are already present within the final report, which acknowledges that some of the respondents in the consultation process referred to 'communities of great ethnic diversity and to communities where much of the population felt disenfranchised' (Advisory Group on Citizenship, 1998: 78). As we have seen, Osler and others criticized this failure to engage more directly with the experiences of inequality (Osler, 2000a) and Faulks took up the point later by arguing that 'the main weakness of the Report is its failure to tackle the issue of structural disadvantage and its implications for equal citizenship' (Faulks, 2006b: 128). Whilst it is certainly the case that one can fit debates about structural inequality into the Crick framework if one wants to, it is equally the case that Crick did not place such concerns at the heart of citizenship himself.

One might argue, as did McLaughlin, that because of the limitations of space and the need to create a clear framework, the Crick Report cannot really be criticized on these grounds. This view rests on Crick's own argument that the framework existed for educators to do what they wanted with, and that the exhortation to consider controversial issues invited educators to engage in critical interpretations (McLaughlin, 2000: 552). However, one might also argue, as did Gillborn, that the failure to be more explicit rendered citizenship education a mere 'placebo', which would do little more than cover up aspects of the institutional racism experienced by many Black people in Britain, not least in schools (Gillborn, 2006).

It is clear from the foregoing discussion that the abstract model of citizenship discussed in the Crick Report left some major issues unexplored in relation to thinking about the experience of citizenship for members of different communities in a multicultural society. It is equally clear from the growing significance of political debates around identity and belonging that this became an area that would be tempting for politicians to return to – and this became the main focus of the Ajegbo Review, which was given the following remit:

- Review the teaching specifically of ethnic, religious and cultural diversity across the curriculum to age 19.
- In relation to Citizenship, explore particularly whether or not 'modern British social and cultural history' should be a fourth pillar of the Citizenship curriculum (Ajegbo, 2007: 14).

The review sought to sidestep the politicians' rhetoric regarding Britishness – indeed one of the bullet points in the summary at the start of the Review reported that many of those consulted were uneasy with the term (Ajegbo, 2007: 8) – and instead the Review favoured a discussion of identity and diversity in Britain. Thus it avoided the controversial task of identifying Britishness and British values, which was subsequently pursued by the Ministry of Justice through a nationwide consultation on the governance of Britain and the nature of Britishness.[7] Starkey has argued that, despite the criticisms of Crick (discussed above) and academics' calls for a more thorough analysis of identity and diversity, it was actually the security agenda which led the government to review this area of citizenship education policy (Starkey, 2008). This resonated with the broader policy developments in which general notions of 'community' gave way to a sharper focus on belonging and identity, criticisms of multiculturalism and the promotion of community cohesion. As Cantle has argued *faith* in particular 'will play an increasingly important role in determining identity and has been something of a political obsession since 9/11 and the London and Madrid bombings' (Cantle, 2008: 25).

This context is borne out in the Ajegbo Review text, which included 29 references[8] to cohesion (27 in relation to community cohesion and two in relation to social cohesion) whilst the Crick Report included just one reference to 'civic cohesion'. The Review made clear connections between teaching about citizenship and diversity and the Education and Inspections Act (2006), which imposed a duty on schools to promote community cohesion. It also made reference to the notion of community (not linked to cohesion) in a variety of ways. Within 104 references to community or communities it is used as a suffix to the following terms: local, religious, subject, school, whole, wider, global,

---

[7] This was available at the time on a dedicated website http://governance.justice.gov.uk.

[8] I have included all the text in the Review except for the schemes of work in the appendix. Because some key terms were repeated in these schemes, I felt including these would distort the overall totals.

white, Muslim, traveller; and as a prefix to the terms: representatives, leaders, languages and relations. Clearly this variety illustrates a difference with the Crick Report, which tended to use the term community in a more abstract philosophical sense, to reiterate the civic republican roots of Crick's vision or to simply refer to 'local community/ies', without specifying what they might be.

As one would expect, given the brief of the Review, there are many references to identity and diversity and other related terms.

- There are 107 occurrences of the terms 'ethnic' or 'ethnicity'.
- The terms 'diversity' or 'diverse' are used 350 times.
- 'Racist' or 'racism' occur 34 times.
- The terms 'minority' or 'minorities' are used 45 times.

Whilst avoiding any particular view of Britishness, the Review argued that it was important for government to think about how a common and inclusive sense of citizenship could be fostered:

> What is evident is that in order to acknowledge diversity effectively, the curriculum needs to provide resources that promote 'collective identities' and challenge ideologies that build the social constructs of 'the nation' and 'national identity' to the exclusion of minority groups (Ajegbo, 2007: 38).

In practice, as well as avoiding direct engagement with the notion of Britishness, the Review also sidestepped the debate about the extent to which government and schools should seek to promote a common 'core' civic identity and tended to focus on the inadequate nature of many schools' current provision in relation to teaching about diversity. The Ajegbo Review incorporated a consultation exercise in schools and the following quotation from a pupil in one of these schools provides a clear summary of the position adopted by the Review's authors:

> We don't learn about different people in the UK, we just learn about people with different cultures around the world (Ajegbo, 2007: 41).

There was a strong assumption running through the Review that learning about one's own identity (much is made of the notion of multiple identities here) and the diversity within the UK (at local, regional and national level) are the most important areas for action. One of the key concerns therefore was that many schools appeared not to engage with the notion of diversity as it is played out in real people's lives within the UK as a whole and within the local area served by the school.

In pursuing this point the Review criticized the paucity of teaching about black and multiethnic UK history and the 'lip-service' approach adopted to Black History Month (Ajegbo, 2007: 41). It also developed a theme about the absence of opportunities for White children to reflect on and value their own identities, arguing that 'some indigenous white pupils' experience of identity issues in the curriculum is that they have negative perceptions of UK/English identities' (Ajegbo, 2007: 6). This theme was developed throughout the Review and several quotes from pupils were used to illustrate the problem:

> 'We spoke to one white British pupil in Year 3, for instance, who, after hearing in a class discussion how the rest of the class came from countries such as the Congo, Portugal, Trinidad and Tobago and Poland, said that she "came from nowhere"' (Ajegbo, 2007: 30).
>
> 'A girl in one of our case study schools said, "I do feel sometimes that there is no white history. There's either Black History Month or they do Muslims and Sikhs. We learn about that but we don't learn about white people, so we feel a bit left out as well"' (Ajegbo, 2007: 30).
>
> 'You're bored with it, you're just British' (Ajegbo, 2007: 31).
>
> 'I'm not from a Caribbean country or an exotic country or even France or Spain. I'm from nowhere like that, I'm just plain British' (Ajegbo, 2007: 31).

In responding to the feelings of the pupils quoted above, the Review's authors argued that:

> It makes no sense in our report to focus on minority ethnic pupils without trying to address and understand the issues for white pupils. It is these white pupils whose attitudes are overwhelmingly important in creating community cohesion (Ajegbo, 2007: 30).

This is an important formulation as it implies that the main obstacle to community cohesion lies within the white British population's lack of under-standing of diversity and in their lack of a positive ethnic identity. This lead to the recommendation that:

> Teachers need to be able, in different contexts, to promote the identities and self worth of indigenous white pupils, white working class pupils, mixed heritage pupils and minority (and sometimes majority) ethnic pupils, and at the same time to be aware of religion and the multiple identities we all live with (Ajegbo, 2007: 66).

As noted above, the Review tended to focus on building self esteem for one's own identity and a deeper understanding and appreciation of the identities of others.

It also argued that a critical awareness of how we construct multiple or hybrid identities is important. The Review did not quite state it so boldly, but one is left with the impression that somehow a positive personal identity, combined with an understanding of the complex process of identity construction and an awareness of how this process plays out in other people's lives, should lead to increased community cohesion. On this reading it appears that the common citizenship to be achieved through this process is actually an appreciation that we are all involved in the same struggle to construct our identities and that we can respect one another for the different ways in which this process plays out. This logic is reminiscent of the Commission on Integration and Cohesion's discussion of multiple identities, which asserts that research in Northern Ireland suggests that 'people with more complex and multiple sources of identity are more positive about other groups, more integrated and less prejudiced' (discussed in McGhee, 2008: 102).

Cantle argued that we need to go further than merely learning about ourselves and one another and stated that one of the tenets of community cohesion was that such an understanding should be learned through 'strong and positive relationships... developed between people from different backgrounds in the workplace, in schools and within neighbourhoods' (Cantle, 2008: 188). This was reflected to some extent in the Ajegbo Review's recommendation that schools should develop 'linking' programmes to enable pupils to work with others in different contexts and learn from and with them (Ajegbo, 2007: 63). Although as we have already noted, the Ajegbo Review also claimed that shared action would follow from identity formation and feelings of solidarity, rather than vice versa.

The Review tended to focus almost exclusively on the nature of identity but it did not engage with other social and economic dimensions to the lived experiences of different communities (Jerome and Shilela, 2007). There was one single reference to 'inequalities' in the entire review and that occurred in a discussion of why 'anti-racist' education went into decline. Anti-racists were described as 'keen to provide the politically correct explanation of why colonialism and imperialism have resulted in a world in which racism, class inequalities and sexual oppression are ubiquitous around the world... they became easy to lampoon because of their insistence on white guilt and political correctness' (Ajegbo, 2007: 26). Leaving aside the accuracy of this caricature of anti-racists and their demise it seems significant that this should be the only reference to inequality. In the following section the authors argued that whilst these 'old hierarchies' must not be ignored, we have entered a new period in which Eastern European immigration has stopped immigration being seen in simple racial terms, and in which white working class boys' underachievement has emerged as a particular problem and religion has become more significant (Ajegbo, 2007: 27).

Gilroy has argued that the most significant source of alienation and marginalization experienced by some people in Britain in the period under discussion was not the differences in identity and values but was actually the erosion of traditional forms of welfare and the market oriented policies initiated by the Thatcher governments and continued under the banner of the Third Way by Tony Blair and Gordon Brown (Gilroy, 2004: 135). One does not have to share this view entirely to recognize the validity of introducing elements other than values and identity into the analysis of contemporary citizenship and community relations. Indeed, in the same year as the Ajegbo Review was published, the Commission on Integration and Cohesion published its 'Interim Statement' which acknowledged these insights and recognized, as Ajegbo did not, that:

> Integration and cohesion policies cannot be a substitute for national policies to reduce deprivation and provide people with more opportunities: tackling inequality is an absolute precondition for integration and cohesion (Commission on Integration and Cohesion, 2007: 21).

This demonstrated that reports undertaken for the government *could* engage with this dimension and that difference need not be reduced to the realm of identity and values. This seems to suggest that although the Ajegbo Review tackled issues of identity and diversity in a more thorough-going way than the Crick Report, and advised teachers much more explicitly about what constitutes good practice in this area, it is nevertheless vulnerable to some of the same criticisms levelled at Crick – that the issues of difference were not sufficiently related to the reality of inequality (see for example Faulks, 2006b). This absence inevitably leads one to question the extent to which such accounts of citizenship education sufficiently accommodate the real experiences of citizens.

The implications of this kind of approach can be seen by comparing an early draft version and the final published version of the revised Citizenship programmes of study (as part of the new National Curriculum for 2008). The text below was not published by the QCA but was circulated between members of the working party and represents the consensus achieved at the end of the first day of discussions.[9] It is perhaps telling that this early draft produced by

---

[9] I was a member of the working group and it is significant to note that the initial redrafting took place a full year before the publication of the Ajegbo Review, indicating that some changes in relation to diversity and identity were already being considered.

teachers, other educationalists and QCA officers in February 2006 acknowledged that in Citizenship pupils should learn about racism and inequality as part of the required knowledge and understanding:

Identities and communities

- The diversity of national, regional, religious, and ethnic identities in the UK, and the need for mutual respect and understanding in communities, and ways of *challenging racism and inequalities.*
- Britain as part of Europe and the world as a global community and the political, social, environmental and economic *impact of global inequality*, and the importance of sustainable development (personal records of working group minutes, my emphasis).

In this version of the programme of study, the concept of inequality was foregrounded. Some on the working group felt that this emphasis was important, both because it described the reality of our society and because a citizenship education programme which fails to acknowledge the reality of citizens' lives seems likely to be seen as an irrelevance. This draft was revised through an additional re-drafting process within the QCA and DfES, and in the programme of study published for further consultation on the QCA website early in 2007, the relevant text had been revised in such a manner as to minimize the reality of inequality. The re-drafted programme of study required teachers to teach pupils about:

- The *shared* values and changing nature of UK society, including the diversity of beliefs, cultures, identities and traditions.
- Reasons for migration to, from and within the UK and the impact of movement and settlement on places and communities.
- The UK's role and interconnections with the European Union and the rest of Europe, the Commonwealth, the United Nations and *the world as a global community* and the political, economic, environmental and social implications of this.

The final version for implementation from September 2008 included some slight rephrasing but the meaning was largely unchanged – significantly, references to inequality were absent in the Key Stage 3 programme of study, although the term was used in relation to global inequalities in Key Stage 4. There were also additional requirements, which derived more or less directly from the Ajegbo recommendations, and which were outlined in a sub-section of 'key concepts' where 'Identities and diversity: living together in the UK' was explained as including learning about the complex and changing nature of identity, diverse communities in the UK and the links between them, global connections and community cohesion. As we noted with the Crick Report, whilst it is possible to interpret the form of words in a critical manner, it is also easier not to. What is obvious from these changes is that citizenship education was much more clearly drawn into the wider policy nexus promoting 'community cohesion' and the debates about 'identity' the government was pursuing in relation to Britishness.

Summary

Crick and Ajegbo illustrate the ways in which official conceptions of citizenship education developed over the decade from 1997 to 2007, and provide some clarification of the purposes of the Citizenship curricula in 2002 and 2008. The three discourses, which combine to define the new citizen, were constant themes in the schemes of work and were more clearly identified as key principles in the 2008 version of the curriculum.

Thus it is clear that official conceptions of Citizenship included a commitment that pupils should appreciate their rights and their responsibilities as citizens, although there was some confusion about quite how this should play out in relation to issues of school governance. Although student voice and school councils were endorsed by the DCSF in 2007 (Whitty and Wisby, 2007) they were not statutory and so learning about rights and responsibilities would remain, for many pupils, a preparation for citizenship rather than a direct experience. The commitment to active citizenship was also a clear area of continuity and marked the Citizenship curriculum out from other subjects as particularly challenging for schools to implement fully. Consequently we have seen how the QCA clarifications and inspection guidance have in some ways minimized the expectations, in order to make them more manageable for schools. Finally, we have explored the ways in which the community and diversity discourse has developed. Here one can see most clearly how citizenship education policy was influenced by shifting conceptions in government about diversity and identity, and about citizenship and belonging.

The new citizen represented in the 2008 curriculum was expected to under-stand the complex processes through which individuals construct their sense of self through multiple identities, and through a critical appreciation of this process they were expected to come to respect others on the same journey and learn to live with the differences that emerge. They should also endorse a shared core of values to sustain community cohesion and develop a sense of common identity, although the government failed to clarify exactly what would constitute such an identity. Wisely perhaps, the QCA chose to steer clear of politicians' calls for the promotion of national identity by carefully phrasing the curriculum so that students learned about 'what it means to be a citizen of the UK' (QCA, 2007). It is likely this aspect of the overall project would have been controversial, even without the on-going prevarication about what values and identities were to be promoted; but in the event, there was some evidence that many schools opted to *explore* notions of Britishness and identity in the light of the Ajegbo Review, rather than set out to teach any explicit model of identity (Hand and Pearce, 2009, Jerome and Clemitshaw, 2012).

In thinking about McCowan's (2008) framework for policy analysis, there were some very clear and consistent elements in the government's model of citizenship. There were also some tensions and limitations evident in the conception of the ideal citizen, which were reproduced, and sometimes exacerbated, in the curricular framework and guidance.[10] Whilst the impetus behind the construction of the new citizen was clear, the precise formulation was less so and in the following chapters we turn to consider how such issues were interpreted in schools.

[10] The inclusion of active citizenship in teaching and assessment frameworks does make the English policy less problematic than the Brazilian one analysed by McCowan. In his case study he noted a clear contradiction between the democratic content of the curriculum and the traditional teaching methods adopted for 'transmitting' the content. In England the existence of active citizenship in the curriculum held out the possibility of greater 'harmony' between ends and means.

Part Two

Implementing the Vision

5

Citizenship – More and Less Than a Subject

'A subject at last!'

Crick opens his 'Essays on Citizenship' (Crick, 2000a) with these words, although at the time of writing this was true in only a limited sense. Citizenship had just been included in the revised national curriculum for 11–16 year olds (QCA, 2000), but schools were given two years to prepare for the implementation (a process which took much longer in some schools). The NFER was funded by the government to evaluate the implementation of Citizenship in an eight year longitudinal research project, and OfSTED also issued reports on how the subject was developing in schools. The evidence demonstrated that there is a difference between being a subject on paper and a subject in schools. This chapter explores this difference and outlines the role that teachers played in those early years of developing and nurturing Citizenship as a school subject.

Translating any educational initiative into classroom reality involves a range of bureaucratic, managerial, financial and pedagogic hurdles with the potential for misunderstandings and reinterpretations at each stage. The discussion in Chapter 2 acknowledged the various stages at which significant re-interpretations of curriculum policy occur – first between the statement of the vision and the construction of curriculum guidance, then in the translation of that guidance into school programmes, and finally in the students' engagement with the subject. Along the way policy-makers at all levels draw on evidence about the policy area, come to a view about the political role of policy and interpret it in the light of their prevailing concerns and the restrictions imposed by their local context. Significantly, Trowler (2003) draws attention to the inevitable 'muddling through' as policy works its way through conflict and compromise at each level of interpretation and implementation. Policy is also characterized by a 'lossy' transmission to and within schools, in which documents literally get lost, but are also filtered, summarized and reinterpreted as the policy works its way through the system, thus losing significant detail. Creating a new school subject would seem to be a particularly tricky example of policy implementation and to highlight some of these challenges we will focus on two key areas, the vision for citizenship education and the creation of a subject identity. We then turn to consider the implications of these challenges for creating a group of teachers who can lead the subject.

The vision for citizenship

'…..a subject but also more than a subject' (Ofsted, 2006: 10).

As we saw in Chapter 4 the Crick Report outlined the case for citizenship education in England and proposed a version influenced by civic republicanism. Much was made of the emphasis on skills and on participation, distinguishing the new English model from a drier civics model (Advisory Group on Citizenship, 1998: 25), and this gave Citizenship in England its most distinctive characteristic. It is the pupils' interaction with the real world, which is hinted at in the idea of Citizenship being 'more than a subject'. How then did this vision translate to the classroom? In 2006 the OfSTED publication 'Towards Consensus?' summarized some of the main themes emerging from inspections of Citizenship teaching in schools. It asked, (somewhat rhetorically):

> There is plenty to argue about in citizenship. Why was it introduced, really? Is it about good behaviour or asking awkward questions? Can the ambition of citizenship education be fulfilled? Did the National Curriculum get it right? Why have many schools been slow to develop strong models of provision for citizenship? Is the infrastructure yet in place? (Ofsted, 2006: 5).

Superficially it seemed that those who observed the teaching of the subject in the first few years could not discern a particular vision for the subject. Had the active nature of Citizenship in schools been diluted, lost or was it yet to emerge?

The Citizenship programmes of study for 11–16 year olds were significantly smaller than the other eleven subjects and appeared last in the printed version of the national curriculum (the subjects were not in alphabetical order and the order was left unexplained – although it does start with English, Mathematics and Science). The document itself was a very quick read – 'no other curriculum subject was stated so briefly, left so much to the individual teacher in different schools in different circumstances' (Crick, 2002c: 499). Crick presented this strong 'bare bones' approach as both a virtue (allowing freedom for schools) and a necessity (the difficulty of a government specifying political content).

To compensate for its brevity Crick suggested that teachers should read the programme of study alongside the Crick Report and he believed that this would enable them to read through the programme of study to the truer vision in the report, 'teachers are not blind horses' (Crick, 2002c: 500). Much, it seemed, was being placed on the shoulders of teachers.

In relation to Trowlers' description of policy implementation as a 'lossy' process we might consider how likely it is that teachers read the Crick Report before implementing the Citizenship programmes of study. Indeed, once the schemes of work were drawn up and disseminated within some schools, it is possible to imagine some teachers (especially those who were teaching outside of their perceived subject expertise) who would not even be aware of the programmes of study, just the lessons they had been asked to teach. The answer to this question was provided by the first NFER longitudinal report, which stated:

> While the majority of teachers (74 per cent) claimed to understand the aims and purposes of citizenship education, over one-third (38 per cent) were uncertain about the detail of the new curriculum that would be introduced in September 2002. There was limited familiarity with the key citizenship curriculum documents, such as the Curriculum Order and Qualifications and Curriculum Authority (QCA) schemes of work, and little or no familiarity with the key policy texts, notably the Crick Report and Post-16 report… College leaders and tutors were even more uncertain about the content of, and background to, the citizenship curriculum (Kerr et al., 2003: viii).

It was perhaps optimistic to expect the first wave of Citizenship teachers – none qualified in Citizenship – to read the Crick Report and understand the vision presented. The vision needed to be contained more explicitly in the programme of study itself, which was being used as the starting point (and ending point) for many teachers. In terms of defining the subject, the brevity of the programme is not a strength but a weakness. However compelling the Crick Report's statement of its case, there was simply not enough 'bandwidth' in the few pages of the initial programme of study to translate this vision clearly. Thus whilst Crick's intentions for leaving teachers space to interpret the curriculum might be seen as laudable in some ways, it did also assume that teachers would be able to identify the key purposes of the subject. Perhaps this was an unfounded assumption given that most of the people responsible for Citizenship would inevitably have been specialists in a subject other than Citizenship.

In particular many schools did not understand the nature of active citizenship.

Active citizenship is admittedly not easy to define, as discussed in Chapter 4 (see for example Annette, 2000), however, the brevity of the programme of study meant that the distinctive nature of Citizenship, the element that made it 'more than a subject', was conveyed to teachers in a single sentence.

> [pupils should be taught to] negotiate, decide and take part responsibly in both school and community based activities (QCA, 2000).

It is not surprising that some teachers failed to fully grasp the idea from this alone. Indeed, one of the early subject reports from Ofsted noted that the active strand of citizenship was being misinterpreted.

> The implementation of citizenship as a National Curriculum subject has been beset by problems of definition. Issues around the subject title itself have been discussed above. Within the programme of study, too, there is much that is taken out of context or misunderstood... A major issue lies in the nature and relationship of the three strands: 'enquiry and communi-cation' and 'participation and responsible action' activate the 'knowledge and understanding about becoming informed citizens'. Enquiry in science and participation in sport, meritorious as they are in their own right, are not about National Curriculum citizenship, unless they are dealing with material from the citizenship programme of study (Ofsted, 2005a).

Based on the brief wording of the programme of study, schools, it seems, were passing off team work in sports as active citizenship.

The lack of understanding about the nature of active citizenship was present in the inspectors too, such that OfSTED needed to publish advice to their own team. The following extract is taken from a newsletter circulated to OfSTED inspectors, which provides institutional updates and issues arising from inspections:

> Some inspectors have been crediting work as citizenship when it is not part of the National Curriculum programme of study. For example, work in other subjects on developing enquiry and communication or on participation has been accepted as citizenship. Collaborative work in PE may be done well and be of considerable value to pupils, but it is not participation in relation to one of the knowledge topics in the first strand of the citizenship National Curriculum' (Ofsted, 2003).

Beyond the programme of study teachers were issued with further guidance and schemes of work to help introduce the subject. But even here the notion of active citizenship was not clearly defined.

> Citizenship activities…*may* also address aspects of knowledge and under-
> standing about becoming informed citizens, and of developing skills of enquiry
> and communication (QCA, 2001: 1, my emphasis).

The use of the word 'may' draws attention to the possibility that such activities
'may not' address such knowledge. As we have seen, such unclear guidance led
some to pursue Physical Education as a possible candidate for active citizenship,
regardless of the lack of connection to knowledge. Some of the other suggestions for active citizenship included:

> Activities such as reception duties, office support and acting as guides for
> visitors. They have a clear job description, and criteria against which they and
> others can assess their achievements in the role… the running of sports and
> other school activities… Playing 'the real game' (a careers education simulation)
> (QCA, 2001: 2–3).

Although these examples are chosen to make a case they are themselves clearly
indicative of confusion around the idea of active citizenship. This confusion
continued throughout the period of implementation and in a 2009 chief
examiner's report for one of the exam boards offering Citizenship short course
GCSE the comments on coursework still pointed out that some schools were
using work experience and sports activities as the basis of 'active citizenship'
coursework, which was hampering students' chances of gaining good marks
because in many cases they were simply inappropriate (Edexcel, 2009: 9).

In conclusion then, although the Crick Report did indeed set out a clear
model for citizenship education, and Crick's subsequent publications elucidated
this, there was a lack of clarity in the curriculum documents and guidance,
which teachers would use as their starting point. Crucially therefore the difficult
process of introducing a new subject into the curriculum in secondary schools
was marred by confusion about what do and how to do it. Whilst one may
agree with Crick that one should not treat teachers like 'blind horses' it does
seem that the introduction of the national curriculum for Citizenship created
a situation in which many teachers felt they were left stumbling around in the
dark, occasionally led further astray by QCA and OfSTED, before eventually
being reined in.

It can also be argued that as so much was being left to teachers it was crucial
that a substantial and enthusiastic body of teachers existed in schools to articulate the vision in an engaging and relevant way to pupils. This though would
have required a more radical and more thorough approach to teacher education,
which will be discussed later in this chapter.

Subject identity

'Civics… is to political literacy… as biology is to sex. It is not hard to imagine which students would prefer to consider' (Crick quoted in Davies, 2003b: 6).

Section 4 of The Crick Report included a number of 'essential recommendations' but the issue of subject identity was left unexplored. The key recommendation was that schools should have a responsibility to enable pupils to achieve the learning outcomes outlined in the report, but the mechanism for this should be left to schools, allowing for local initiatives and school-specific solutions. The report stated that schools should spend 'no more than five per cent of curriculum time' on achieving these outcomes and listed tutor time, general studies, blocks and modules as suitable alternatives to a regular weekly period (Advisory Group on Citizenship, 1998: 22). In addition, the report indicated that subject combinations should be explored, as should connections to whole school issues. This represents another meaning to the phrase that Citizenship is 'more than a subject', that is, it would be statutory but not rely on gaining a traditional subject 'slot' on the timetable.

On one reading then the Crick Report did not seem to be particularly wedded to the notion of subject identity at all, preferring to specify general expectations (outcomes), whilst remaining neutral on the curriculum (or other) methods to achieve this. There was no specific mention, in the main body of the report, of Citizenship as a separate subject in its own right, indeed the report specifically rejected the implications of becoming a subject (in the sense defined in the English national curriculum) by arguing against detailed programmes of study and assessment (Advisory Group on Citizenship, 1998: 22). Whilst an enthusiast might interpret this as a brave new approach to the curriculum, it is easy to imagine many teachers seeing Citizenship (as described in the report) as somewhat 'less than a subject', lacking as the model did three of the main formal characteristics of subject identity – a detailed programme of study, a place in the timetable, and a means of assessment. The only section in the report which acknowledged the complexity of creating and implementing a new subject was the discussion of the feedback from consultation exercises. Here there was a clear acknowledgement of the debate between those who argued 'subject status' was essential to ensure this initiative did not go the way of the earlier cross-curricular Citizenship theme and the opponents who feared an interest group was paving the way for another separate subject, which would compete with others for curriculum time (Advisory Group on Citizenship, 1998: 73–7).

It is clear that the commitment to becoming a subject extended only as far as subject status was seen as necessary for Citizenship to become an entitlement in schools, but there was little interest in, nor attention paid to, how this would work within schools, which are of course primarily organized around 'subjects'.

Perhaps the confusion over this crucial issue, or at least the explanation for the idea that Citizenship could stand alone within the curriculum as a different kind of entitlement, reflected in part Crick's own roots. McCowan has argued that in this regard it is significant that Crick was first and foremost a political theorist with a commitment to political education, rather than an educationalist with a passion for politics (McCowan, 2009: Ch.3). It is not surprising therefore that he had a tendency to focus on the broader vision for Citizenship, whilst leaving the practicalities of pedagogy and school organization to others to work out. In relation to the Advisory Group he led, of course there were some relatively detailed recommendations about how Citizenship might be integrated within schools, but these do not acknowledge the problems that were so evident in the comments from people working within education, where the nature of subject identity is much more sharply outlined.

In brief then, the final report included clues about the problems that would flow from creating a new subject (rivalry with other subjects; absorption into PSHE; lack of status among teachers, parents and pupils; problems establishing a foothold in the timetable) but it failed to work through how those problems could be overcome. Instead, there was a faith that teachers would somehow work it out in practice if they were required to do so.

This faith in teachers to find a solution failed to seriously acknowledge the warnings of professionals who were consulted by the Advisory Group and also ignored the clear warnings from a previous attempt to integrate citizenship education across the curriculum. An earlier version of the national curriculum included five cross-curricular themes that were intended to permeate across the core and foundation subjects as well as being taught through discrete provision where necessary. The research into the failure of these themes to establish a foothold in most schools was discussed in Chapter 2, but in brief Whitty et al. (1994) argued that it was very hard for them to succeed in a school environment where strong subjects dominated the timetable, resource allocation, teachers' identities, and ultimately students' expectations. Students had little awareness of the themes as distinct entities from the host subjects and no distinctive teaching methods or recognition and realization rules emerged. Further, many teachers saw the themes as a distraction from their 'core' business.

The five themes themselves centred around the personal and social lives of pupils to a greater extent than the more traditional academic subjects. In this regard the recognition rules of the host subject became a problem. For example, Whitty et al. noted that students felt reluctant to talk about how they brush their teeth in a Science lesson, feeling that such talk would be inappropriate. Even though the teacher was trying to incorporate a cross-curricular theme the pupils were not used to using their own lives as a starting and ending point for learning in Science and so did not feel at ease with changing the implicit rules governing discourse in the subject.

Theoretically then, in the 1990s Citizenship did not flourish as a cross-curricular theme because, in part, its content demanded a specific discourse. In practice it did not flourish, at least in part, because teachers on the whole were not enthusiastic and saw it as counter-productive to their core business. It is not surprising then that four years into the implementation phase, with schools free to use a cross curricular model and only 500 specialist teachers trained, OfSTED found that the permeation model was not successful:

> While it should be acknowledged that citizenship can be taught through other subjects and can be of benefit to them, cross-curricular work in most cases results in an uneasy and often unsuccessful compromise (Ofsted, 2006).

Compared to other subjects, Citizenship is not robustly *classified*, which is to say that its boundaries with other subjects are not tightly drawn. Indeed Crick suggested that if the 'order is read carefully' then much of the content can be taught through other subjects (Crick 200:10), and such advice is only possible where the classification is weak and the subject's boundaries are blurred. In one sense this blurring is inevitable as the more a subject relates to current social issues and is made relevant to the lives of students then the greater the overlap with Citizenship. This causes a problem for Citizenship in terms of establishing a clearly differentiated role in the secondary school curriculum. It seems that Citizenship, if weakly classified and loosely framed (and it can be argued it must be so to retain its topicality and relevance), can merge readily with cross-curricular or whole school 'ethos' conceptions. Once again it seems the subject was set up in a way that made it hard to make headway against the backdrop of an established collection of strongly classified and strongly framed subjects.

One way for the subject to survive in this environment would be to create distinctive recognition and realization rules in the minds of students. In this way the weak classification and framing might be overcome if students were able to develop a sense of a subject identity through its methods and language. For example, at one school students understand that Citizenship is centred on ideas of 'change action', which emphasises the active citizenship dimension. Another school encourages students to express their opinions on display boards, which then form the basis for on-going discussions on topical issues. In these schools students had begun to develop a sense of a subject, an expectation of the methods used and the discourses expected from them. In these schools Citizenship is taught by specialist teachers who have developed a distinct pedagogy for the subject, and it is to these teachers that we now turn.

Teacher education

'And teachers, if I may preach before being practical, need to have a sense of mission about the new subject, to grasp the fullness of its moral and social aims' (Crick, 2002d).

In the consultation conferences, which discussed the recommendations in the Crick Report, pre-service and in-service teacher training emerged as issues that should receive closer attention by the Advisory Group, as they would be essential in determining the success of the initiative. This was the second most frequently mentioned issue in the responses to the initial report submitted to the Advisory Group (Advisory Group on Citizenship, 1998: 75–9). Subsequently the only explicit reference to teacher training was that (a) teacher trainers, among others, should receive a 'clear statement of what is meant by citizenship education and their central role in it' (Advisory Group on Citizenship, 1998: 23) and (b) that a standing Commission on Citizenship Education should be established to work out the details of, and monitor progress in, the implementation of Citizenship, including the requirements for teacher training (Advisory Group on Citizenship, 1998: 24).

In a section entitled 'The Way Forward' there was some more detail about the perceived implications for teacher education – both pre-service and in-service. Here the report advised that the national standards for qualified teacher status (QTS) should 'pay due regard to the importance of citizenship' (Advisory Group on Citizenship, 1998: 30), which was significant because these standards were the generic criteria all pre-service teachers had to meet in order to gain employment as qualified teachers. The report also called for the creation of a special commission to liaise with the general body responsible for funding and regulating pre-service and in-service teacher training in England, the Teacher Training Agency (this agency was re-named the Teacher Development Agency in 2005 and will be referred to henceforward as the TDA). The commission's role would be to provide guidance on how to interpret the standards to ensure trainee teachers developed the knowledge and skills necessary to teach Citizenship effectively, although this body was never established. The clear expectation here was that there would not be specialist training courses, as reference was made to subjects which are likely to have substantial common ground with Citizenship, such as English, History and Geography, as well as subjects in the 'other' category of pre-service courses, which included Social Science, Politics and Philosophy programmes.

In practice one aspect of these recommendations was implemented and the standards for Qualified Teacher Status were amended to include a reference, for *all* qualifying teachers to be familiar with the requirements of the Citizenship programmes of study (this was omitted from the 2008 revised standards). However, this was accompanied by the funding of specific Citizenship training places for a limited number of trainee secondary teachers every year. This clearly went beyond the Crick Report's recommendations, but one could argue this was an essential step in creating a community of expert subject specialists who could develop distinctive pedagogical approaches to citizenship education and begin to establish a professional community. Although most pre-service courses in Citizenship by 2012 were single subject courses, in the first instance many institutions started joint courses (often History with Citizenship) to explore the connections between the subjects and, presumably, to make the new subject easier to integrate into existing course structures (Lewis, 2003).

Further recommendations in the Crick Report included the adaptation of other training and accreditation programmes for middle managers and headteachers, and the provision of courses and materials to help qualified teachers to develop the knowledge and skills to become Citizenship teachers. Specifically, the report argued that the TDA should provide some resources for teachers (that were independent of campaigning groups) and the Standards Fund in the Department for Education should provide resources to support regional training events involving a diverse range of organizations as a way to provide support to teachers.

In practice, one can see some of these recommendations being implemented through the TDA's funding of citizED as a Professional Resource Network (www. citized.info), and the DfES' funding of a series of regional conferences to launch citizenship education to teachers, which involved a range of citizenship organizations. In addition the DfES started a Citizenship website (now defunct), where resources and case studies were disseminated, as well as providing funding for the Association for Citizenship Teaching, to provide support and professional development for teachers of Citizenship. It took some time for the DfES to make a more concerted effort to provide in-service training for teachers who assumed responsibility for teaching Citizenship after they qualified in another subject, and when the courses came they suffered from a lack of take-up, indicating perhaps that many people had adapted to teaching Citizenship without any perceived need for training. In 2006/7 284 teachers started the course, although the target was 540 (Ofsted, 2009: 9). This lack of take up may echo the early findings of the NFER longitudinal study that staff felt confident in teaching Citizenship despite their lack of familiarity with the curriculum or key reports.

Teacher numbers

Overall the evidence suggests that specialist Citizenship teachers have a big impact on the quality of the subject in schools, and yet there is a widespread view that more should be done to ensure enough qualified Citizenship teachers were being trained (Blunkett, 2009, Ofsted, 2006). A House of Commons Committee enquiry into Citizenship recognized this in its report:

> During our inquiry, the one area that has stood out quite clearly as critical to the future development of citizenship education is the adequate training of teachers, lecturers and leaders (House of Commons Education and Skills Committee, 2007: 29).

The demand for more Citizenship teachers can be understood from a brief analysis of the numbers involved. Each year since 2001, 180–230 pre-service teachers started a Citizenship Post Graduate Certificate in Education (PGCE) course (these one-year courses were the most common route to qualify as a secondary school teacher). Assuming an average of 220 per year this means only about 2,200 Citizenship training places have been made available over the ten years to 2011 – just enough to train two thirds of the required total, if the aim was to have one qualified teacher in each of the 3,360 state maintained secondary schools in England. However, the number of training places available and the number of qualified teachers working in the education system are quite different. If one assumes a failure/dropout rate during the course of 10 per cent per cent[1], the first decade of Citizenship PGCE courses up to 2011 would have

---

[1]   This is likely to be optimistic, for example in 2006/7 the drop-out rate for Citizenship teachers was 20 per cent according to Smithers and Robinson (2008) and the TDA website showed that actually 18 per cent of Citizenship trainees failed to complete QTS, although the situation was better in 2005/6 when 86 per cent qualified, and in 2004/5 the figure was 87 per cent.

produced around 1,980 specialist teachers, although the actual non-completion rate is often much higher than assumed here (Smithers and Robinson, 2008). Not all of these would have entered teaching (assume 3 per cent do not each year) and a fair number will leave the profession each year (assume 2 per cent of teachers leave the profession each year). This would mean that there are currently a maximum of 1,565 trained Citizenship specialist teachers in secondary schools – still fewer than half the number of schools where Citizenship is supposed to be taught.

Teachers and subject identity

The PGCE courses, on the whole, have been heavily oversubscribed and have attracted well-qualified applicants (Ofsted, 2004b, Ofsted, 2005b), although, because Citizenship is not an established academic discipline at university, students are drawn from a range of subjects that have relevance to the Citizenship programme of study.[2] The fact that Citizenship PGCE students have no shared academic disciplines may also mean that the final cohort of qualified teachers may lack the academic homogeneity of other subjects. On some levels this presents no problem, and can even be a strength, however the underlying cause behind the lack of homogeneity might also be the root of some issues surrounding the subject's identity.

Consider the issue of first order subject knowledge. Citizenship students will have different areas of expertise and might not feel confident in teaching unfamiliar topics. This though is not unusual, and many History PGCE students will teach medieval history having last studied the topic as pupils at school and Science teachers are unlikely to have degree level knowledge in Physics, Chemistry and Biology. So Citizenship teachers, superficially, are no different in having to teach unfamiliar topics. Besides, the topical nature of the subject means that they should be frequently teaching new material anyway, and further, the light touch nature of the subject deliberately permits greater focus on some areas than others, allowing teachers to focus on their strengths (Crick, 2000a: 118). However the academic homogeneity of PGCE students in other subjects does make a difference. A History PGCE student might not know much

---

[2] The first degrees of the last 100 students starting their Citizenship PGCE at the Institute of Education, University of London are as follows: 15 Law, 15 Sociology, 13 Politics, 7 History and Politics, 6 Philosophy, 6 Sociology and Politics, 4 International Politics/Relations, 4 Education, 4 Public Policy/Administration, 3 Criminology, 3 Economics, 3 European studies, 3 Anthropology, 3 Media, 2 Classics, 2 Politics, Philosophy and Economics (PPE), 2 Humanities, 1 Development studies, 1 African studies, 1 Osteopathy, 1 Sport, 1 Youth and Community studies.

about castles, however she will be likely to have experienced History as a taught subject during her secondary, further and higher education. This will have some impact; the student will be familiar with the subject's teaching methods and discourse – in other words, the second order knowledge. A Science PGCE student too will be familiar with experiments, test tubes, observations etc. Their school mentors also will have a clear idea of subject identity and can help develop their teaching accordingly. In these subjects the student's lack of subject knowledge is mitigated by their prior and ongoing immersion in a subject discipline, which outlines the approaches, methods, and equipment that should be used in teaching unfamiliar material. By contrast in Citizenship, PGCE tutors have had to engage with this afresh, asking 'what subject knowledge is needed to teach citizenship education?' (Davies, 2003b).

Simply because Citizenship did not exist in most schools, the Citizenship PGCE student has generally lacked these mitigating factors which provide teachers with a clear sense of the subject. They did not study Citizenship at school, sixth form or university and their mentor did not undertake Citizenship at PGCE level. Indeed, frequently, in the early years of the Institute of Education's PGCE course, students, on their first week in placement schools, were introduced to staff and pupils as the 'experts' in citizenship education. In this context the teaching of unfamiliar material takes on a different complexion; without recourse to an established pedagogy or discourse students often resort to generic and basic methods of teaching. For example, instead of setting up a Mock UN Security Council on a topical issue a student might simply transmit the 'facts' and abstract structures of the council via PowerPoint. The student may not have experienced a United Nations role-play at school or university and their school mentor may be similarly disadvantaged. The subject pedagogy has not been experienced first-hand and so the student simply copies the generic teaching methods observed in the placement school. Of course the role of the PGCE courses was, in part, to establish and develop the very pedagogies that would help forge subject identity. If the student teacher experienced a mock UN debate during their PGCE course then this could become part of their teaching and understanding about the subject, and in turn part of the pupils' experience and expectations, although as Parker and Hess (2001) have illustrated, this transfer is far from straight forward, especially when the style of teaching is not already established in school.

Behind the issue of establishing a suitable repertoire of teaching methods and a subject specialist discourse lies a more fundamental difference between Citizenship PGCE students and their counterparts in the more established

academic domains. Historians and scientists have not only experienced the subject in their education but in doing so they have also developed the appropriate 'lens' with which to view and analyse the world. Science teaching encourages pupils to think like scientists and to view the world from this perspective. Likewise the historians. In both these subjects PGCE students may lack the first order knowledge, however they have experienced the second order knowledge and further have developed the appropriate lens which can provide a focus and direction for their teaching.

Here the academic heterogeneity of the Citizenship students becomes an issue. Some may be familiar with analysing an issue from a sociological perspective; others might be accustomed to seeking the underlying philosophical issues; others still may think like lawyers about the problem. It is not clear what the Citizenship 'lens' is, and this in part is because citizenship is a widely contested notion. So for the History student teacher the subject knowledge on certain topics may be initially missing but the pedagogy has been experienced and a subject lens is lived and experienced by the student. For the Citizenship student teacher, the subject knowledge is missing, so is the pedagogy and it is not clear what the lens should look like.

The fluidity of subject identity and lack of an obvious 'lens' also raised questions for the university tutors leading Citizenship PGCE courses. Should these develop a distinctive definition of Citizenship – perhaps one reflecting the strengths of the course tutor or the nature of the university? It would have been hard to avoid this entirely, as any course leader still had to choose exactly how much emphasis to give to any particular element. This variability was more evident at the beginning of the period, as course designers were exercising their individual judgement in the absence of substantial models of good practice in schools. Hence one PGCE model emerged based on the principles of (1) Story, (2) Trust, (3) Power and (4) Success (Sunderland, 2003), themes which were a long way from the key organizing ideas foregrounded in either the Crick Report or the programmes of study. This pattern was also seen in the programme of in-service courses which were offered to teachers who had qualified in a subject other than Citizenship, but who wanted to 'convert'. The OfSTED evaluation of these programmes highlighted how different course had different emphases, noting that some focused more heavily on subject knowledge, others on pedagogy and others still on the theoretical underpinning of the subject (Ofsted, 2009).

Conclusion

This chapter has highlighted some of the challenges that marked the introduction of Citizenship into the national curriculum. The first decade of implementation has demonstrated some enduring facts about the school curriculum and the culture of schooling and Bernstein's earlier analysis reminds us that one of the most significant factors shaping the fortunes of curriculum innovation is the nature of the curriculum which already exists. Whilst brave visions of 'new types' of subject or subjects which are 'more than subjects' make excellent rhetorical devices they may flounder when confronted with the more prosaic nature of school organization. School pupils might well ask of any subject: What are we doing? Who are we doing it with? Where are we doing it? And, how does it relate to other subjects? And these are all questions that can be answered with some certainty for other subjects in school. The following chapters take a closer look at how these issues have developed in schools, starting with an account of Citizenship from the teachers' and students' perspectives.

6

Teaching Citizenship

This chapter discusses teachers and the ideas and experiences that inform their interpretations of Citizenship. It is divided into several distinct sections, the first of which summarizes some of the wider evidence about the role of the teacher as an active agent in the construction of the curriculum. The second section outlines the two case study schools where I collected data for this study and the third section provides an overview of the formal Citizenship policy documents in one of the case study schools. Having considered the formal policy documents, the chapter moves on to the longest section which is concerned with identifying what Citizenship teachers think about Citizenship and what they aim to achieve. This final section is based on a series of interviews with teachers in the case study schools. Subsequent chapters return to the beliefs, actions and values of these Citizenship teachers in relation to the three themes of rights and responsibilities, community and diversity and active citizenship; here the discussion focuses on broader issues relating to purpose and context.

Citizenship teachers as active curriculum constructors

Whilst policy makers often tend to envisage teachers as 'conduits', who will transmit policy into the classroom, in fact they may be better perceived as 'gatekeepers' or 'controllers' (Sim, 2008). On this view the teacher is a *curriculum agent*, whose practice "is intellectual, moral and inventive" (Parker, 1987, in Sim, 2008: 263). In her study of Citizenship teachers in Singapore, Sim found that some teachers adopted positions which were essentially *conforming* to the policy makers' intentions, whilst others *reformed* the policy, through active reinterpretation. In his case study of enterprise education in Scotland, Deuchar described a similar process, in which:

'The teachers studied were perhaps beginning to 'dress' enterprise in a new set of clothes that resembled many of the characteristics of the Citizenship agenda, as a means of taking the edge off of the models of business enterprise education and profitability' (Deuchar, 2006: 544).

Deuchar notes that the freedom for teachers to make curriculum decisions in relation to Citizenship is circumscribed by wider policy constraints, such as the imperative to promote higher standards and the generally authoritarian approach to decision making in schools. Nevertheless, he maintains that through the decisions they make about how to present content in specific ways the teachers still exercise their role as curriculum agents. In some ways these countervailing pressures can actually create opportunities for agency. For example, in her study of teachers committed to global citizenship education, Schweisfurth found 'the complexity of teachers' work means that they constantly need to make judgements about where to spend their own energies, and the learning time of their students' (Schweisfurth, 2006: 49–50). This need to make individual decisions leaves significant power in the hands of teachers.

As we saw in the previous chapter, in England the minimal prescription in the Citizenship programmes of study left plenty of scope for teachers to actively interpret the curriculum in ways that would make sense in their own context. As Crick explained it:

> 'The virtue of the order is that the generality of its prescriptions will leave the school and the teacher with a good deal of freedom and discretion, more than in the other statutory subjects' (Crick, 2000a: 118).

This was for two reasons: first he felt it would be inappropriate for the state (directly through the DfE or indirectly through the QCA) to be overly prescriptive in relation to politically or morally sensitive issues; and secondly he felt it was important for Citizenship to be interpreted in ways that responded to the local context. Given this, Citizenship teachers' own views about politics and citizenship are likely to be significant in shaping their interpretation (Walkington and Wilkins, 2000).

Keddie's case study of a single teacher, whom she refers to as Mr C, demonstrates the potential of this freedom for a teacher who is fully committed to building on this foundation. Mr C is a political activist who uses his experiences around the world as teaching material, and who also creates opportunities for his students to engage in campaigns. Keddie notes that Mr C's personal commitment to promote equality and inclusion affects both his teaching style and decisions about what topics to teach, thus realising the transformative potential of citizenship education (Keddie, 2008). Keddie argues that because many teachers will not turn the Citizenship programmes of study into a transformative experience, this reflects a flaw in the curriculum and necessarily limits the impact of citizenship education. This criticism seems to rather miss the point, which is simply that teachers will exercise their agency in relation to the curriculum in ways which reflect their own personal beliefs, commitments and understandings. This has been illustrated by surveys of Citizenship teachers in England, which demonstrated that their personal scepticism about a political issue, for example in relation to patriotism, led them to resist 'promoting' messages with which they were uneasy (Davies et al., 2005; Hand and Pearce, 2009; Jerome and Clemitshaw, 2012).

Other studies have confirmed that different political beliefs tend to lead teachers to construct Citizenship rather differently. Leenders and her colleagues have demonstrated in their research in the Netherlands that teachers' own beliefs shape their classroom practice (Leenders et al., 2008) and Myers' research in Brazil demonstrates the impact of teachers' own political activism on their practice (Myers, 2009). Osler also notes other influencing factors in her small scale study of Citizenship teachers in England, for example she observes that the History specialists she spoke to tended to focus predominantly on the national picture, whilst the Citizenship specialists tended to focus on local issues (Osler, 2010a: 17). In this chapter I consider some of the ways in which five teachers have sought to shape Citizenship in their schools and to explore the beliefs that have shaped their interpretations of the subject.

Two case studies

I collected data in two secondary schools in order to gain a deeper insight than could be gleaned from the national research that had already been conducted into the implementation of Citizenship. Both the case study schools were chosen because they were deemed to be strong examples of institutions which had taken Citizenship seriously, and where it was likely I would be able to engage with respondents who had substantial experience of Citizenship. I was influenced in this decision by Michael Apple's argument that researchers should consider where to spend their time wisely, and that there was much to learn from schools where one could study success (Apple, 2008). This felt like an approach that was politically worthwhile, and also pragmatically important, as I was primarily interested in using the case study element of the research design to explore the Citizenship related experiences of participants in schools, not in accounting for the absence of such experiences. This approach was therefore influenced by the positive attraction to understand what was happening in schools where Citizenship was being taken seriously, and the negative motivation to avoid engaging in what has been called 'misery research', where researchers spend time explaining why something is not happening (McLaughlin, 2008). Given that I work in a university that has a network of schools which help to train new teachers in Citizenship, I approached schools I judged to be potentially valuable case studies. This was on the basis that substantial citizenship education was happening, that there were specialist teachers, and that the work they did was generally deemed to be of a high quality.

Oak Park School

Oak Park is the only state secondary school serving the small town of Oakton in the South East of England [the school and town name are fictional, to ensure anonymity]. In the 2001 census[1] the town population was 21,000, and other data showed the population was relatively affluent. There was low unemployment, relatively low rates of migration (96 per cent of residents were white and 92 per cent were born in the UK), a relatively high socio-economic profile (49 per cent of residents were in intermediate or professional employment categories compared to the national level of 36 per cent), and 82 per cent of households lived in owner-occupied housing (national level 71 per cent).

In terms of GCSE outcomes the school had a mixed record in the years preceding this research. The number of students achieving 5 or more GCSE grades A-C (including English and Maths) improved between 2007–10 from 27 per cent to 53 per cent and the Contextual Value Added (CVA) measure improved from 965 to 1009, demonstrating the school achieved a significant turnaround.[2] In 2007 the school was one of 638 schools in England[3] that had fallen below the government's minimum target of 30 per cent gaining 5 GCSE grades A-C (including English and Maths), but in 2010 it was identified by the government as one of the 100 most improved secondary schools in the country. In that year (the year during which the data for this case study was collected), there were 800 students enrolled, the number of students with an identified

---

[1] The data presented is drawn from the Census Profile for the town, but this is not referenced to ensure anonymity. Similarly, data about the school is drawn from a range of on-line publications but has not been referenced to avoid identifying the school.

[2] The norm is 1,000 and CVA scores below 1,000 indicate students achieve less well than similar students in other schools, whilst scores over 1,000 indicate students do better than the average.

[3] There are approximately 3,200 secondary schools in the country, putting this school in the bottom fifth for GCSE scores.

special need was slightly higher than the national average and the number receiving free school meals was slightly lower.

The Citizenship department was one of a small number of departments entering almost all students in Key Stage 4 (KS4) for a compulsory GCSE exam. Despite this policy of universal entry for the Citizenship exam, and whilst the school as a whole seems to have struggled to achieve overall outcomes comparable to national averages, Citizenship outcomes were significantly better. In 2009 and 2010 73 per cent of students gained a grade C or above in Citizenship, which was consistently ahead of English (71 per cent in 2010 and 66 per cent in 2009), and Maths (59 per cent in 2010 and 49 per cent in 2009). One can also compare the school's results in these exams against the national attainment in each subject: in 2010 Oak Park's students achieved higher than most students being entered for Citizenship across England (national average A-C for Citizenship was 56 per cent compared to Oak Park's 73 per cent), comparable figures for English are 63 per cent national/71 per cent school; and for Maths 56 per cent national/59 per cent school. This comparison demonstrates not only that Citizenship attainment is fairly high in the school, but also that standards achieved in Citizenship appear to be relatively high when compared to those achieved in other schools around the country.

The Headteacher who oversaw these improvements was in post from 2004–10 and was superseded by a member of his senior management team during the academic year 2009–10. The vision for the school for this period included a clear commitment to Citizenship, and one of the three points which summarized the school's mission included the aim for every student to become 'responsible and successful citizens'. The incoming head reiterated this commitment in her first letter to parents when she committed to sustaining an inclusive community school with 'participation and active citizenship at the heart of all we do'.

Given this firm commitment, it was surprising to discover a lack of organizational stability for the Citizenship department in the school. The interview with Chris, the Head of Department, demonstrated that, despite the support of the Headteacher, Citizenship had variously been located within a faculty with other Humanities subjects, functioned as a stand-alone subject department, been line managed alongside PE, and was being returned to the Humanities faculty in 2010–11, where Citizenship was being combined with Religious Education (RE) and Personal, Social and Health Education (PSHE) in a single timetabled slot. The Citizenship teachers in the school had different perceptions of these changes, as is illustrated in the interviews discussed below. In this brief overview of the school, it is worth noting however, that even with supportive Headteachers, subject specialists and GCSE success, the issues around curriculum identity and status were still being dealt with at Oak Park and that Citizenship had still to find a settled curriculum home.

The Head of Department indicated, during conversations throughout the period of data collection, that the school's evolving policy on Community Cohesion had influenced the way that Citizenship was seen. In this regard it is significant that her own post was changing and she was moving on from her middle management (curriculum leader) responsibility to take up a role in senior management, combining Community Cohesion, work experience and careers. Chris characterized her new role as combining the community outreach work she had developed with the outgoing Headteacher's responsibility for 'doing the stats' (23/2/10)[4].

The Heath School

The Heath School is also a state secondary school serving a large catchment area around a small village, Heathway, in the South East of England [the school and town name are fictional, to ensure anonymity]. In the 2001 census the village population was just over 9,000 and a quarter of the residents were retired. The socio-economic profile of the area was similar to Oakton, with very low levels of unemployment in the village, a relatively affluent population, and higher than average levels of owner-occupation. However, because the school was so big and the village so small, significant numbers of children travelled from a large catchment area to the school, which gave the school a very different relationship with its local community – some residents saw the school as a source of inconvenience and were quick to complain if students misbehaved in the village.

The school is a large secondary and in the year I collected data there were 1,200 pupils with over 200 students in the sixth form. Fewer than 2 per cent of the pupils had identified special needs and only 3 per cent received free school meals. Between 2007–10 the number of pupils gaining 5 or more GCSE A*-C grades including Maths and English rose from 59 per cent to 69 per cent, whereas the national average was 46 per cent to 54 per cent. Nevertheless, the government measure of Key Stage 2 to 4 contextual value added indicates that the school's success largely reflects a high achieving in-take; the CVA score

---

[4] Some quotations are drawn from field notes, written up shortly after each visit to the school. These are therefore approximations of the actual conversations and are indicated by the bracketed dates of the conversation. All other quotations are taken from the formal interviews, which were recorded and fully transcribed, and are therefore verbatim reports.

fell from 997 in 2006 to 983 in 2010, which led to a reduction in their overall OfSTED grade. Conversely, the sixth form results demonstrate significantly above average CVA, in excess of 1,020. The school prides itself on its distinctive international ethos and as well as offering the International Baccalaureate in the sixth form, it also runs a wide ranging programme of international visits and exchange trips for all pupils to complement its diverse language offer.

The school operates a comprehensive admissions system for local young people, many of whom come to school from surrounding villages by bus. It also selects additional pupils with international family links, and in the past these pupils have been selected by letter of application from parents to the Headteacher. According to the Headteacher recent changes in the admissions policy have led to an increased number of pupils from inner city areas and Black and minority ethnic communities. There are approximately 15 per cent of pupils speaking English as an additional language, although few are at an early stage of learning English.

The Headteacher is a supporter of Citizenship and teaches the subject himself, the Citizenship Coordinator in the school is also the International Director, and is responsible for coordinating the trips and visits programme, and there is one other specialist Citizenship teacher. Before Citizenship was introduced as a specific curriculum subject the school had a similar programme in place to promote learning about the international dimension. Over recent years the status of Citizenship as a subject had grown and in the year in which the data was collected the school had brought the PSHE teaching under the subject title of Citizenship, to ensure Citizenship had a better level of recognition among the students, and it was also implementing plans to ensure all Citizenship was taught by subject specialists.

Doing policy work in Oak Park School

In many ways The Heath School's Citizenship policies derive largely from an interpretation of their internationalist ethos. Although I shall allude to this in the discussions below, it seemed of more general interest to interrogate the policies that had been developed in Oak Park, because in many ways they are likely to be easier for others to relate to. Consequently, the following discussion is based on my interpretation of several policy documents at Oak Park School. The first two were attributed to the Head of Department ('Citizenship and PSHE Policy' and the 'School Council Policy') and the third ('Equality, Diversity and Community Cohesion') was attributed to the Headteacher. The policy documents were analysed to identify the ways in which the school characterized citizenship education and the ways in which it was linked to other policies in the school. Braun et al.'s work in secondary schools illustrates the complexity involved with studies of how schools 'do' policy work (Braun et al., 2010). They draw attention to the intricate work involved in writing school policy, as external policy documents are received, de-coded, discussed, connected with other initiatives and local knowledge of the context, and re-coded in a form which is intended to inform subsequent developments in the school. Starting with these policy documents therefore enabled me to think about the formal institutional responses to citizenship education policy, and in doing so illuminated what I described in Chapter 2 as 'leap 2' from curriculum guidance to school practice. It is important to remember though that policy is embedded in the practice within schools as well as in the formal policy documents themselves. This section focuses on the written policies which represent one way to think about what teachers set out to achieve in their work. The final section of this chapter is also important in thinking about Citizenship policy because it is concerned with teachers' interpretations of what was happening in their schools, and as a consequence it provides an important insight into how policy actually developed in the case study schools.

Oak Park's formal account of its Citizenship provision is currently recorded in a document called the 'Citizenship and PSHE Policy'. I accessed this document in April 2010, but it had a footer indicating it was due for review in January 2009. The fact that this was still a current document indicated that there had been no recent review of the policy, and this seemed to be confirmed by the headings listed in the assessment section, which did not reflect the 2008 revisions to the national curriculum. Therefore the first observation one can make about how the school interpreted Citizenship policy is that some of the external changes in the curriculum had not been fully implemented which would indicate that, at the policy level at least, the Citizenship reforms had not made a significant impact on the vision for Citizenship. In one sense, this would seem to favour an interpretation that the school had developed its own vision for citizenship education and was using the programmes of study to support it, rather than re-shaping policy around the curriculum. Whilst this might indicate that the school was likely to achieve some consistency, it also provides evidence that there is disconnect between changes in government policy and the corresponding policy statements in school.

The 'Citizenship and PSHE Policy' set out the school's Key Stage 3 (KS3) plan, which was delivered in a weekly lesson plus additional events. The lessons covered 'crime, culture and diversity, sex education and the environment', and although this clearly combined PSHE and Citizenship topics there was no clear differentiation between the two subjects. In Key Stage 4 (KS4) all students studied the short course General Certificate of Secondary Education (GCSE), where topics included 'responsibilities in the workplace, globalization, fair trade and the criminal justice system'. Reference was made to mapping Citizenship across the curriculum, although this cross-curricular approach was not mentioned by any of the staff in interviews. In thinking about the ways in which actual provision was developing in the light of this policy overview it seemed significant that, in the year after the case study data was collected, the school website no longer listed Citizenship as a subject in the KS3 Curriculum Plan. Instead PSHE, Community Participation and Cultural Diversity were listed as examples of 'enrichment' activities, and Citizenship and RE were listed as subjects which students *may* also begin studying and which led to short course GCSE. Citizenship remained part of the core curriculum at KS4, although it was also combined with PSHE, sex education, careers, enterprise and work experience. This implies that, whilst the formal policy statement remained consistent, there were changes related to subject identity and status.

The 'Citizenship and PSHE Policy' connected the subjects to students' own interests and experiences, real life issues, and 'activities that can help not only their school and local community but as far out as the global community'. It also mentioned the skills of investigation, critical thinking, discussion and the 'skills to challenge stereotyping'. In relation to the three discourses promoted in official policy about citizenship education one can see here the emphasis on community and active citizenship, but nothing relating explicitly to rights and responsibilities. The school's vision was effectively one rooted in a commitment to being a community school, and the value of Citizenship was seen in the subject's potential to connect with the young people's lives and experiences and engage them in their community. Whilst the global community was mentioned, it was also qualified by the phrase 'as far out', which served to underline that the global connections are distant from the young people. Whilst on one level it is geographically true that local is close and global can be distant, the geographical reading sits uneasily with the conceptual implications of a deeper understanding of the interconnections that exist between people regardless of geographical location. An approach to the global dimension that focuses on interdependence is more likely to establish the global community as just as real a context for action as the local community. This approach echoes that described by Osler in her research with teachers where she found a tendency to start local for what appear to be sound pedagogic reasons, but then remain local for pragmatic reasons, with occasional forays into a depoliticized global community (Osler, 2010a).

In its engagement with the discourse of community, relating as it does to identity and diversity, one may also note a tendency to view problems as personal rather than political in the discussion of stereotyping. The document stated that Citizenship and PSHE will equip students with 'the skills to challenge stereotyping and assumptions and make decisions based on education and fact'. The clear assumption here is that stereotyping arises from ignorance or error and that all students would want to eradicate it. This glosses over the possibility that prejudice exists for other reasons and for some this may be a political choice. The final statement in the policy takes a slightly different perspective and stated that, 'above all it equips our young people with a respect to view positively the difference in others, whether they arise from race, gender, ability or disability'. This is an interesting construction in that the language obfuscates the nature of the intention. In the same way that challenging stereotyping was described as a *skill*, respect was seen as something with which students could be *equipped*, rather than a personal commitment or orientation they could adopt for themselves. It seems the language employed in the policy document takes the political problems of respect and prejudice and turns them into neutral educational aims – developing skills and providing young people with the equipment required to view the world in certain ways.

The limited notion of community was also reflected in the document's account of GCSE coursework, which was described as being linked to a community event and the examples given were (i) running a Macmillan coffee morning (raising money for a cancer charity), (ii) planning mufti days (non-uniform days, usually run to raise money for charity) and (iii) taking an active role in assemblies to raise awareness of issues that affect them. Only the third option opened the possibility of action akin to campaigning, and this reflected the statement in the opening section that Citizenship enables students to 'participate in activities that can *help*…' (my emphasis).

The Head of Citizenship also produced the 'School Council Policy' and she focused on the connection between taught Citizenship and this method of student involvement in many of our conversations. There were annual elections, which were conducted with proper ballot boxes, time out of lessons for voting, and the results were counted and announced by a local council official. Those elected to represent their peers received training to support them as they assumed their responsibilities and there were procedures for de-selecting representatives who failed to fulfil their role. The school council was described as providing a democratic forum where 'issues of concern to students can be discussed *in order to improve life*' at the school and where 'activities can be organized for students *in order to benefit* the school community and the wider world' (my emphasis). This statement of purpose echoes the emphasis, discussed above, on activities which are *helpful,* and therefore reflects Crick's account of the *good* citizen (helpful and compliant) as opposed to the *active* citizen (critically informed, politically engaged and seeking change).

This interpretation is supported by the examples provided within the document. There were several clauses in the policy relating to procedures to ensure the school council could hear issues from their peers (open forums, comment boxes, minuted meetings with standing items, feedback to assemblies) but the requirement to survey the student body was reserved for 'any major whole school decisions that arise, for example the colour of paint for the corridors'. This was the only specific example of an issue the council might deal with, and the fact that this example was used to illustrate how the council might be involved in *major* decisions, indicates perhaps that it was not envisaged that the group would be involved in anything much more significant than the colour of paint. This tendency to limit the agenda of school councils is well documented (Whitty and Wisby, 2007), although other research provides evidence that school councils can be effectively involved in 'the core business of the school, which is teaching and learning' (Davies and Yamashita, 2007: ii).

The third policy document, 'Equality, diversity and community cohesion', was attributed to the Headteacher[5] and aimed to establish a proactive approach to discrimination (Osler and Starkey, 2005)[6]. The policy established the curriculum as one significant area for action and in doing so it expanded and clarified the points made above in relation to the 'Citizenship and PSHE Policy'. In confronting prejudice and discrimination in the school the policy stated 'we are aware that low self-image and ignorance can cause prejudice and stereotyping' and therefore it sought to promote action through 'positive educational experiences and support for each individual's point of view... to promote positive

---

[5] Although it has been amended to reflect the school context it appears to draw heavily on a template for a school policy – an Internet search for some of the early phrases turns up many similar examples from different schools.

[6] Osler and Starkey discuss the need for such policies in the wake of the Stephen Lawrence Enquiry and the tone of this policy statement appears to indicate a progressive stance being adopted.

social attitudes and respect for all'. Whilst all curriculum areas could contribute, Citizenship and PSHE were assigned a major role. Later, in the section dealing with rewards and sanctions, the policy recognized that where unfair, unjust or discriminatory acts take place, and where the perpetrators 'committed the act without intending to cause harm or were themselves subject to unkind treatment by the victim, then a teaching intervention should be considered a priority, under the express understanding that no repeat of that type of behaviour would be tolerated again'.[7] Where such acts have been committed purposefully, then sanctions 'may apply'. This discussion goes further than the 'Citizenship and PSHE Policy' document and confronts the possibility of wilful and deliberate prejudice, but it was still focused on the potential of education to promote positive outcomes for all – victim and perpetrator alike.

In pursuit of such positive outcomes teachers were encouraged to teach in a manner which paid 'due regard to the racial and cultural sensitivities of all members of the class', and to select resources that reflected the diversity of the wider community, acknowledging that the actual school community is not very diverse at all. As the Headteacher put it, although 'the school *benefits* from having a small number of staff and students from other backgrounds… the small level of ethnic diversity within the local community' meant the school had to aim to 'reflect the cultural diversity of the wider community to promote awareness and understanding'.

The policy established an explicit link between the PSHE and Citizenship curriculum in particular and the school's commitment to tackling racism. It was limited though in the way in which it envisaged such discrimination, and it described incidents which were clearly examples of bullying or poor behaviour from one individual or group towards another. Thus the policy was limited to discussing how to deal with incidents which might arise through ignorance, or where one might say the victims of discrimination were themselves 'unkind' in the first instance. Thus, racism and other forms of discrimination were seen, in the school context, as examples of unkindness, and as such were dealt with in the same way as other low-level behavioural problems which might arise when children fall out or argue, albeit with a stern warning that future incidents would not be tolerated. Other forms of prejudice related to the 'sensitivities' of minority ethnic children in the classroom, thus the policy aimed to avoid offending these sensitivities. This is weaker than asking teachers to include

---

[7] This text appears to have been developed in the school and does not appear to be part of the template.

children and reflect diversity in their teaching because children should feel included in all aspects of school, and the appeal to some children's sensitivities seems to place the problem with these *sensitive* children, rather than the potentially excluding curriculum or teacher.

Thus the policy dealt with two forms of prejudice or discrimination – individual behaviour and cultural representation. In focusing on these dimensions the policy was similar to the previous documents in that the political roots of inequality in society were ignored. There was nothing about how the school would teach about the fact of structural socio-economic inequality or the unequal distribution of power, instead diversity was seen as something to be celebrated, and prejudice was seen as something arising from ignorance or oversight, and occasionally by wilful unkindness. It was thus rendered amenable to teaching solutions, and Citizenship took its place as the curriculum area where much of this teaching would take place. As we have already seen, the 'Citizenship and PSHE Policy' committed the Citizenship department to do this by dispelling ignorance through teaching relevant facts and critical thinking skills about diversity and aiming to equip young people 'with a respect to view positively the difference in others'. Thus whilst the policies linked up in an admirably comprehensive manner, the overall approach towards diversity and discrimination was one which avoided critical political interpretations in favour of re-defining the issues until they became amenable to relatively straight forward teaching. This interpretation reflects Fisher's argument that the Citizenship agenda in schools tends to promote a way of thinking in which 'individualised understandings of success are reinforced whilst the complex processes of exclusion are neglected' (Fisher, 2011: 53).

This seems to provide some support for Gillborn's claim that citizenship education may act as a placebo and thus enable teachers and schools to appear to take action whilst failing to tackle fundamental issues related to inequality (Gillborn, 2006). As discussed above in Chapter 4, whilst the Citizenship programme of study *could be* interpreted as providing a space to engage with the nature of inequality, this set of school policies indicates that it is also possible to interpret Citizenship in a way that avoids such a critical perspective. Whilst the Ajegbo Review set out to clarify this area of Citizenship, its focus on diversity and identity rather than inequality meant that such interpretations could remain unchallenged. As we shall see when we turn to the data collected from teachers and students in the school, this lack of critical engagement with inequality and prejudice is consistent from policy to classroom practice.

Interviews

Having said something about the ways in which Citizenship has been discussed and defined in one of the schools, I now turn to the Citizenship teachers in both case study schools, and to a consideration of how they described their own practice, what this reveals about their understanding of Citizenship and how this reflects the issues raised in the school's policy documents. During the data collection phase of this research there were many informal conversations with teachers at the school, and these were recorded soon after each visit, in my field notes. The bulk of the following discussion is based on formal interviews I conducted with the Citizenship teachers:

- Chris was the Head of Citizenship at Oak Park. She had taught at the school for nine years, and had recently been appointed to a senior management role, leading Community Cohesion. Chris was employed originally as an unqualified teacher and the school funded her to complete a degree and a Graduate Training Programme (GTP) to achieve qualified teacher status. She had only taught at Oak Park School and had run Citizenship since its inception. As well as teaching Citizenship she taught Health and Social Care.
- Penny was the other main Citizenship teacher in the department in Oak Park. She had been teaching at the school for four years; she completed part of her teacher training placement at the school and had subsequently only worked at Oak Park. As a result of the changes happening during the period of data collection Penny resigned from the school shortly after this interview was completed. As well as teaching Citizenship she also taught Health and Social Care and Sociology.
- Katrina was coming to the end of her first year working as a teacher in Oak Park. Like Penny, she completed part of her training at the school and was then employed. She had already handed in her resignation by the time of the interview, to take up a position in another school. She taught predominantly Humanities but was considered part of the Citizenship team, although this only accounted for about a third of her teaching timetable.
- Mary was Head of Citizenship and International Director at The Heath School. Her background was in Geography, but she had taken responsibility for Citizenship when it was introduced, partly because it was seen as so closely aligned to the work that had already been established to promote the international dimension in the curriculum.

- Jenny was the other specialist Citizenship teacher at The Heath School. She trained in the school as a Citizenship specialist, on the GTP route, and had recently been given the new role of Key Stage 3 Citizenship coordinator.

Penny and Katrina were interviewed together and the other teachers were interviewed separately.[8]

The interviews were recorded and fully transcribed, and the transcriptions were then annotated to indicate connections between them, and to identify significant themes. This was done partly by looking for connections to the three discourses being considered in this analysis, and partly through applying some of the questions identified by Ozga, discussed in Chapter 2 (Ozga, 2000). In essence these relate to how the text (interview transcript) generates a narrative, what drives that narrative, what significant ideas feature in this narrative, and which ideas are marginalized or absent. In addition, Ozga urges the analyst to consider who features in these accounts, how subjects and agents are constructed, how they relate to one another, and how individuals and groups of people relate to institutions, the community and state. The themes which emerged from this analysis are:

1 Subject and status
2 Young people and their parents
3 Teaching and learning

In addition teachers spoke about the three discourses discussed in the preceding analysis of policy – rights and responsibilities, active citizenship and community and diversity. These themes are included in the later chapters which deal with each discourse separately.

Subject and status

The National Foundation for Educational Research (NFER)'s longitudinal research commented on the changing fortunes of Citizenship within single schools over time (Keating et al., 2009). Whilst the decade of policy developments in some schools appear to follow a straightforward trajectory, from confusion, to experimentation, to consolidation and deeper development, in many other schools progress was much more erratic, with successful models

---

[8] These interviews lasted approximately an hour each and took place towards the end of my time in the school, after I had built up a fairly good idea of the school's provision and the students' experience.

being dropped or changed for reasons beyond the Citizenship department's control. The NFER report authors discuss status, leadership, resources and a range of other factors to account for the variability. However, because the reports are inevitably rather broad overviews, it is not possible to understand fully what is going on in these schools. Oak Park and The Heath School provide usefully contrasting case studies in this regard. Teachers at The Heath School describe a relatively smooth trajectory for Citizenship, whilst at Oak Park the story is much more mixed.

Both members of staff in The Heath School mentioned the whole school ethos as being particularly supportive of Citizenship. The school had previously identified three core aims, which were referred to as the pillars of the school, and it had recently adopted citizenship as a 'fourth pillar', and both teachers referred to this in their interview responses. Mary, as Citizenship coordinator, summed up the development in her first answer:

> 'We've always had the international dimension but now that's being interpreted as international citizenship. And so every time the head talks about the school he talks about internationalism, which is one of the things I'm doing, but he talks about citizenship as well, so it is right up there, whenever they talk about the ethos of the school. I mean, it is a value driven school, we know that, but now it's said, they use the word citizenship, which maybe in the past we didn't'.

Mary also stressed the importance of the recent change in Headteacher, and felt that the commitment of the new Headteacher to Citizenship had driven this new explicit reference. This new focus had led to other changes, for example a governor had asked to come to school to find out about the work of the Citizenship department.

Jenny also acknowledged that there were some problems associated with developing Citizenship within a school that already had a strong tradition in areas that were related to the new subject:

> 'If you're building a new house you can just build from scratch and that's it, and you can kind of do everything the way you want to, but we've already got some really good existing foundations and some really good features that we would really like to keep but we've got to tinker them within what's already in place'.

Mary supported this when she said, 'we've had to put on a bit of a straightjacket because we've had to deliver some aspects that we weren't before'. She illustrated this with reference to her role coordinating an international dimension to the curriculum across the whole school. Citizenship lessons had become a key point of articulation between the ethos and cross curricular dimension, and the taught core curriculum of the school, 'in Citizenship we can really say, this is a subject and it's all about the stuff the school's about'. But she also acknowledged there was some risk with this change, and that other teachers might think this work was taken care of outside of their departments:

> 'I think it runs that slight risk of saying, 'well they're looking after that, they're doing that.' And I suppose my challenge is to keep the international dimension alive in subjects... So the message I'll be giving people will be, 'yes, we're now delivering international citizenship but departments still have to continue,' and I will continue to do that through funding, I've got an international development fund which helps. A little bit of money always helps'.

In their responses relating to this theme there was a feeling that the school was moving into a new phase of its development and that the necessary alignments were being made between Citizenship and the school's distinctive identity. Mary was also keen to build on this capacity for the Citizenship department to become a focal point for whole school issues by taking some leadership on the Every Child Matters agenda, and she had recently run a training workshop for all staff on how the Citizenship agenda linked with this policy initiative. On one view then, the Citizenship department had aligned itself to be a crucial link between the school's perception of itself as a 'values driven school' (Mary's term) and the formal curriculum.

The school's assessment systems for Citizenship reflected the broader links Mary made in her own role. Students had to write a series of statements which reflected on their achievement in a range of fields, including their work in Citizenship and PSHE, and their active citizenship experiences (including membership of clubs and teams), but these were accompanied by statements on their language learning and international citizenship, which in this context was defined as the visits and exchange programme. This system for maintaining a wider, school-specific assessment process was designed to ensure that students and teachers continued to see Citizenship as something that happens across the whole school and not just in a single subject.

The Citizenship department was evolving to reflect this wide remit. Mary had been joined by another Citizenship subject specialist, Jenny, and was also recruiting a third specialist. They had also been allocated new teaching rooms, a resource base and an office for the first time. Mary felt this was important in raising the profile and status of the department for students and colleagues, but she also felt that this brought other issues to the fore in terms of how she and her department were viewed by colleagues. Mary recognized the tension between having a higher status in the school, but being removed from the debates about achievement and raising standards that concerned the other heads of department in the school:

> 'I think there's probably a little bit of resentment sometimes amongst other departments, that Citizenship is given this profile and yet we're not a subject that are delivering big results and maybe they think that's not fair but... that's hard lines [laughs]... you know, I'm sitting on things like the head of departments forum but I'm not having to join in discussions about how we raise GCSE levels and actually from my point of view that's quite nice. It's nice to run a department where I'm not answerable like that...'

This suspicion of resentment was accompanied by a negative response to Citizenship from many colleagues in the school. Because much of the programme in Key Stage 3 had been delivered by teams of non-specialists, this had led to some problems. Mary described the planned move to specialist provision as:

> '[Gaining] our access to Key Stage 3 and what we've gained is the argument to say that we need people that know what they're doing and we don't just want people that have got time on their timetable.'

The feeling was mutual, Mary suspected, and when asked what the impact of Citizenship had been on other colleagues, she felt they were largely 'thrilled' at the prospect of not having to teach Citizenship any more 'because they hate it'.

Both Jenny and Mary were sure that the resistance from staff who have been involved in teaching Citizenship in the lower school was largely due to non-specialists' lack of expertise.

> 'And it's because they don't... it's not because they don't like what we do, it's not because they don't like what we teach, it's because they haven't got the skills to teach it.' (Mary)

> 'I sometimes feel "Oh, this is awful" when I've had a meeting with people who are non-specialists and are, are struggling with a group and are quite... and sometime a little bit cynical about it, and not wanting to teach it, it's not their subject, they don't feel comfortable, they're out of their comfort zone.' (Jenny)

Such sentiments reflect general inspection findings, which recognize that, 'in those schools where most teachers are involved... the quality of teaching is also influenced by the very different attitudes towards the subject held by staff, including some unhealthy scepticism'(Ofsted, 2006: 31). Both teachers at The Heath School felt their provision was moving in the right direction, away from a wide team including non-specialists, and towards a small specialist team, with identifiable Citizenship lessons, and an attempt to give the subject a high status by developing a whole-school system for connecting assessment and the school ethos.

Given that the interviews in Oak Park coincided with negotiations concerning the Citizenship team's relocation within the Humanities faculty it is not surprising that the teachers in this school had a very different perception to those in The Heath School. Whilst Chris, as head of Citizenship, felt the changes could be taken in her stride, Penny and Katrina were more frustrated by the changes.

First, there was a fear that the identity of Citizenship would be lost as it became part of a new combined subject, especially one identified as PSHE. This new development was seen as particularly frustrating by Penny because it was interpreted in a longer time frame, in which she had seen several other changes to where Citizenship fitted into curricular structures:

'The one thing that has been an issue with Citizenship is that we've been pushed around... Since I've been here we've been part of Humanities, PE, our own faculty, Performance and Personal Development which is Drama, English, no Drama, Maths, PE now and now we're going back to Humanities and we're sort of changing... We don't know whether we're coming or going some of the times... it's really quite difficult.'

The frustration was echoed by Katrina who described Citizenship as being 'batted from pillar to post'. What seems interesting about this discussion is the recurrent issue of where Citizenship fits into broader curriculum structures. One might assume that the introduction of a new subject into the school curriculum would be initially difficult, but thereafter each school would achieve its own solution. This school case study illustrates in quite stark terms what an on-going problem this can represent, even where Citizenship as a subject is felt to have enjoyed the patronage of the Headteacher. [9]

The move to Humanities was seen as particularly problematic in terms of the relative status between the subjects within that faculty. As Penny continued:

'I'm going to be the only Citizenship teacher, specialist, and they have three Geographers, and not everyone does Geography but everyone has to do Citizenship and not everyone has to do History but everyone has to do

---

[9] This pattern of changing organization, management, curriculum location, and delivery pattern was also evident in some of the NFER longitudinal research case study schools, see for example Keating et al. (2009).

Citizenship, and yet they don't visualise that they just think anyone can teach it and what we've seen is that those classes that don't have a Citizenship teacher or someone that actually enjoys the subject, because you don't have to be a Citizenship teacher to enjoy it or value it, those classes suffer so much... And yet GCSE, all the year groups are going to do GCSE but they don't value that, and it's a full GCSE but they don't value it, so if they don't value it the kids aren't going to value it'.

It is evident that, despite the relative success of Citizenship with the students, Penny still felt somewhat marginalized within the school and a little beleaguered. This played out in rather concrete terms in the disparity between teaching loads, which leads to a significant assessment burden – here it is worth noting that Penny taught seven GCSE classes and that the Citizenship course included 60 per cent coursework/controlled assessment, all of which had to be marked by the class teacher. This amount of GCSE teaching and assessment is unusually high.

Penny was also worried that Citizenship's status was being threatened as part of the whole school's commitment. There were rumours that the new Headteacher would be downplaying the role of Citizenship in the whole school. And these rumours were themselves linked to broader political speculation about the future of the subject under a Conservative Secretary of State for Education. Michael Gove had visited the school during the election campaign and had been asked about his views on Citizenship. Penny put her speculations about the Headteacher in this context by insisting:

'The Conservatives admitted themselves that without Citizenship politics would not have been as popular or prominent and that it wouldn't have been as successful as it has been this year, umm but they're very, they're very driven by the classical subjects such as History and Geography and they think that the students need them...'

So for these two young teachers there was a sense of status anxiety operating at several levels. First, they did not feel their efforts were being recognized in the school. Teaching seven exam groups is certainly an unusually onerous task, and Penny felt this was not being recognized by colleagues, especially senior management. Second, Citizenship's identity was being lost, as the teaching was about to be subsumed into PSHE. Third, as the staff move into the Humanities faculty, there was resentment and distrust related to the fact that there were more specialist staff in the other Humanities subjects, whilst Citizenship remained a subject which was perceived not to require specialist staff. Fourth, there was a suspicion that the new Headteacher would downplay the role of Citizenship in the whole school, and therefore marginalize the subject further. And finally, there was a fear that Citizenship would lose ground to other Humanities subjects under a new government.

By contrast, Chris, the Head of Department in Oak Park, struck a very different chord when she reflected on the journey of Citizenship within the school's curriculum. She felt that Citizenship had made the journey from lack of status to full acceptance:

'Doing something that was considered not to have a place in the curriculum, that was quite tricky professionally to deal with, and then of course came the more, you know, the better teaching and learning side and, you know, we had clear schemes of work, we had short-term, mid-term, long-term plans in place and we suddenly became like any other subject in the school, like any other foundation subject and we got accepted… In this school, I feel like we have a place like every other subject and I think we couldn't have said that four years ago and I think that's great'.

For her then, Citizenship had already achieved a level of recognition and parity, which Penny and Katrina felt had yet to be achieved, and which was becoming unachievable.

In relation to the move to a Humanities faculty, Chris recognized this was not ideal but given the other structural changes, through which Citizenship had flourished, she felt it was not an insurmountable problem:

'I think it's survivable, you know it's, it's built its foundations and I think you know if it has a year where we have to share our time with PSHE, possibly RE, then I think we can survive that. I don't know if it's the best thing for the subject, I'd like to have seen it gather more momentum, but you've got to work within the restrictions that you have as a school'.

Here then is a much more positive picture of the changes about to unfold in the school. Whereas the two younger teachers felt beleaguered by an array of negative developments, Chris was able to interpret these as just short term set-backs, and as further examples of how the changing curriculum context required Citizenship to adapt in order to survive and thrive. There was a definite sense in her responses that Citizenship had achieved parity with other subjects, and that this was embraced by (most) teachers and students, and therefore issues of faculty or curriculum structure were seen as less problematic.

Penny and Katrina's concerns echoed those in the wider literature about Citizenship. Katrina argued that the school should continue with discrete

Citizenship lessons and build up the assessment so that students could get a full GCSE, and Penny argued for greater recognition of subject specialist knowledge, or at least of teachers who are willing to invest time and effort to support citizenship education. These were the main characteristics of effective citizenship education identified in the NFER national evaluation (Keating et al., 2010) and they also resonate with earlier OfSTED reports, which argued for more discrete provision and higher status assessment (Ofsted, 2006). The reasons for this may well be related to Bernstein's analysis of curriculum codes (Bernstein, 1971a), which indicated that the status of subjects is related to the strength of their collection codes, i.e. the extent to which there are clear, shared expectations and markers of what constitutes the subject, including specialized knowledge, routines and staff. As we saw in Chapters 2 and 5, Bernstein's analysis has been used on multiple occasions to analyse the fortunes of citizenship education, in relation to cross curricular themes in the early national curriculum (Whitty et al., 1994) and the more recent implementation of Citizenship as a subject (Adams and Calvert, 2005; Hayward and Jerome, 2010). This evidence would suggest that Penny and Katrina's concerns were well founded.

They were certainly real enough for them both to have left the school by the end of the academic year in which the interviews were conducted. Penny resigned in anger at the changes and then looked for another post; Katrina had already been offered a job in another school by the time the interviews took place. In addition, as we have noted, Chris was moving on into a wider senior role in the school, meaning the department was due to lose almost all of its subject specialist teachers.

Young people and their parents

When discussing the young people they taught, all the teachers talked about special 'breakthrough' moments in their teaching. Penny discussed Mark, a year 11 boy, who had established his own charity, with Penny and Chris as trustees, and which had already started providing part-time youth work in the area and was currently bidding for a full-time youth worker and a dedicated building.

> 'He is so excited about it the whole time and it's really good to see how he's come out of his shell. He's not the brightest kid in the class but he's showed such commitment and dedication that he's already found a route in life where he wants to go and loves Citizenship'.

Here one can see the connections between Citizenship in school and the desire to enable young people to become active members of their community. In doing so, both Penny and Chris were willing to go beyond the remit of teacher and take on the responsibilities of trustees for Mark's charity.

Katrina gave an example more rooted in the classroom, but still linked to the potential of Citizenship to be transformational in some way. In a lesson on international aid, some girls raised the issue of immigration, and expressed their opinion that people should go back to their own countries if they were not happy in the UK. A rather quiet and shy boy intervened:

'He put his hand up and he said "it's attitudes like this that started the holocaust movement, it's people, individuals with views like this that started the mass genocide of a whole race of people" and it was, it was so, it was like a goose pimple kind of a moment, he doesn't say boo to a goose this boy and he is very, very conservative... And these girls you know are loud as you can get and he put his hand up and students in the class, you know they started clapping and they were so excited. He said this is what is wrong with our country today because you don't see the bigger picture and he kind of, he started to get on his soapbox a bit, but I didn't want to say what he had to say I wanted to see how many of the students would sit by and just listen to what was going on because that is more worrying for me, the students that kind of think this is OK, yeh I agree with her, as opposed to saying something and he did say something and I was so proud at that moment. It's not to do with me, you know obviously that's his parents, but you know it was such a goose pimple moment... I'll never forget that moment because it's so true'.

Katrina's goose pimple moment was linked to the fact that the boy spoke up against strongly expressed dominant positions (the 'loud' girls) and in many ways the boy's action is an archetypal act of citizenship (Isin and Nielsen, 2008). It is telling that in the same interview Katrina reflected on Niemoller's famous poem, which she has taught in her History class:

'First they came for the communists and I did not speak out because I was not a communist.
Then they came for the trade unionists and I did not speak out because I was not a trade unionist.
Then they came for the Jews, and I did not speak out because I was not a Jew.
Finally, they came for me and there was no one left to speak out' (Quoted in Ishay, 2008: 217).

It reflects perhaps how we weave together stories about ourselves and our practice that the boy is described in terms that resonate with the powerful message Katrina had been teaching through Niemoller's poem. However, the 'goose pimple moment' is one that appeals to the ideal Citizenship moment, as it implies a breakthrough, a moment of real engagement with an individual – education as transformation rather than simply remembering or understanding. On her presentation, the breakthrough is significant not simply because someone questioned the easy anti-immigration views of one of the girls in the class, but because it represented a more profound discovery of a voice and a confidence to use it, and a refusal to be cowed by the vocal, dominant group.

Jenny, from The Heath School offered a similar example from her teaching to illustrate this goose pimple moment:

> '...and I remember distinctly with one Year 11 class I had this, I taught them for a year and a half and they really didn't like each other to start with but by the end of the year we'd built up such a good relationship, because we had all these discussions about different things that matter to them, that by the end, when we were saying, well, what are you going on to do next in your life... one girl who had hardly said anything, didn't get on with the others, and when she said, really what she wanted to do was go off and... be an RSPCA inspector, she was going to this course and that course and everybody in that room, and this is the kids who had sort of been, you know, maybe not viewed so favourably round the school, they all just got up and applauded her because they could see the value in what she wanted to do, they could see that she had principles, they knew that she was sticking to them, and that just meant so much, that this relationship had formed from this group, and I knew it was all to do with those lessons we'd had...they could go away from here and realise that even if they didn't really have a lot in common with these people in the room, they could still appreciate them for what they could offer, umm, and that was, that really was "Oooh" [spine tingling] that was wonderful'.

Throughout the interview Jenny was concerned with the relationships she could nurture in the classroom. She often talked about building students' confidence and enabling them to build relationships with those outside of their normal peer group. Here one can see very clearly that Citizenship is valuable not just because of what it teaches young people in terms of knowledge and skills but because of the contribution it makes to their development as people, their attitudes towards themselves and others, and thus their sense of place in the world. In this sense, Citizenship's contribution to positive identity formation seems central to her construction of the subject.

All the teachers drew on stories about individual students to justify their enthusiasm for the subject, and in doing so they often relied on a contrasting group of students. This is just the other side of coin – once one draws attention to the outstanding individuals, one makes certain intimations about the crowd from whom they stand out. Whilst in the extracts discussed above there was a positive sense that most students supported Citizenship in the schools, there was also a shared discourse between these teachers about the challenge of teaching particular children. In Oak Park, because the intake was overwhelmingly drawn from the local area, this was largely related to the teachers' characterization of Oakton as a place to grow up.

Chris drew a distinction between students who had travelled abroad and those who had not, and she characterized the latter group as being impoverished by their lack of broader experience. She appeared to see Citizenship as a subject where she could, to some extent, address that gap in their experience and educate them to have a wider perspective. The following extracts draw on this central theme:

> 'I think, you know, if you've got a child who spends a lot of their time travelling with their parents they kind of have a citizenshippy type education through travelling… but then if you've got children who never leave the village in which they live it's nice to teach them about the big wide world… and it's the ones that don't [travel] who kind of never look outside of where they live, they've got no perspective in life about where their role is and how lucky, whatever, they are…'

On this reading then, Citizenship is a partial antidote to the parochialism of living in Oakton. A 'citizenshippy type education' implies a level of global awareness and an ability to appreciate one's own position in a world marked by inequality and diversity.

Citizenship is also required to make up for another source of ignorance:

> 'There are other children who, you know, I suppose the hardest to reach are the young people who have fixed views and whose parents have fixed views and there is a fear I suppose from their side of change and embracing multiculturalism and anything different in life, they're the harder children to reach'.

Whilst the initial reference is to 'fixed views' as the problem, it is apparent that it is the *views* rather than their *fixedness* which are deemed to be problematic. Hence multiculturalism, change and anything different are conflated here as being rejected by some young people (partly because of their parents), and this was linked to some extent to the nature of Oakton, where one does not encounter significant diversity. Whilst these children may well present a challenge, there is also an opportunity for Citizenship to function as an ameliorative intervention.

Chris acknowledged that for some students (those with parents who take them abroad and who talk to them about the news round the dinner table) there may be less justification for citizenship education, but for those who do not have these advantages, Citizenship lessons can go some way to compensating for the perceived deficit.

Katrina and Penny referred to this parochialism as living inside a bubble and saw one of their main teaching tasks as improving the students' 'understanding about what goes on outside of this bubble'. Penny pointed out:

> 'It's called a valley for a reason, it's a very small town [Katrina laughs]… they have arguments between who lives up on the hill and who doesn't'.

And Katrina continued:

> 'And Cranmore[10] is like, "Oh my god, it's like hell, it's the worst place you could go to", that's as diverse as it gets, and, "we can't go to Cranmore," and for me, I'm like, Cranmore? What are you talking about? But that is as diverse as it gets for them and it's a bad area and it's really rough… A lot of them are from like kind of middle to… [Penny middle class] middle classes or like, upper working class kind of, that kind of bracket where their, their kind of understanding of, you know, what deprivation is and what poverty in the UK is about is very, very, very, very kind, kind of [Penny slim] slim and narrow'.

Here one gets the distinct impression that these children are being positioned very differently from their teachers. Katrina was bemused by the intense localism in Oakton. There was a clear divide between herself and her experiences of Cranmore, and her students, who were caricatured as being afraid of the urban, multicultural suburb on their doorstep.

In The Heath School there were some differences in the way Jenny and Mary perceived the students. Mary was partly concerned with a resistant core, which was largely made up of the more deprived local students, who came from families in social housing. She felt these students were likely to be more challenging, and often presented difficult attitudes. She was also aware of another set of potential problems from the more affluent students who may 'bring from home such negative vibes, such negative views… about people who aren't as clever as them, people who aren't as rich as them'. The end result is that she felt frustrated that, 'even after you've taught something they still come out

---

[10] Cranmore is a fictional name for the nearby outer London suburb, which is two rail stops from Oakton. It has a BME population of 40 per cent, and whilst it feels very urban compared to Oakton, it has lower rates of unemployment, poverty and crime than the London average.

with the same old stereotypes... and you think, have I, have I done anything, what have I achieved?'.

There are aspects of Mary's responses that indicate she holds a view of the students as recipients of learning, rather than active participants. Jenny on the other hand admitted that the students drawn in to the school through the local comprehensive intake did struggle with the school's commitment to language learning, but in relation to Citizenship she felt there was not a pronounced problem.

> 'I've never found a particular difference, in teaching this subject, you know, there being a difference in response. Because you know, it could be that possibly, you know, the children who sometimes aren't so academically able are really interested in doing this sort of active citizenship part, even if they don't, you know, are not worried so much about GCSEs'.

In contrast to Mary, for whom Citizenship was largely about preparing students for the future by addressing gaps in knowledge, Jenny valued the Citizenship clubs she organized as an adjunct to her teaching because, 'it's a social time, but it's also putting hopefully what they're learning in lessons into practice'. For her, not only did the clubs provide an opportunity to extend and apply the learning in class, they also catered for a particular type of student:

> 'They don't need to be particularly academic, which maybe they feel, if you had to be on student council you'd have to be, you'd have to be articulate, or if you, if you did something else, you'd have to be able to write very well. But here they can still contribute with ideas and with their sheer *niceness* which is what most of them really just are, they just want to help and they want to feel valued and I think that's what this particular aspect offers them that maybe they wouldn't get elsewhere'.

This builds on Jenny's earlier emphasis on Citizenship as an opportunity to develop identities and relationships and suggests she is also using the subject as a means to promote social inclusion, and in particular as a means to meet some particular children's social needs.

At the beginning of this chapter I discussed research about the ways in which teachers construct their own political views about Citizenship and bring these ideas to bear on their practice. The views discussed here seem to illustrate some strong teacher perceptions being brought to bear on conceptu-alizing Citizenship in their particular schools, although these are not always overtly political and often reflect wider beliefs about the school's context and the children. Similarly Mead (2010) argues that OfSTED have adopted different agendas for Citizenship, depending on the nature of the schools being inspected. Those schools with poor results and struggling with poor pupil behaviour received reports which tended to discuss Citizenship as a mechanism for regulating behaviour and promoting better relationships in the school; whilst those schools with higher grades tended to receive more general comments about Citizenship provision. This implies that education professionals (teachers and inspectors) interpret Citizenship in specific ways in response to their interpretation of the school context. Whilst Mead noted this could be linked to measures of school effectiveness (which are often aligned with socio-economic status), it is also possible to interpret the teachers in Oak Park as having identified parochialism as a problem in this school, and then formulating Citizenship as an educational response. In The Heath School the diagnosis of each teacher is different, and the different intakes blurs this process to some extent, as different groups of students are seen as requiring different types of intervention. The significant observation seems to be that, whatever the nature of the deficit to be remedied, Citizenship may be being used to address perceived social problems in the school. This in turn reflects a broader dimension in New Labour's citizenship policy (see Chapter 3) relating to what has been called the 'responsibilization' or 're-moralization' agenda (Manley Scott et al., 2009). It also indicates one significant reason why we might expect Citizenship to vary between schools.

The discussion above has already made allusions to the ways in which the Citizenship teachers perceived the parents. In Katrina's account of the students' political maturation, one measure of success was that the children departed from their parents' politics, although she also recognized that, in the example of the boy standing up against prejudice, parents could also provide a moral compass for their children – she attributed his actions to his parents rather than her teaching. For Penny parents were there (as are friends) to be questioned as one becomes more politically mature. She also discussed them as a source of transport for the children who were otherwise trapped in Oakton because of the poor bus service.

In her conversations about children Chris initially divided parents into two broad categories: they were either the source of valuable citizenship educational experiences (conversations round the table and travel); or the source of fixed opinions, which are antithetical to the inclusive multiculturalism being promoted by the school. But Chris also believed that even these parents could be converted to value citizenship education. She explained that she and the other Citizenship teachers always spent a few minutes explaining Citizenship to parents at open evening and:

> 'Actually what we get from that is a very positive response and we get an awful lot of, I wish I'd been taught that at school, this is a really exciting subject, and what often happens is that we get, say, students from Year 9 whose parents come to see us and they'll say things like, we really love Citizenship, you know ever since they've been doing Citizenship we have to watch the news and we always have a debate at the dinner table so I think parents are seeing you know a positive side to it'.

Chris perceived the requirement for students to discuss Citizenship in school as having a ripple effect into their homes, thus at least some of the parents who may not have given their children these valuable experiences may be drawn into doing so. Whilst acknowledging that Citizenship 'doesn't matter' to some parents who are only interested in the core subjects, she also said that she thought it would eventually just 'become part of the world we live in' and that she could help to bring this change about by explaining the subject and encouraging parents to get involved.

Whilst parents were characterized by teachers alternatively as sources of educational support, and potentially as obstacles to citizenship education, they were wholly missing from these interviews as active partners. This omission is underlined by Vincent and Martin's account of how parents have been involved systematically in education as partners elsewhere (Vincent and Martin, 2005). Whilst Chris mentioned the Parent Staff Association, and spoke about her conversations with parents, none of the teachers interviewed talked about parents being involved in citizenship education in a more systematic way. This is perhaps even more surprising given that Chris talked consistently about the school's identity as a community school.

Teaching and learning

Many of the comments discussed above relate to the teachers' understanding of teaching and learning in Citizenship. All three teachers were optimistic about the potential of citizenship education to make a difference. As Chris put it, Citizenship holds out the possibility of:

> 'Getting people engaged in the world in which they live and a part of it and being positive… I like engaging kids in politics and helping to potentially shape the future of the country just by educating young people'.

There was a clear belief that this could be achieved through a combination of classroom activities and whole school (and beyond school) activities promoted by the teachers. Whilst, as we shall see in Chapter 9, some of the important issues were left for 'implicit' coverage, there was also a commitment to use Citizenship classes to engage directly in some controversial issues. The teachers all reported drawing on a range of local, national and international case studies to stimulate discussion about conflict, and rights and responsibilities. The point of these discussions was summarized by Chris who argued:

> 'I just think that Citizenship deals with a lot of issues where if you don't deal with them in the classroom, umm assumptions grow, myths grow and then they're too old to get rid of those'.

There was a sense in all of these interviews that school represents an opportunity to engage children in conversations that they might not ordinarily have, and to develop greater sophistication in their understanding of difficult political and ethical problems. There was also a clear expectation, as was evident in the responses discussed in relation to community and active citizenship, that this enhanced understanding should lead to a propensity to action.

The two younger teachers in Oak Park talked about the challenges posed by discussing these ethical dilemmas in class. They felt a tension between the desire to open up difficult issues for discussion and the subsequent pressure on them to maintain order and a respectful ethos in the classroom. It was evident though that they were aiming for a self-regulating classroom, and they felt that as students got older they came to play a part in resolving these tensions. One suspects that part of this argument's appeal is that it provides a resolution to the problems for Penny and Katrina which is congruent with their overall faith in participation. If the answer to the problem of student participation is that the students regulate themselves, the tension therefore is ultimately resolved by the young people's own responsible participation. It seems unlikely that this self-regulation could replace the occasional need for teachers to intervene and to 'manage' the discussion to some extent, but it is important to note how the teachers sought a resolution which retained the central tenets of participation intact.

The strength of that faith is evident in Chris's statement on the matter:

> 'I'm a true utter believer that raising participation levels will raise attainment, because I think if people have any kind of emotional responsibility to their school, to their teacher, then I think you've got a child who wants to please, who wants to do well for themselves, for other people, I also think you've got… citizenship'.

Here one can perceive a strong communitarian ethos binding together the disparate elements. Participation was not just perceived as an end in itself (although elsewhere Chris argued that it should be valued in and of itself), it is also useful because the participation created a sense of responsibility to others. In social capital terms, this might be seen as promoting bonding social capital, creating stronger connections between people (Gamarnikow and Green, 2000). This is expressed partly through the young person coming to understand that others have expectations of them, and so they want to succeed both for their own fulfilment and also because they want to fulfil others' expectations. This constitutes a fairly complex model of how Citizenship might support broader educational goals; on Chris's reading, the various elements hang together through a harmonious set of connections.

Conclusions

The accounts presented in this chapter illustrate the ways in which official policy has been received and actively re-interpreted and enacted within the schools. Through the simple fact that some policy documents have not been updated and some policy developments have simply been ignored, this process demonstrates a time lag, or even what Trowler referred to as a 'lossiness' inherent in the policy process (Trowler, 2003). In this way potentially significant policy developments may simply fail to have an impact on schools. The struggle for status and curriculum identity also demonstrates the structural constraints which have an impact on the implementation of curriculum policy. However, the detailed account of teachers' sense of the subject, and what they do in the name of the subject, reveals that there is still significant agency for these individual teachers to shape the subject, through the messages they convey through Citizenship, the opportunities provided for the students and the content which is included or excluded. The next chapter considers the students' experiences of the subject, and in turning to how the subject has been experienced by young people we can examine the extent to which these teachers' views have had an impact. We can now say something about what teachers think they are doing, but the next question is what impact does this have on the students?

7

Learning Citizenship

This chapter is about young people and their experiences of Citizenship. The first section considers the methodology developed in this research project to ensure young people were involved as co-researchers, not just subjects. The next section provides a brief discussion of some of the wider evidence about young people and Citizenship. The rest of the chapter considers some of the initial themes which emerged from the two case study schools and includes findings from focus groups, interviews and surveys. Whilst this chapter considers fairly broad issues about how students have experienced Citizenship in school, there is a more detailed discussion in subsequent chapters about young people's views of rights and responsibilities, active citizenship and community and diversity.

Developing student researchers

I outlined the rationale for working with student researchers in Chapter 2, and the reasons partly related to the potential insight to be gleaned from working with young people and partly to a values commitment to recognize students' voices. Ball's recent work on education policy implementation (Ball, 2010), which I refer to below, is theoretically impressive and interesting because of the focus on what teachers actually do when they enact policy, but it remains limited because the young people are largely absent from his account. Whilst he and his colleagues do a good job of exploring teachers as both the objects and agents of curriculum policy, the young people, when they do appear, appear as objects, that is to say they have policy done to them. To this extent, students are still too often 'the missing voice' in education research (Cook Sather, 2002). By contrast, as Bland and Atweh have argued, if we really want to understand phenomena in education we need to listen to student voices, and engaging the students in research about these issues not only provides us with the opportunity to listen to them but also holds out the possibility of connecting them to activities aimed at improving education and their experiences within school (Bland and Atweh, 2007: 339).

My rationale for the approach adopted was based on six principles:

1. Young people can act as ethnographic researchers.
2. Young people can design child friendly research instruments.
3. Young people have easy access to respondents.
4. Young people can bring insights to the interpretation of data.
5. Research serves an educational purpose for the young people involved.
6. Research honours Article 12 of the UNCRC and recognizes student voice.

In the following comments I will address each of these briefly, and use them to reflect on the experiences in the schools.

1. Young people can act as ethnographic researchers

Entering my case study schools I was aware of the limitations of the time available to me as an outsider to try to get to grips with the complicated relationships and ways of working in the schools. Recruiting a group of young people who knew the ropes, understood the subtle status issues between subjects and teachers, and who had experienced the ethos of the school, enabled them to act as ethnographers in a way that I could not. Bland and Atweh discuss this aspect of working with students in the following terms:

> By attending to the voices of… students as presented through their [research] participation, schools have obtained an insider perspective on student issues and the ways in which their policies and practices impact on students. For instance, statements made to… student researchers about racism and teacher attitudes towards indigenous students… were very unlikely to have been made to teachers (Bland and Atweh, 2007: 343).

These advantages also seemed apparent in my own research, and, interestingly, they became most apparent in the later conversations about racism and diversity. It was useful for me to see the ways in which the young people struggled to interpret their interview data, and also struggled to articulate this in the research group, and ultimately this gave me an understanding of the ways in which young people in the school engaged with the issue and experienced race.

Ethnography usually seeks to develop an insider perspective and to gain data from natural settings which provides some sort of access to the shared cultural meanings of the group (Punch, 2009:127). Given that the students were already insiders, they had access to the setting and to the shared meanings of the school already. One of my roles through the research group's discussions was to help them to think afresh about what they knew, saw and heard. One illustration of the value of this approach emerged in their discussion of the differences between teachers. The students spent much time discussing their teachers and this emerged as very significant in their discussion of Citizenship in both schools. This had not occurred to me before embarking on the field work, thus my appreciation of the role of teachers in shaping students' perceptions was almost entirely due to my co-researchers' perspective.

2. Young people can design child friendly research instruments

Inspired by Kellett's account of training young children fairly formally in research methods (Kellett, 2005a), I devised some short training sessions, which resulted in a research instrument for subsequent use in each school. Because the Citizenship provision in each school was different and the young people were interested in different issues, the research instruments were unique to the context. The training session on questionnaires resulted in the draft questionnaire in each school. In Oak Park I also had time to train the student co-researchers in interview techniques. We devised questions together, addressing the issues that had arisen from the questionnaire results, and they practised using their digital voice recorders and trying out the questions. We reviewed the initial phase of interviews after a week and then they collected 25 formal interviews from across the year groups in the school.

Whilst the input of students did not render the questionnaire design foolproof, it did reduce the number of problems in the research instruments. The wording which worked less well was almost entirely devised by me, whereas the questions devised by the students worked well. This was particularly evident in the interviews, where some of the research group became quite adept at phrasing and re-phrasing questions and asking follow up questions to make sure they collected data they felt was useful.

3. Young people have easy access to respondents

The issue of access was not merely linked to the availability of fellow students for interview, it was also evident from many of the recordings, that interviewees were often much more at ease with the student researchers than I would have expected them to be with me as an adult from outside the school. Some of the exchanges felt very informal, and there was joking and laughter, which freed up the conversation. Having said that, the student researchers did report finding it more difficult to get young pupils to open up beyond short answers, and this was an area we began to discuss during our de-brief in the middle of the interview period. Their discussion indicated that they were very aware of the issues arising in interviews and were able to adjust their style appropriately. In some cases, for example, interviewers re-phrased questions, provided examples to prompt respondents into elaborating on short responses and made the interview feel more discursive than interrogative.

4. Young people can bring insights to the interpretation of data

I summarized the questionnaire data in graph form for the students and they identified what they considered to be the most important issues for feed back to the school's management, and (in Oak Park) which issues they felt should be explored in greater detail in interviews. It was particularly useful for me to hear what sense they made of the numerical data. For example, as an outsider, once one has noted that there are differences between year groups in terms of how much students enjoy the subject, it is difficult to know exactly what to make of it. The student researchers developed hypotheses, related it to their own personal experiences of Year 7 and Year 9, and tested their ideas out in interviews. To this extent it was helpful to get immediate responses to data, which were able to roam beyond the confines of the specific questions asked.

5. Research serves an educational purpose for the young people involved

I explained to the participating students and their teachers that one of the planned benefits of participation would be that the project would help them to reflect on Citizenship and develop skills of advocacy, as defined in the Citizenship programmes of study. It certainly appeared to me that the students were able to engage with increasing confidence in interviews, and were able to present their views cogently to the management group in the school. The data in this and subsequent chapters also indicate that the student researchers seem to have been able to organize and express their thoughts in relation to aspects of Citizenship with increasing clarity through the research.

6. Research honours Article 12 of the UNCRC and recognizes student voice

Because the research project in the school culminated in the students presenting their findings and recommendations to the school management group, this did enable them to formulate and express their opinions on citizenship education. As part of their presentation, they were also able to report back on some levels of dissatisfaction they felt, which were also evident from interviews, relating to the ways in which the school council had been operating. Thus in both the pilot school, and the case study school, the students were able to express their opinion of the mechanisms that existed to enable them to express their opinions in the school – a process one might refer to as meta-student voice.

Overall the methodology provided a valuable framework for future work on policy implementation in schools, particularly curriculum policy. In her response to the students, the Headteacher of Oak Park school indicated that she felt there was some benefit in this approach to curriculum review and that she would like to explore the model further. Of course, the student researchers were already well aware that the important decisions about merging Citizenship with PSHE and relocating it to a broader Humanities faculty had already been taken ahead of their presentation of the findings. Therefore I would not claim that this project substantially altered the balance between management decisions and student voice in the school. I do feel, however, that the methodology adopted offers the potential of involving young people in reviewing their school experiences in ways which can avoid them being co-opted into managerialist procedures (Cook Sather, 2007). Ultimately, the extent to which this potential is realized depends on the goodwill of the adults involved, and the seriousness with which they treat the findings and recommendations. This echoes Lundy's argument that, for student voice to have a meaningful impact, others have to listen and act on what they have heard (Lundy, 2007). The approach adopted supports the wider evidence that involving young people as active agents in educational research enables them to think through the issues and articulate a message that has value to them and to others in education; the rest of the process is in the hands of school management (Osler, 2010b).

Evidence about young people and citizenship education

Much of the literature about citizenship education characterizes young people in terms of their perceived deficits and identifies a range of problems including apathy, ignorance, excessive individualism or anti-social behaviour. Whilst we know how easy it is to construct random general knowledge tests to catch people out, we nevertheless feel something is wrong when we read that more children recognize Simon Cowell than the Prime Minister (Mensa, 2007). As we saw in Chapter 4 the Crick Report considered some of the evidence for this disconnection between young people and the mainstream political culture and concluded that, whilst 'things may not be getting dramatically worse, they are inexcusably and damagingly bad, and could and should be remedied' (Advisory Group on Citizenship, 1998: 16).

Weller (2007) considers some of the sources for this debate about young people's disconnection from mainstream adult society and argues that there are a number of different traditional concerns that feed into it. There is a literature concerned with young people's lack of competency that sees them as both incompetent to take on some of the tasks associated with citizenship and in need of protection and guidance. One might characterize children as vulnerable and innocent, or as 'the beast in the nursery' (Phillips, 1998), but as Weller points out, the inevitable conclusion to both views is that they are citizens-in-the-making, and therefore the appropriate thing to do for them is to train them up for the adult world. This is exacerbated by the expansion of the concept of childhood and the emergence of adolescence, both of which serve to exclude children and young people from the 'adult' category of citizen. In fact, a more flexible approach would acknowledge that young people become competent in different ways at different paces and can therefore assume some of the roles and responsibilities of citizenship at different times.

The empirical data often shows young people have variable levels of knowledge about politics and variable take-up rates of opportunities for participation. However, there is also evidence that young people are often actually very interested in controversial public issues whilst remaining sceptical about the role of formal politics in dealing with those issues (White et al., 2000). Thus, the extent to which one views young people as active citizens depends as much on our definition of citizenship as it does on the young people themselves (Osler and Starkey, 2005c). However Weller's analysis stretches the concept of citizenship a little too far and attempts to describe young people's negotiations of the playground and other social spaces as manifestations of teenagers' citizenship.

There is a risk here that the concept of citizenship can become distorted and less useful if one tries to insist that it can be used in all circumstances.

Drawing on more readily identifiable definitions of citizenship, Ruth Lister has argued that whilst the young people she spoke to had varied ideas about citizenship, there was a tendency towards communitarian conceptions of citizenship, along the lines of promoting good citizenship, and taking personal responsibility and behaving in pro-social ways (Lister et al., 2003). More recent work by Osler indicates that this broad orientation can be combined with a basic sense of justice or fairness to enable young people to develop fairly critical perspectives and to articulate a demand for greater social justice in their schools (Osler, 2010b). In a similar vein, Wood has argued that the young people in his research engaged critically with officially sanctioned models of citizenship to make judgements about the fairness or appropriateness of models of good citizenship (Wood, 2009: 303). The national longitudinal evaluation of Citizenship demonstrated that young people's sense of citizenship is also powerfully influenced by their parents and the communities with which they identify. An early implementation report concluded there was strong evidence that Asian and Black young people more strongly supported voluntary activity in their communities, whilst children from homes with more books and more highly educated parents reported a greater sense of empowerment (Cleaver et al., 2005).

Whilst many of the conclusions from the longitudinal evaluation are discussed in the next three chapters, we can say something about the overall impact here. In 2010 two key reports were published by the Department for Education, which shed some light on national developments since the introduction of citizenship education. Both reports were produced by NFER, the first represented the culmination of an eight year longitudinal evaluation project, tracking the impact of citizenship education in England (Keating et al., 2010); and the second provided a national snapshot for the International Civic and Citizenship Education Study (ICCS) (Nelson et al., 2010). These provide significant additional measures of impact to complement the more usual Ofsted reports, which tend to be rather focused on what schools do, rather than the impact they have (Ofsted, 2004a, 2006, 2010). However, before discussing the headline findings, it is important to say something about the design of these two surveys, as there are some issues that will affect how one might interpret their conclusions.

The Citizenship Education Longitudinal Study (CELS) drew on quantitative data from a cohort of young people who were tracked from Year 7 (11 years old in 2002–3) to Year 13 (18 years old in 2008–9); and an additional survey of 2,500 students across 300 schools every two years. This was accompanied by a qualitative case study approach to look more closely at 12 schools during the research period, which incorporated interviews with managers, classroom teachers and students. Whilst the longitudinal element was the most anticipated aspect of the research it has been flawed in practice by two limitations. The first is an editorial decision which means each annual report focuses on a particular theme, and the final report makes no attempt to present a holistic appraisal of the research, and one has to refer back to previous thematic reports to see complementary aspects of the data, which of course reflect analyses from different years. The main limitation though appears to be linked to a declining participation rate throughout the life time of the project. In the original survey 18,583 11-year-old pupils responded, but eight years later only 1,325 18-year-olds remained in the survey. The report authors give no indication of how or why the numbers reduced, nor is there information on the characteristics of the students who dropped out of the research. Whilst much of the data analysis focuses on the relationships which can be established between various background and experiential factors and outcomes, there must remain the possibility that the 93 per cent of young people whose views are not represented by the end of the research could have very different experiences and views in relation to citizenship and citizenship education. One suspects there is a bias in the 7 per cent who chose to continue their involvement, both in terms of their attitude towards citizenship education and their continuing with schooling. The authors do not appear to have isolated these 1,325 respondents and compared their answers with earlier responses; instead, the overall cohort averages at the beginning and end of the research are reported. Therefore, conclusions drawn about the changes over time must be seen as problematic and less conclusive than they appear.

The ICCS report for the IEA follows an earlier international research project, the International Civic Education study (CIVED) (Kerr et al., 2002). The research utilises questionnaires, largely consisting of multiple choice responses and focusing on three main areas (Nelson et al., 2010: 6):

- Content dimension – incorporating four domains: civic systems; civic principles; civic participation and civic identities.
- Cognitive dimension – incorporating two domains: knowing and reasoning/analysing.
- Affective-behavioural dimension – incorporating four domains: value beliefs; attitudes; behaviours and behavioural intentions.

Because of the timings of these two IEA projects, the publications provide another useful source of information about young people's citizenship learning and attitudes before and after the introduction of citizenship education in the national curriculum in England. Unfortunately, the usefulness is slightly reduced due to some basic changes in methodology. For example, multiple choice questions in the ICCS research had the option of 'don't know' removed, and final results are reported as proportions of valid responses, omitting questionnaires with no response, thus inflating the numbers reported in the ICCS survey compared to those in the CIVED report . Also, the students in the sample for the ICCS survey were on average 8 months younger than the original CIVED study, and answered the survey in Year 9 as opposed to at the beginning of Year 10 (Nelson et al., 2010: 5). Nevertheless, the surveys cover some similar issues, which enables one to identify some relevant comparisons, and there are a small number of questions where the wording has been retained (Nelson et al., 2010: 10).

The key finding in the CELS report was that more citizenship education was positively associated with improvements in a range of citizenship outcomes. Positive outcomes were more likely where a number of conditions were met:

- Citizenship education took place in discrete timetabled slots comprising more than 45 minutes per week,
- Specialist teachers developed the curriculum they were teaching,
- Citizenship was formally examined,
- Students experienced Citizenship consistently throughout their schooling (Keating et al., 2010: vii).

This adds significant detail to the Ofsted report from the same year, which also noted that students' Citizenship entitlement was more effectively met in schools that had regular Citizenship lessons rather than one-off events, such as suspended timetable days (Ofsted, 2010). The CELS report stated that the impact was greatest in relation to personal efficacy (young people's sense that they could make a difference and influence others), although there were also improvements both in intentions to participate in the future in elections and community groups, and in present levels of participation, for example, in school elections, signing petitions, and raising money for charities (Keating et al., 2010: v–vi).

Of particular interest for this chapter, given the focus on the potential difference between teacher intentions and student perceptions, the report authors employ a measure of student's *received* citizenship education, rather than data collected from teachers and school leaders about the amount and quality of Citizenship *provision* in their schools. They state that using teacher reports of Citizenship, analysis reveals little impact on outcomes, but using young people's perceived level of citizenship education there is indeed some impact between levels of citizenship education received and citizenship outcomes (Keating et al., 2010: 48–9). This also resonates with some of the findings in the ICCS report, where Headteacher reports of an ethos supportive of diversity are occasionally negatively correlated with positive citizenship outcomes.

In the CELS research young people who said they received a lot of citizenship education tended to have higher scores in relation to future voting intentions and to broader measures of political and civic participation than those who said they received little or none. This difference held across the longitudinal research as long as there was a lot of citizenship education in the year of the survey, in other words, it had to be sustained otherwise the impact tailed off quite quickly. Strangely perhaps, given this, the positive relationship between Citizenship and self efficacy did not persist into the final survey, when respondents were 18 years of age. The report authors simply note this and do not seek any explanation, but it may be possible that the much smaller cohort has had an impact.

The penultimate annual report from this research project indicated that the characteristics of 'successful' Citizenship schools were still found in only a minority of schools (Keating et al., 2009). Thus the main conclusion from the CELS research seems to be that citizenship education *does* have a positive impact, where it is delivered under certain circumstances, but those circumstances do not prevail in most schools. Therefore the implementation of citizenship education has had a limited impact across the country *because* it has had a patchy implementation.

Case study schools

There is not much evidence about how young people have experienced Citizenship during the subject's implementation in schools. There is a tendency to focus on the measurable outcomes of citizenship education, hence the longitudinal surveys tend to focus on questions about the extent of curriculum coverage and tests related to knowledge and skills or levels of active engagement. Because the two case studies were constructed with the students, the data collected reflect the students' own preoccupations and interests. Whilst the evidence relating to rights and responsibilities, active citizenship and community is dealt with in subsequent chapters, the rest of this chapter deals with other issues which emerged from the students' conversations. The first topic the students raised with me, and talked about at length, was their teachers, and this emerged as a significant issue in defining the subject for them. The second issue they talked about was the content of their Citizenship classes. And the third issue which arose related to the various reasons the students gave to explain why they were experiencing Citizenship classes at all.

Teachers

In the Heath School Citizenship was delivered in discrete modules, each taught by a different teacher. During our discussions of each of the modules a great deal of time was spent talking about the relative merits of the teachers, as well as judgements about the content of each module. The students' recollections and enjoyment of the modules were closely bound up with the teachers they associated with each topic. The importance of students' perceptions of teachers' reputations has been described by Perry as 'educational seduction' and there is some evidence to suggest that students rate teachers more positively in response to knowledge of reputations, even where there is little evidence through lessons directly experienced (Perry, 1977).

Similarly in Oak Park, one of the first issues to emerge was the importance of the teacher with whom students associated the subject. This was vividly illustrated when I asked Robert in one of the student meetings what came to mind when he thought of Citizenship and he answered, 'When I think of citizenship education I think of Mrs C and world peace for some reason...' Because this issue had arisen so quickly in both schools, it seemed useful to investigate it further in Oak Park, where there was more time available. Subsequent discussion with the student researchers about what made some teachers better than others identified their level of enthusiasm for the subject and so in the questionnaires students were asked, 'How enthusiastic would you say your Citizenship teacher is about the subject?'. There was a strong connection between the students' perception of teacher enthusiasm and the specialism of the teacher, with the three specialist teachers rated as more enthusiastic than the non-specialist teachers. Students were asked to rate their teacher's level of enthusiasm on a scale of 1–5, with 3 representing a fairly neutral 'OK' and 4 and 5 being positive. Miss P, whose timetable is largely made up of Citizenship teaching, and Mrs C who runs the Citizenship department, were rated 4 or 5 by three quarters of their students respectively, whilst the comparable figure for Miss K, the newly qualified Citizenship teacher was 71 per cent. The non-specialist teachers were rated significantly lower, with Miss D being seen as enthusiastic by 13 per cent of her students and Miss H by 43 per cent.

There was a clear assumption in the discussions of the student focus group that enthusiasm was linked to students' own appreciation of the subject, so a further question asked simply, 'Do you enjoy Citizenship?'. Overall there was some disparity between the two questions, as only a third said they enjoyed the subject (rated 4 or 5), 48 per cent said it was OK, and 19 per cent indicated they did not enjoy the subject (rated 1 or 2). Mrs C was the only teacher for whom a majority of students (58 per cent) said they positively enjoyed their Citizenship lessons, and perhaps more importantly there was only one person who said they did not enjoy Citizenship with Mrs C. Whilst the most popular response was that the subject was 'OK', there were also significant numbers of students who said they did not enjoy the subject at all. However, there was still a correlation between those two variables,[1] with the majority of students who said they enjoyed Citizenship also rating their teacher's level of enthusiasm highly.

The questionnaire also included questions about the quality of the teaching ('How well do you think Citizenship is taught?') and the extent to which students felt the subject was going to prove useful to them ('Do you think Citizenship will benefit you in life?'). Two thirds of respondents felt that Citizenship would benefit them and only 13 per cent disagreed, with the remainder indicating they had no opinion. In relation to the quality of teaching, 39 per cent agreed it was 'OK' and a further 48 per cent indicated the subject was taught well or very well, with 13 per cent indicating it was not well taught. Students who believed the subject was well taught were more likely to perceive a benefit to the subject. In both questions, Mrs C stands out from the rest of the Citizenship teachers: in relation to the quality of teaching, 67 per cent said she taught well or very well, and in relation to the perceived benefit of Citizenship, 85 per cent of students taught by her agreed they would benefit from studying Citizenship. Most of the other teachers were generally in line with the average, except Miss D, a non-specialist, whose teaching was rated very low, with only 27 per cent giving the highest grades.

These findings provide qualified support for the hypothesis that the teacher makes a significant difference to how the subject is perceived. This was reinforced in all the conversations between members of the student research

---

[1]   Kendall's tau b test yields a moderately high correlation value of 0.432, which is significant at the 0.01 level (2 tailed)

group. In the first meeting, as students were discussing what makes Citizenship so enjoyable, one member of the group said 'I think that's down to Mrs C because you can tell she really, really cares about it… She's like really passionate about it and it kind of rubs off' (Shelley, Oak Park Meeting 1). The strengths of Mrs C were underlined by contrasting her qualities with other teachers. Amelia noted, 'our English teacher, he has helped our levels a lot but he doesn't respect you… you know he's raised our levels from like 5c to 7 but he's just not respectful and that's when you don't enjoy the lessons' (Amelia, OP Meeting 5). In the interviews students were not asked explicitly to comment on their teachers but two people did make relevant comments, with one intimating that respect and control were an issue for another Citizenship teacher: 'Miss P is OK but it's hard because loads of people don't listen to her' (OP Interviewee 3, year 8). Another student drew the connection between changing attitudes towards Citizenship over time, and the change of teacher: 'It's improved so much, like drastically, Year 7 and 8 were so basic we kind of did it in primary school and the teacher was crap… but Year 9 Citizenship, it involves you a lot more and I prefer that' (OP Interviewee 27, Year 9).

This data complements the wider research discussed in the previous chapter, which demonstrated that teachers have a significant impact on shaping the subject in the classroom. The data collected from the students indicate that the teacher is one of the most important factors in determining the extent to which the subject is valued by students. The school case studies certainly reflect the connection established in the CELS longitudinal research between specialist teachers and positive outcomes. It also suggests that one of the reasons for this may simply be that specialist teachers can make the Citizenship lessons more enjoyable and bring a greater sense of enthusiasm for the subject.

Topics

For the students in the Oak Park research group, several strands had coalesced to make Year 9 Citizenship better than previous years. This led them to assume that Citizenship simply got better as one progressed through the school. However, the student questionnaire revealed a more complicated picture – whilst Year 9 seems to mark a high point in the school, Year 7 results were also fairly high, and Year 8 and Year 10 seemed to be characterized by less positive responses. For the students in the research group though, they associated Year 9 Citizenship with a coincidence of better teaching, more engaging lessons and more interesting topics.

The students in the focus group believed Year 9 was better simply because the topics covered were more interesting than Years 7 and 8. Reflecting on his experience of Year 7, Tony recalled, 'the only thing I enjoyed in Year 7 was contraception, babies and stuff... that was the assessment, making posters about contraception'. Amelia also shared some of her interview data, relating to teaching about animal rights in Year 7. It is interesting to note that all of these topics – animal rights, sex education, personal problems – are not Citizenship topics, that is they do not relate explicitly to the programmes of study for Citizenship. This might indicate that Year 7 work in Oak Park was actually weighted towards PSHE topics, and it is these that are remembered as being of less interest. Exploring why the Year 9 topics seemed to be of greater interest, it became apparent that more obvious Citizenship content was cited:

> When you go up through the years you learn about stuff that you can be more involved in, like politics, you can vote for who you want to run the country when you are 18, and that's the sort of thing, when you get into the details of it, that we're interested in (Tony, OP Meeting 5).

This point about being able to appeal to growing personal interest was picked up later in the discussion:

> What they end up doing is like taking people who are actually by Year 9 already interested in politics, they enhance their thing by taking them on trips and stuff but if you took them on trips in Year 7 then they'd become interested a lot quicker and then you'd have a lot more people who are interested (Mary, OP Meeting 5).

Here then, Mary built on Tony's argument that politics is more inherently interesting because it connects with students' real lives and interests. She argued that this was not merely a reflection of maturity, enabling teachers to engage with different topics, and instead suggested that an earlier opportunity to engage with the more serious side of Citizenship would enable people to get switched onto the subject sooner. This echoes the case made by Alan Sears when he argued that there is evidence to suggest young people are both more interested in, and more able to engage with, complex Citizenship concepts than teachers are often willing to acknowledge (Sears, 2009). It also resonates with Henn and Foard's research which found enthusiasm for relevant political education even amongst young people who did not vote and who received little or no citizenship education (Henn and Foard, 2011).

By contrast, the students in The Heath School were slightly sceptical about their experience of being taught about politics. One group said this module 'was not relevant to [students] our age' but probably 'good if you are studying government [in the sixth form]' (Heath School, Focus group 1). Some members of the group acknowledged, 'we need to know about it', but went on to ask, 'how do we make it more interesting?" This was echoed in another discussion where politics was described as 'dull' but acknowledged as important, as one of the students said, 'it was dull but then, what can you do about it?'. (HS, Focus group 2). Interestingly, this group said their teacher introduced the module somewhat apologetically, acknowledging that politics switched off most people. In a later discussion with the head of department, she predicted that politics would be students' least favourite module, partly because they 'don't expect to get their heads down and produce good quality work'. This seems to indicate that the teachers in this school also felt that politics was a subject where students need to simply learn what is important, even though it may be dull.

When they turned to consider their other modules, one group in particular spoke about the shock and emotion they felt when they watched videos or read information about some of the global issues and human rights abuses they covered in class. One boy recalled, 'I think the real eye opener was when Annie Lennox did that song and there was the video behind her and every person in the video is now dead from AIDS' (HS, Focus group 1). They felt the videos were much more effective than simply hearing messages from the teacher – they made them feel 'how lucky we are' and also encouraged them to think about what they might do themselves about it. The students in the focus groups had all been involved in a model United Nations day, which is a simulated UN General assembly meeting to discuss a rights-related issue. Students came in to school 'dressed up' in formal clothes, sixth formers organized the event and led the sessions, and the day also included testimony from a Burmese refugee. For all students the apparent absence of teachers and the strong element of student control made the event particularly enjoyable and effective as a learning experience. The participative element was deemed to be the most significant factor. When the students contrasted their learning in the rights module with the politics one someone said it was important that 'we haven't had to use it [politics], but we have had to use human right knowledge in the UN day' (HS, Focus group 1). Thus the modules were being judged by a combination of factors including teacher effectiveness, relevance, interest and usefulness.

One group of students in The Heath School argued that the school should give students information to help them form their own opinion, rather than try to overtly convince people to care about citizenship issues. The students in this group said they had been motivated by their own experiences in the school, but there was also a feeling that, for those who want to do something, there are limited opportunities. They knew that the school had a twinned school overseas, for which there were occasional fundraising activities, but one boy argued that one might reasonably expect more from a school with such international links. When asked how well the school prepared them to be citizens in our society there was a general feeling that that The Heath School probably did more than other schools, because of its distinctive ethos. Nevertheless, students felt 'there's no way we can practice what we've learned' (HS, Focus group 1).

In thinking about how they would like citizenship education provision to be developed in the future, several students argued that they wanted more activities along the lines of UN day. When asked to think what this might mean for more traditional timetabled classes they thought it would be important to spend more time learning about global issues. They also felt that normal lessons could build in more independent research and link to debates and role plays. Summing up this part of the discussion one of the students said simply, 'we need to be more active in the lessons' (HS, Focus group 1) and others argued for more lessons based on conversations rather than worksheets and teaching that builds on the interests of students. This emerged in Oak Park too, where discussion about the most popular teacher alighted repeatedly on her skill in drawing all students into discussions, and using these as learning opportunities.

Justifications for Citizenship

In both schools the student questionnaires included a question asking why they thought the school taught them about Citizenship. The questionnaire provided no further prompts, students were given a blank box to write their answer into, and these responses were grouped together to identify similarities between them. They provide one way of gauging students' overall understanding of the nature and purpose of Citizenship. In The Heath School for example, where the school ethos embraced an international dimension, many of the student responses reflected this and the most common answer related to learning about the world. Given the head of department's very strong focus on 'community' in Oak Park – she referred frequently to Oak Park school as a community in its own right, and as a community school – one might expect this to come through as strongly as the international dimension in The Heath School. In fact, only four responses (out of 230 which could be coded) talked about 'community' explicitly, which is very low, given that more than this (13 respondents) gave frivolous or negative responses to the question, such as 'because they want to try and kill us with the most boring stuff this school has to offer' (Respondent 83). In fact, what emerges is a rather general understanding of Citizenship; the most frequently cited reasons were coded as *preparation for life* (59 responses) and *how the world works* (56 responses). After these the number in each category becomes relatively small, with the third most frequently mentioned category being global issues (25 responses[2]) and then knowledge about politics (17 responses).

The category *preparation for life* reflected a number of responses which used this or very similar phrases. Some students also referred to the subject as providing help with employment, although very few of the responses spelled out exactly what the connection to employment might be. A few of these responses will serve to illustrate the kinds of ideas that were referred to:

To prepare you for life so you can understand how our world works and understand everyday life' (OP Respondent 44)

'For us to know more about the decisions we will have to make when we are older' (OP Respondent 56)

'To help you to know about life and what will happen when we get older' (OP Respondent 214)

This notion of school preparing young people for life is a common trope and it was also the second biggest category in The Heath School student survey. It reflects expectations of schooling as a functional institution for the socialization of youth into society. This carries with it implicit assumptions that young people are *not yet* members of society, and thus limits the type of citizenship that might be deemed suitable. In doing so it reflects Weller's criticism that Citizenship embodies a tendency to see young people mainly as citizens-in-the-making (Weller, 2007). On this assumption, citizenship education is education to prepare young people for a future citizenship status, rather than a process

---

[2] There was some difficulty allocating responses between the two categories of *how the world works* and *global issues* because of the frequent and vague use of the word 'world' to indicate society in general. This is why I have chosen to retain the vagueness in the category title, because it does reflect the nature of the responses. However, I felt it was important to create a 'global' category in addition because some uses of the word did imply a more specific meaning. For example one response stated "it is important know diffrent that happen in the world or about pollatics so that we then now more about the world" (Respondent 43) which was coded as *how the world works* rather than as *global issues*. By contrast the answer "so we know more about the world and the countries" (Respondent 182) was coded as *global issues*. In order to try to simplify the process I coded each answer once, in an attempt to capture the main idea, which does mean subsidiary mentions of other factors (politics for example in response 43) are not reflected in the coding, as the main category was deemed to be *how the world works*.

in which young people are viewed as citizens in their own right during their time in school. Of course, this is a question of degrees, rather than absolutes, but it does seem significant that so many of the young people in these two schools used these ideas to justify citizenship education, rather than to approach citizenship education as being essentially about the here and now. By contrast, only a handful of students gave an answer which was predominantly about themselves as active citizens and only one of these in Oak Park was unequivocal about their current status as an active citizen, for them the school teaches Citizenship, 'so you can help and make a difference' (OP Respondent 110).

The other most popular category related Citizenship to learning *how the world works* and included a range of assertions about the potential value of citizenship education. Some of these already reflect the mindset discussed above, which relates citizenship to a future status, and therefore positions citizenship education as part of the preparation for this role:

'So when your older you can understand why and how things are changing' (OP Respondent 96).

'So you know more when your older' (OP Respondent 161).

'So we are aware of everything around us, when we are adults, it gives us common sense' (OP Respondent 239).

But others are less specific about time, and indeed about precisely what it is that is being learned:

'To learn more about society and life in general' (OP Respondent 184).

'To educate us in the real world with media and stuff' (OP Respondent 213).

'So we know about the world around us and issues that may affect us' (OP Respondent 288).

'There are those in the class who don't understand anything about the world around them and what goes on in it' (HS Respondent 81).

In the vague terminology they use, it appears that many of the students espouse a view of Citizenship which is akin to some form of life skills lesson, where the aspiration is a broad general knowledge, somehow associated with the kind of general knowledge and skills that might be useful in adult life. Students wrote about 'real life', 'everyday things that affect you', 'stuff we should know', 'the world around us' and the 'outside world'.

There are some similarities between these popular categories of response in terms of how they establish a distance between citizenship and citizenship education. Whilst those answers that position citizenship as a future concern clearly insert a temporal break between school activities and real citizenship, other types of response seem to insert a form of spatial break between school and real citizenship. Hence these are still essentially models of citizenship in which citizenship education is perceived as a preparation for activities which will happen elsewhere. 'Society and life in general', like 'the real world' and the 'world around us' are implicitly contrasted with the school, which it follows is a place for citizenship education, but not for citizenship. In Kerr's terms (Kerr, 2000), these students seem to see citizenship education not so much as education *through* citizenship, but rather education *about* citizenship and *for* citizenship, a citizenship which is in turn defined as part of out-of-school life.

Conclusions

Some things, once said, seemed obvious all along; the issue of who teaches Citizenship is one of those things and yet this scarcely features in the broader literature about Citizenship. From a student's point of view, one of the most important defining characteristics of a lesson is who teaches it – is your teacher interesting? Are they good? Are they nice? Do they make their lessons fun? The NFER and OfSTED data suggests that specialist teachers tend to improve the quality of teaching and learning, but the student answers here indicate that one of the reasons why this happens is simply that they appear to care more about the subject and they bother to engage with the subject and the students more enthusiastically. This is also evident in the discussion about what the students learned, as some topics can be viewed as difficult and boring in one school, whilst they are exciting and motivating in another. The NFER evaluations show that, year on year, political literacy emerges as a problematic area for teachers to make interesting, and this certainly seemed to be the case in The Heath School; but in Oak Park many of the students thoroughly enjoyed their politics lessons and argued that they should have received more of it earlier on. This lends weight to the suggestion that it is not topics that are inherently difficult to teach, it is the teachers' approach to them that makes them problematic.

These observations are important not just because they remind us of what school feels like for a young person, but because they also remind us about some important issues relating to the nature of school subjects. It may be that the subject itself can act as a motivation for many young people, but motivation is also likely to be determined by who teaches it, where and how. However, Citizenship is supposed to do more than establish itself in the curriculum; it is supposed to be a means to an end – a step towards establishing a new norm of citizenship identity and behaviour. The young people's responses hint that, in establishing itself as a subject, Citizenship may run the risk of losing sight of the bigger goal. The young people's justifications for Citizenship reflected a rather passive model of 'learning about' and 'preparation for' citizenship. To a significant extent, this process was seen as a rather general preparation for adult life and students seemed content that the lesson was designed to help them understand the world around them a bit better. This is a laudable aim in its own right, but unlikely to promote high levels of participation or a commitment to civic republican ideals.

At the end of Chapter 4 I drew some conclusions about the type of citizens that might be promoted through the Citizenship curriculum. There we noted the unresolved tension between seeing Citizenship in school as a reflection of young people's current status, and as a preparation for a future status. As we have seen in the discussion about students' own justifications for the subject, it appears that for many students in these two schools, Citizenship was about their future role rather than their current one. This has implications for their learning about rights and responsibilities, and their experience of active citizenship, which are considered in Chapters 8 and 10. There were also unresolved questions about community and diversity. For example, there was a clear intention that Citizenship should promote a form of collective identity to strengthen the ties underpinning our democratic society, but there was no clear guidance about exactly what might constitute that shared identity. The teachers discussed this area at length and it was evident that the unresolved tensions in broader debates about this issue remained largely unresolved in the school. Whilst teachers wanted to promote a better understanding of diversity and an expanded sense of identity they seemed reticent about tackling these issues head on, and largely fell back on notions of embedding implicit messages in their teaching rather than teaching about them explicitly. Chapter 9 discusses these issues in relation to the case study schools which will enable us to ascertain the extent to which the young people felt they were being given opportunities to engage with and think through these issues.

8

Rights and Responsibilities

There was a tension in New Labour's approach to rights. On the one hand the Human Rights Act indicated a desire to promote a culture of human rights and to embody international principles more explicitly in UK law; but on the other hand there was a move towards a view of rights which saw them as increasingly conditional on the rights-bearer's acceptance of a contract, in which a series of duties were also specified. In Chapter 3 I discussed the increasingly contractual view of the relationship between rights and responsibilities and addressed the ways in which this has been described as a 'responsibilization' agenda, in which citizens are educated, coerced and ultimately required to demonstrate an appropriate level of responsibility. We also saw how this reflected the broadly communitarian foundations of much of New Labour's thinking and how, when we consider the specific duty to participate in public life, this also resonated with a stronger civic republican philosophy characteristic of Blunkett and Crick's approach to citizenship. In the discussion about citizenship education policy in Chapter 4, these themes were all present and there was an additional tension between a tradition which saw children as rights-bearers, and a more conservative view, which tended to see rights as a topic to learn about, as a form of preparation for future citizenship.

This chapter picks up the theme of rights and responsibilities where that more general discussion about policy left off. We first consider some of the national evidence, and then move on to look more closely at practice in the two case study schools.

The evidence about young people, rights and responsibilities

As detailed in Chapter 7, there are several sources of information about the impact of Citizenship over the decade of implementation. These reports include data about young people's understanding of a range of political issues, including rights and responsibilities, and about their attitudes and beliefs. The English case studies, which formed part of the International Association for the Evaluation of Educational Achievement (IEA) international studies, demonstrated that levels of knowledge appear to have fallen between the initial CIVED survey in 2002 (Kerr et al., 2002) and the ICCS one, in 2010 (Nelson et al., 2010: 35). This period spans the first eight years of Citizenship as a national curriculum subject so the decline seems unexpected to say the least. However, the report authors attribute this decline in part to the fact that younger students responded in the ICCS survey in England. This point may well be valid, but we also have to remember that the first cohort of Year 10 students had no experience of national curriculum Citizenship, whilst the Year 9 students who participated in the second research project had experienced three years of Citizenship. In questions relating to civic knowledge, English students scored above the international average and young people in England also scored more highly on questions relating to civil institutions (ranked 10th) than those relating to state institutions (ranked 19th). The results were rather different in questions relating to what is described by the ICCS researchers as 'civic principles' where England ranked 22nd in questions about equity, freedom and social cohesion (Nelson et al., 2010: 27–8), and it is this area which seems most useful for shedding light on young people's attitudes towards rights.

Perhaps the most significant finding in relation to these questions is the positive correlation between young people's civic knowledge and positive support for democratic principles. The report authors favour the interpretation that gaining knowledge may lead to greater support for these principles and, whilst proving causation remains more difficult than correlation, this does seem to be supported by the longitudinal Citizenship Education Longitudinal Study (CELS) research, which demonstrated the positive impact of substantial specialist citizenship education. This is also in line with previous work completed by Niemi and Junn, who found that civics teaching in the US was positively linked to improved knowledge and attitudes relating to democracy (Niemi and Junn, 1998).

The CELS research also tracked young people's attitudes towards certain citizenship issues, most of which involve students in taking some view on how rights are implemented. Here there is what the authors refer to as a 'hardening' of attitudes towards immigrants and other social issues (Keating et al., 2010: 29). The report does not always put the findings into the broader context of attitudes in the adult population, but these comparisons are useful for understanding the significance of the findings. This can be illustrated with reference to two areas, where attitudes are said to be hardening.

Example 1 Refugees and the right to asylum

Whilst the United Nations recognizes the right to seek asylum as a fundamental human right we have also seen in earlier chapters that this was a controversial policy area throughout the New Labour period in office. In the longitudinal CELS survey, the proportion of respondents agreeing that 'Britain does not have room to accept any more refugees' rose by 20 per cent (comparing respondents answers at 11 years of age with those at 18) but was less than 50 per cent overall. The national Citizenship Survey shows that between 2006–10 there was a consistently high number of adults (76–8 per cent) who believed immigration should be reduced (over half said 'by a lot') (DCLG, 2011: 16). This might indicate that the young people in the research project change their opinions as they grow older, but are only really coming into line with the prevailing attitudes in the country. It also indicates that even by the age of 18 young people may have different opinions on this issue than the population at large – opinions which seem to favour the rights-claimant.

Example 2 Benefits and welfare rights

Similarly, the longitudinal survey documents a 30 per cent increase (from 28 per cent to 58 per cent) in those agreeing 'the government should cut benefits for the unemployed to encourage them to find work'. The British Social Attitudes Survey shows adult attitudes to such policy areas have also changed over the New Labour period in office, with an 8 per cent rise (between 1998–2009) in the number of people saying single parents of school age children should work; 25 per cent stating they would be prepared for single parents to lose all benefits if they refused to attend a job centre to look for work and a further 57 per cent agreeing to benefits being cut (NCSR, 2010). In a separate analysis spanning a longer period, Taylor-Gooby has identified: an increase of 12 per cent in the proportion of adults who believe poverty is caused by individual laziness, an 8 per cent reduction in those attributing it to social injustice (between 1994–2006), and a 20 per cent decrease (between 1985 and 2006) in the proportion believing the state should spend more on welfare payments to the poor (Taylor-Gooby, 2009: 176–7). This example also seems to suggest that there may be a combined effect at work, with attitudes changing as respondents get older, but effectively simply moving closer towards the opinions of the adult population. In this regard it appears there is a genuine change occurring in the British public's attitudes towards welfare rights.

The CELS report authors' claim of 'hardening' attitudes caught the attention of journalists in the media coverage of the evaluation report (see for example Bailey, 2010); however, the comparisons with other social surveys indicate that the attitudes among the young people are moving generally in the same direction as broader social trends. This said, the faster rate of change is compatible with the view that young people are shifting their opinions more quickly as part of their political maturation. One should also note that whilst questions of unemployment benefits or asylum relate to specific rights, they are also genuinely open political questions. It is possible that a citizenship education programme in schools might not engage with these specific areas at all, as the exact policy areas covered in lessons is a decision for teachers, rather than a curriculum requirement. Where discussion of these issues does occur it is likely that Citizenship teachers would approach them in the spirit of informed discussion, rather than attempting to promote a specific partisan approach. Even if teachers were to set out to promote their own political opinion in these policy areas, opinion polls show that, whilst the teaching profession has tended to favour Labour, the numbers doing so has declined rapidly between 2005–10, so the opinion of teachers is far from uniform (Vaughan, 2010). In other words, there is no reason to expect that a successful Citizenship programme would lead to a particular interpretation of specific rights.

More interesting perhaps are the questions relating to areas where one would expect teachers to teach about the core content (the rule of law and human rights) and to take a definite values stance in support of the principles. Here students take a firm stand in relation to values. For example, when asked whether 'people should obey a law, even if it violates human rights', one of the biggest shifts occurred in the research (as 11-year-olds, 22 per cent disagreed with the statement, but this increased to 60 per cent when they were aged 18), i.e. 60 per cent of respondents put the defence of human rights principles above the narrower principle of being a law-abiding citizen. Thus the sound-bite of hardening attitudes glosses over other developments which indicate that that young people are increasingly keen supporters of broad democratic rights.

The ICCS research also included questions about attitudes towards principles, such as democracy, and here there is some ambiguity in the responses, which seem to have an in-built tendency towards agreement. Hence, whilst 90 per cent or more of respondents agree that people should be free to express their political opinions, to protest against laws they perceive to be unfair and that political rights should be respected, 69 per cent also believe that the government should control the media when there are threats to national security, and 58 per cent agree the police should be able to hold suspects without trial (Nelson et al., 2010: 47). Clearly such responses beg more questions than they answer. Whilst there is general support for some of the core ideas associated with democracy such as freedom of expression, media diversity, free elections etc. there is also significant support for government intervention, which might be seen as threatening such fundamental freedoms. The range of responses indicates that the young people surveyed do not hold an absolutist stance in relation to such freedoms, and are willing to compromise in certain circumstances, but the reasoning behind these decisions is not investigated in this research. Ultimately one is left to assume young people are balancing individual general rights and collective security in specific circumstances, although there must remain a possibility that they simply hold contradictory views on related issues.

There is also another interesting source of evidence about how young people understand rights and responsibilities. During the same period in which Citizenship was introduced in the curriculum, UNICEF were promoting a Rights Respecting Schools Award (RRSA) programme to provide a framework for schools which decided to promote children's rights more rigorously. One large local authority sought to introduce the approach across all its schools and Covell and Howe conducted an evaluation of their efforts (Covell and Howe, 2008, Covell et al., 2008). They concluded that in those schools where the approach had been fully implemented, pupils were more likely to say they enjoyed school, they were more likely to participate in activities in the school and teachers reported improvements in the children's behaviour around school (Covell and Howe, 2008). Whilst children in all schools knew that they could not simply do as they pleased, the evaluation report indicated that the moral reasoning behind such opinions develops, so in schools where the rights approach had not taken root children were more likely to cite adult authority as a key reason for them moderating their behaviour, whilst in rights respecting schools more children spoke about the need to avoid infringing other people's rights (Covell and Howe, 2008: 9).

In reviewing the literature on rights based approaches to education, Covell et al. argue that:

> Children who are taught about their contemporaneous rights and respon-
> sibilities in classrooms and in schools that respect those rights by allowing
> meaningful participation are children who display moral and socially respon-
> sible behaviours and feel empowered to act (Covell et al., 2008: 323).

These conclusions are still contentious though and Trivers has argued that the benefits are largely the result of the rights and responsibility agenda being used as the basis for behaviour management programmes, rather than informing genuinely explorative or empowering rights based education (Trivers, 2010). However, the emphasis on participation also resonates with earlier research conducted by Hannam (2001, 2003) who observed that secondary schools could successfully combine high levels of student participation with improvements in attendance, punctuality, behaviour and achievement.

Teachers

Although rights and responsibilities have been identified as one of the key discourses relating to the formulation of citizenship education policy at government level, and in the national curriculum, this was relatively marginal in the teacher interviews. Those references which emerged were largely related to responsibilities, rather than rights, which is not uncommon among teachers (Howe and Covell, 2010). The formal language of schools, particularly in relation to behaviour policies, often favours talk of responsibilities, and the development of individual responsibility is clearly a key theme given that educational success is often attributed to individuals taking responsibility for themselves. Katrina introduced the theme in her interview at Oak Park:

> 'What is your responsibility as a citizen of the UK? Or what is your responsibility as a citizen of Oakton? Or of the school, in terms of…? You need to… if you're not part of the problem then you're part of the solution (sic). I teach history about the Holocaust at the moment and there's a fantastic poem[1] that was written at that time umm, about, like if you don't stand up for the trade unionist you don't… I'm not sure, I can't remember the poem off the top of my head or who wrote it, however the students can then, they, they're bringing Citizenship in there because they're like… if you are not part of the solution then maybe you are part of the problem and being a bystander, linking it back to bullying, persecution, prejudice, all of those kind of things…'.

Katrina's statement focuses on responsibility, and particularly on the individual's moral responsibility for their actions (or inaction) in society.

Chris, Oak Park's head of department, argued that her approach was not to foreground teaching and rights and responsibilities to but to diffuse it through other topics:

---

[1]   This is the Niemoller poem quoted in Chapter 6.

'I think rights and responsibilities underpins a lot of the work we do rather than we teach it explicitly, we teach it through everything'.

When asked for specific examples, like Katrina, Chris also focused on responsibilities:

'As a school we have, you know active student voice, we have active student leadership, you know we have kids engaging in level 1 youth work. We are definitely at a stage where we are getting young people to take responsibility, not just for their school but for their local community and for what happens with young people in the local community umm, and that's a time thing, it's nothing I could specifically say we did this and that changed that it was just over time they feel that they can take on responsibility, they have a positive impact'.

I returned to the question again and phrased it more specifically, asking Chris to explain to me what she hoped students would understand in relation to their rights and responsibilities by the time they left the school.

'Well, I think definitely to know their rights in every sense of the word, umm, it's diff..., umm without listing ideas I think it's quite difficult to, you know I'd like them to know their rights in the law, I'd like them to know their rights in politics, you know and in terms of their responsibilities I'd like them to leave with a sense of an understanding that, you know, rights come alongside respon-sibilities and that they have a role to play in the world in which we live and from the very small scale from having a responsibility in the family to having a responsibility to the world'.

Whilst there was a greater awareness of the specific rights young people have in this answer, there was a quick return to the responsibilities agenda, which in turn moved quickly from the specific to the general. As we have seen elsewhere in this book, this notion of young people growing into adult responsibilities also reflects the model of the 'good citizen' about which Crick was so disparaging (2000a: 98).

The Heath School adopted a slightly different approach, and Mary argued they had a longer history of teaching about this area:

'We used to do something called Minorities and Languages and we talked about the Basques... and did Basque separatism and Northern Ireland and things like that and we... but out of that came the idea that we could change that round and do human rights and I think you found... that that's the one the kids really love doing, they like that particular unit'.

Her colleague, Jenny, reflected this and said this unit was one of the most popular, and that she thought it was particularly important because understanding rights allowed students to think about power and who had power over them and how much power they had to make decisions for themselves or to affect change.

These case study interviews demonstrate the degree of variability between Citizenship teachers in how they understand rights and responsibilities and the degree to which they see them as central concepts to their work. Whilst The Heath School seemed to have a more explicit and clear understanding of how rights are treated in their curriculum, none of the teachers made this a core theme in their interviews. Certainly none of the teachers I spoke to articulated a clear vision for how rights and responsibilities were connected and how this related to the curriculum and their teaching.

Students

In the initial meeting of the student research groups in Oak Park and The Heath School there was some ambivalence about the importance of rights. The students were split into small groups and asked to rank a series of statements about what constitutes 'a good citizen'. The main purpose of this task was to start a citizenship focused conversation but I also asked each group to record their rankings for later analysis. One of the students justified his ranking with the following reflection on citizenship:

> 'Being a good citizen is mostly personal, you know about helping somebody...
> or like telling somebody, like, such as police, if you see something going on, or
> somebody being robbed, or somebody stealing then I think you should tell the
> police' [Robert, OP Meeting 1].

Despite their recognition that rights and responsibilities were moderately important, albeit not absolutely central to citizenship, the general discussions that followed this activity, and which were relatively unstructured to elicit their experiences of citizenship education, did not include rights or responsibilities at all.

The students in The Heath School did not prioritise this theme in their questionnaire, but in the Oak Park survey students were asked if the school helped them to realise their rights[2]. The results indicate a very large majority

---

[2] There is an obvious problem with the use of the word 'realise' in this question, and in a later question about responsibilities. In the workshop designing the questionnaire, the students and I discussed the idea of asking about rights and responsibilities and in this case I decided on the final wording as I was preparing the questionnaire. The word is ambiguous, and I have assumed that it was interpreted as meaning 'realize what they are' rather than the more active sense of 'realizing

who believe the school has helped them to know about their rights (55 per cent chose yes and 31 per cent chose sometimes). This was reflected in the interviews too, and it was evident that many students felt they had learned about rights through their Citizenship lessons:

'Before I was just like, some people would say oh that's my right I have the right to do that and some people don't actually know what they are but I do now' (OP Interviewee 3, Year 8).

Although a few students were unable to name any specific rights when asked for examples, most were able to give one or two – for example the right to education, freedom of speech, privacy, voting, food and water, life. Some also demonstrated a less sound grasp of their actual rights by referring to rather vague ideas, such as the right to be free or even very specific examples which are not rights, such as the right to clean clothing.

One student had confused their rights with advice about good behaviour and qualified his own right to freedom of speech in a novel manner:

'Right to speak when spoken to or whatever it is' (OP Interviewee 25, Year 9).

Others indicated that they had begun to develop their thinking about rights in a slightly more sophisticated manner, but were still struggling to achieve a clear understanding. In answer to the question, 'what sort of things have you learned about your rights?', one person answered:

'You can't take other people's property, the right to live, the right to freedom of expression' (OP Interviewee 2, Year 8).

But when asked whether she agreed with them all,[3] she expanded:

'Some of them yeh, but it's kind of weird how they sort of like overlap each other'.

There is a sense here that the student has remembered some of the rights learned in lessons, but has not developed a related conceptual understanding of rights. She is unable to positively articulate the essentially linked nature of rights (Starkey,

them through action'. Partly because of this, rights and responsibilities were revisited as questions in the follow up interviews, to enable the student researchers to explore students' understandings of the terms in greater detail. In the interviews respondents were asked for examples of rights and responsibilities.

3 I think this subsidiary question highlights one of the values of working with students as co-researchers – I would not have thought to ask if someone agrees with a list of rights, which I take to be self evidently agreeable. Clearly though, the student interviewer felt this was a relevant question and in turn received an interesting and valuable answer.

2007), nor is she able to engage in the debate about how rights are limited in the perpetual search for a balance between an individual's rights and between different people's rights (Alderson, 2008). On this reading rights are social, i.e. an individual claiming his or her rights simultaneously accepts and acknowledges the equivalent rights of others, which leads logically both to a sense of how one's rights are limited and to an associated sense of obligation to others. One might argue that this is too complicated for a Year 8 student to understand, but one should not underestimate the understanding already evident in a 12-year-old who is able to think about this problem for herself, and to notice the 'weird' nature of these overlapping rights.

In relation to responsibilities the questionnaire dealt with these slightly differently. Students were first asked what responsibilities they had in the school, then they were asked whether Citizenship had helped them to realize their responsibilities (52 per cent said yes, 28 per cent no, 20 per cent had no opinion), and finally they were asked about the most important responsibilities of citizens in Britain. Because the first question was concerned with Citizenship classes and had a reduced number of answers available it is not easy to make a direct comparison with the earlier question about rights and the school. However, one notable observation about this question is that 20 per cent expressed no opinion – much higher than those with no opinion about rights (3 per cent). This might imply that students were less clear about responsibilities than about rights, and the other data supports this interpretation. Indeed one should not be too surprised at this finding, given that responsibilities are much more difficult to pin down than rights. Although some writers have produced useful syntheses (Osler and Starkey, 2005b: Ch.9), they are not generally codified in the same way rights are, and there is no commonly accepted language for talking about them.

When asked about their responsibilities in school, there were a range of responses, which indicated that most students were able to reflect on specific responsibilities they felt they had. However, a third of students did not provide a response at all, or said they had no responsibilities, which indicates that not all students are confident with the terminology of responsibilities. Many of the responses related to conventional good behaviour in school, for example following the rules, behaving on trips and in the classroom, looking after pens and equipment and tidying the class at the end of lessons. There were also some answers acknowledging a slightly wider definition of good behaviour, which embraced a social dimension, for example looking after younger students and being a role model. Some students wrote about formal roles they had undertaken in the school to achieve this, for example as representatives on the school council, prefects or peer mentors. Whilst some talked about their responsibility to reflect well on the school, to make the school look good to outsiders, others were much more personally focused and said their main responsibilities were to work hard and succeed at school.

When it came to thinking about the general responsibilities of citizens, a third of students did not provide any answer and, of those who did, the responses were largely related to the model of good citizenship, as opposed to Crick's ideal of active citizenship. Many responses were focused on being a compliant, law-abiding citizen, paying taxes, respecting others and helping people. 13 per cent of responses mentioned voting, but there were few other forms of action mentioned, apart from actions relating to safeguarding the environment, for example recycling and avoiding littering. The list of responsibilities suggested by students paints a portrait of largely pro-social young people who understood, broadly speaking, what is necessary for a harmonious society and there was a strong sense of mutual obligation, commitment to other people's welfare, and an awareness that everyone has a potential contribution to make to a healthy society. This might well be characterized as community cohesion, and some of the suggestions included welcoming newcomers, keeping our surroundings tidy, looking out for others, helping others in need, and protecting others. As one student summed it up: 'to keep world peace and help the elderly' (OP Respondent 56).

The combination of the high numbers not answering these questions, plus the vagueness of some of the responses, led the student researchers to include questions about responsibilities in the interview schedule. Here, the pattern was generally confirmed. Whilst most of those who answered said they had learned about rights and responsibilities in Citizenship, several were unable to give an answer at all when asked for an example of a responsibility. This was an interesting feature of the interviews – immediately after failing to give a response about their responsibilities, interviewees confirmed that they had indeed been taught about rights and responsibilities. Their inability to describe one responsibility they had did not shake their confidence that this was a topic they had learned about.

Those who were able to say something about their responsibilities largely spoke about their personal responsibilities, for example to tidy their bedroom, babysit younger siblings, or walk the dog. A few gave other more general answers, such as 'taking part', or 'being kind'. Only one explicitly connected his example of a right to education, with his responsibility to educate himself.

The student researchers were aware that the level of understanding of rights and responsibilities among the students they spoke to was variable. In the de-brief meeting, following the interviews, one of them pointed this out:

'They knew about human rights but some of them struggled to know any off by heart…I mean like simplify it down, like right to education' (Shelley, OP Meeting 5).

Mary mentioned that some students had in fact mentioned privacy, which she assumed was because of what she referred to as the 'Facebook scam':

'Well there's been this Facebook scam, where the school can access our Facebook they can phone up Facebook and ask to unlock our Facebook and I think that's because certain things have been going on, but like they're accessing random people's ones' (Shelley, OP Meeting 5).

'And that is private, that is our right to privacy… because I got into trouble because I wrote something about Miss L [the new Headteacher] and she made me come and talk to her about it' (Mary, OP Meeting 5).

'Yes, it's child protection… but if the school is worried they're supposed to go to the child protection officer in the school… they can't just do it themselves' (Claire, OP Meeting 5).

In some ways this exchange showed a fairly sophisticated understanding of the concept of rights being applied to a difficult current situation. The final contribution in particular demonstrated an ability to balance a general right (to privacy) to another (to protection) but recognize there are systems and agencies set up to deal with the conflict. Here the students adopted a clear critical stance about the way in which the Headteacher appeared to act as the final arbiter in the case, and to arrive at a solution which the students felt had failed to recognize their right to privacy at all. Now of course one might question Mary's original action – to publish information about a teacher on Facebook, without considering the teacher's interests in the matter – but the point to make here is simply that these students, in this particular example, were able to think about rights in a fairly sophisticated way, recognizing that rights need to be balanced, and that there are agencies for this arbitration process.

Overall, the findings in relation to rights and responsibilities are ambiguous. One of the most striking features is the lack of response from many of the respondents. In the initial student focus group, the subject was largely absent; in the questionnaire, over a third of students did not provide an answer at all; and in the interviews, questions about responsibilities in particular elicited several prolonged silences, or admissions that respondents had nothing to say. And yet, there is an overwhelming sense that students have learned about rights and responsibilities in Citizenship classes. Whilst this teaching had resulted in some awareness of the kinds of rights people have, there was little evidence that this had resulted in a higher level of conceptual awareness about rights per se. In relation to responsibilities, the ideas the students had were largely related to issues of personal morality, and large numbers of responses related to compliant and pro-social behaviour. Clearly there is considerable value to young people demonstrating an understanding of their social role in creating community cohesion, but as noted above, there is little evidence here that these young people are moving beyond a simple model of the good citizen, and embracing a more expansive sense of themselves and others as active rights-bearers.

Conclusion

In terms of rights and responsibilities, the national surveys indicate that young people seem to generally support equality and rights connected to democratic principles – the right to free speech, to access free media, to choose one's leaders in free elections. They also tend to accept the importance of voting as a responsibility in democracy, with high numbers claiming they intend to vote. However, in specific areas of policy, or in specific contexts, many are also willing to suspend or severely limit these freedoms, for example by supporting the arrest and detention of suspects and government control of the media in the name of national security. Such opinions are not untypical of those held by adults in society at large.

Whilst policy makers might be pleased with the general tendency to focus on responsibilities, they might be less impressed by the fact that Citizenship does not appear to be informed by a particularly clear conceptual model of the nature of those responsibilities, nor of the link between rights and responsibilities. In many ways the views of these Citizenship subject specialists do not appear to be significantly different to those generally espoused by teachers, where it is not uncommon to find a rather vague concern with the broad concept of one's moral responsibilities towards others (Howe and Covell, 2010).

Whilst many students in Oak Park school were able to say something about rights and responsibilities, their responses reflected a largely apolitical conception of rights. This was especially so for responsibilities, where examples were often drawn from lists of personal chores. This is clearly an area where the reality is falling short of the policy makers' intentions. Whilst students report having 'done' rights and responsibilities in class, there is little evidence in their responses that they have any clear understanding about this area, and certainly no evidence that there is any significantly political/conceptual understanding being developed though the Citizenship lessons.

In relation to the earlier discussion of the models of citizenship being promoted in policy and the tensions within these debates we might say Citizenship in Oak Park provided some support for a rather vague communitarian model, in which responsibilities were always attached to rights, and these were frequently seen as moral obligations, derived from relationships. In The Heath School, there was more routine teaching about rights, but in keeping with its ethos this was most frequently discussed in relation to overseas contexts, thus rights were used as a framework for understanding conflict and the consequences of underdevelopment. This might bear a closer resemblance to the other strand in New Labour thinking – to promote a human rights culture, although of course this was limited by the tendency to relate rights to other people's troubled lives. There was little evidence of any systematic attempt to deliver on Ajegbo's call to investigate the specific warrants for claims to rights, and to explore the relationship between belonging to a community and one's rights and responsibilities. Neither did there appear to be any particularly clear exploration of the nature of the relationship between rights and responsibilities, nor of the ways in which rights are limited. Oak Park is a case study of how it has been possible to 'do' rights and responsibilities without any clarity about what the underlying purpose might be. This is interesting in the light of the glimpses in the data of young people's readiness for greater rigour and clarity. For example, the 12–year-old interviewee who noted the 'weirdness' of the inter-relatedness of rights and the student researchers who criticized the school's management for not managing the tensions between rights in a responsible way. These examples indicate that these young people are perfectly able to articulate and engage with the more subtle nature of rights and responsibilities, but that Citizenship has not always provided them with the opportunity to do so.

9

Community and Diversity

This discourse, which we have identified as relating to community and diversity is a fairly broad one and includes a number of elements which at times jostle for dominance. Thus for Crick, the point was to create a shared sense of belonging to a common political community, and to see oneself as an active member of it. For Ajegbo, the agenda was much more concerned with acknowledging that there are diverse actual communities which influence people, both as resources to construct their own identities and as contexts for participation. During the period of the New Labour governments the agenda shifted between strengthening communities, because this was seen as a good in and of itself, and building connections between separate communities to strengthen a sense of national identity. This area has proved controversial and touches on a series of sensitive questions – with whom do we identify? Who do we trust? With whom do we collaborate? Where do we feel we belong? And what impact does all this have on how we see ourselves and what we do? Clearly these questions touch on how people feel as well as what they do and so the discussion in the first part of this chapter considers some of the evidence relating to young people's sense of belonging, trust and toleration. The chapter then moves on to consider what teachers and young people in the case study schools said about this dimension of citizenship and what this tells us about citizenship education.

Young people, community and belonging

One solution to this yearning for a sense of national community would be to promote patriotism, and a study towards the end of New Labour's period in office investigated what teachers and young people thought of such an approach (Hand and Pearce, 2009). Almost all of the teachers (94 per cent) and three quarters of their students felt that teaching about patriotism should always include a balance of views and should not include the teacher promoting patriotism. Fewer than one in ten teachers and students felt it was appropriate for schools to promote patriotism and almost half believed that schools should remain neutral on the matter. When asked what approach teachers should adopt when young people express their own views, fewer than one in five teachers felt that schools should support patriotic sentiments when students expressed them but three quarters felt they had a duty to point out the dangers of patriotic sentiments. Hand and Pearce concluded that the most favoured approach by teachers for dealing with issues of patriotism in the classroom was through open discussion and the correction of factual errors – in other words as a controversial issue, rather than as a set of values to be promoted.

Similarly Davies' survey of teachers found that whilst there was strong support for the notion of tolerance and respect for diversity, there was little enthusiasm for citizenship education as a vehicle for teaching patriotism (Davies et al., 2005). Davies interprets this as a reflection of the teachers' personal scepticism about patriotism as well as their professional scepticism that it should be a proper object of education. Wilkins' earlier study of student teachers found similar attitudes, including a profound scepticism amongst student teachers towards the idea of 'British values' (Wilkins, 1999), a conclusion which was replicated in a study of Citizenship student teachers after the Ajegbo Review (Jerome and Clemitshaw, 2012).

The studies focussing on the promotion of national identity seem to indicate there is little appetite for it among teachers. The favoured approach seems to include a more discursive consideration of the nature of diversity. However, when Maylor undertook research in schools to support the work of the Ajegbo Review she concluded that many teachers avoided teaching about diversity, and many of those who did teach about it tended to focus on ethnic diversity and to omit teaching about particular groups entirely (such as those with dual heritage) and therefore failed to explore diversities within broad ethnic categories (Maylor, 2010). Maylor spoke to white British young people who experienced their ethnicity as an absence of identity, seeing diversity as being about others, and about the differences between groups, rather than differences within groups. She argued that the combination of scepticism and avoidance meant that often such teaching about Britishness became tokenistic and failed to overcome problems with teaching about 'the other'. She identified the quest for an inclusive Britishness as the major challenge for teachers wanting to engage seriously with this agenda, which echoed Osler who has also written about the narrowness of definitions of Britishness and the difficulties of connecting this approach to children's own identities (Osler, 2008; 2009). However, the NFER's longitudinal survey data indicated that teachers' fears in this area may be unwarranted as there was overwhelming support in all ethnic groups (around 90 per cent) for statements such as 'I am proud to live in England', and 'I have great respect for England' (Nelson et al., 2010: 56), which indicates there may be some common ground which can be used as a starting point.

The final longitudinal survey concluded that young people in England were more likely than the European average to support equal rights for minority ethnic groups and for women. However, they were less likely than the average to support the rights of immigrants and here there was a significant gap between native English respondents and non-native young people, with the former group being less likely to support the rights of immigrants (Nelson et al., 2010: 73). It is not necessary to seek explanations linked to youth for this finding, as this reflects the general trends in public opinion over time.

When asked about trust, the young people in the CELS surveys had high levels of trust in teachers rising from approximately 60 per cent to 80 per cent (between being 11 and 18 years old), and low levels of trust in politicians (20 per cent of 11 year olds said they did not trust politicians at all, rising to 33 per cent of 18 year olds). Whilst the authors speculate on a process of hardening attitudes as respondents get older, they also note it is likely that these changes merely reflect broader trends in society; for example, trust in politicians markedly declined in this period, especially in 2009 following scandals relating to MPs' expense (Ipsos-Mori, 2009). The national Citizenship Survey showed that in 2010 trust in parliament returned to levels similar to the previous decade, with 2009 as a low point; however, this survey showed that, consistently over the previous decade, only around a third of the population said they trusted parliament a lot or a fair amount (DCLG, 2011: 10). The ICCS data supported this view of young people's trust but also demonstrated a consistent gap between Christian white students' responses on the one hand and members of minority ethnic groups and those with a religious belief other than Christianity on the other hand, with the latter groups demonstrating consistently lower levels of trust in a range of institutions (Nelson et al., 2010: 108).

It would be foolhardy to draw conclusions about all young people across the country, and national surveys are likely to gloss over local issues of mistrust or poor relations between ethnic and religious communities, which are often specific to a local context (Lemos, 2005). It is also difficult to understand fully the implications of surveys which demonstrate that people generally hold tolerant views but are highly sceptical about immigrants rights, as in a society with generally high levels of immigration this may have a corrosive effect over time on the general sense of reciprocity which is required for a sense of shared identity (Taylor-Gooby, 2009). Nevertheless, the data outlined so far demonstrates some of the issues arising in other surveys and studies. It appears there is general support for a teaching approach which opens up the area of identity and community to informed debate, and it would seem that teachers are well placed to oversee such a process, given the relatively high levels of trust. It is also apparent that such debates would be happening between young people whose own identity has a significant impact on their attitudes towards tolerance and inclusivity, and thus teachers face a significant challenge in managing this process to a positive educational conclusion. The rest of this chapter presents a discussion of some of the experiences of teachers and young people in the case study schools, to help illustrate the ways in which these tensions played out in reality.

Teachers

The school as a community and in the community

When asked about the reasons why the government introduced Citizenship into the school curriculum, Jenny, in The Heath School, identified community cohesion as a key objective:

> 'There's two things that I try and tackle in it, I mean sort of, how to try to prevent a break down in society [laughter] that sounds very grand but certainly improving relations between communities and people and different people within that community and to understand one another and I think that's an important value that sort of hits any school, regardless of its ethos and its particular intake. Umm, and sort of the communication that's involved in that, the communication skills that are involved with that, knowing your rights, knowing umm what power you have and what power maybe lies with other people, umm and where you need to head, and uhh, obviously feeling that you're part of something, feeling that you're involved, part of your community and part of your maybe, you know the political system there on a smaller and wider level'.

Clearly this view is very firmly situated within the later dominant strand of Citizenship policy, with the emphasis on equipping young people with the skills to communicate and build bridges with people who are different from themselves. The school is also situated as a site where teachers can develop a model community, in which these values are experienced firsthand.

Because Oak Park positioned itself as a community school and because the Head of Citizenship was also leading on the school's community cohesion policy, this theme emerged in the interviews there as well. When discussing the students, Oakton was seen as a limiting factor, but all three teachers also spoke positively about 'the community' and the relationships between it and the school. Because of her role in senior management, and the length of time she had spent in the school, Chris had the most to say about the connections between the school and community. In reflecting specifically on community connections, Chris claimed the small size of Oakton and the school were beneficial, in that she could 'organize lots of active projects without it getting out of hand'.

> 'I think a community school has been evolving for the last four or five years, what's interesting is that it's not a government initiative that we've suddenly had to take on I think we have been building up to this through the work we have been doing in Citizenship and I think we pride ourselves on being at the heart of the Oakton community and I think people [staff]… believe in the work that I do and the Citizenship team do'.

When the focus was on the community, as opposed to the individual students and their parents, Chris adopted a slightly different emphasis. When discussing students' experiences, she stressed the role of Citizenship in providing vicarious enriching experiences to teach about 'the big wide world'. But when asked to reflect on the community in relation to Citizenship she spoke about the value of local connections and opportunities, and actually denigrated, to some extent, the global perspective:

> 'And I suppose having a good relationship with the local community, the local police, means that we are more likely to tackle issues that affect young people from a sort of a multi-agency approach I suppose. But I also think that it's important that, as much as we can, we get the kids out, and that the local community come in, and that where possible we use local data… It's very tempting to go national or global on it and I think as much as you can you need to keep it as, you need to keep it as local as you can, because then it's real to them you know. Like we get kids involved in carnivals and you know setting up stalls and getting them active'.

In her interview Chris did not resolve the tension between these two different sets of ideas. In theory there is an approach, advocated by the development movement's mantra of 'think global, act local' which resolves these ideas, or at least connects the tensions within one world-view, but Chris did not explicitly connect these two approaches, and instead she alternated between advocating Citizenship as a celebration of community connections, and as the aspiration to move beyond parochialism.

In this we can observe some of the tensions discussed in earlier chapters in relation to broader policy developments. As McGhee (2005, 2008) points out, the government simultaneously sought to value the strong communities which act as communities of identity, whilst also developing concerns that such communities act to exclude others. Thus the government alternated between policies which sought to strengthen communities, and those which sought to build bridges between different communities. These approaches clearly existed in tension with one another – a tension McGhee described as leading to a desire for a form of *cosmopolitanization*, in which strong communities of identity also embraced diversity and tolerance as core constituent values. This issue might be seen to arise from within the communitarian roots of some of New Labour's thinking on community policy, as there is an unresolved issue about the nature of the community to be embraced in such a philosophy (Kymlicka, 2002). Given the primacy of the ideal of 'community', it is significant that the level of analysis remains somewhat contested (Annette, 2008), and so references to community can be interpreted as neighbourhood, social group, nation or political arena. In Chapter 3 we saw how these tensions were unresolved at the policy level and remained the subject of controversial debate among academics. Chris' interview reflects these same tensions and indicates that rather than being resolved at the local level, they may simply continue unabated and thus lead to potentially contradictory impulses in schools.

Her account of how the school's success was achieved was very much focused on small scale change at the local level. An example of participation she returned to several times (both in the interview and in other conversations) was her recollection of a painting project:

> 'The first thing I ever did was allowed a group of Year 11s to paint my classroom and it suddenly just changed, they painted these flags on the ceiling and, everybody that then entered into my room, it was quite interesting that the Year 11s had painted it, and why had they painted it, part of their active citizenship project, we want to do that Miss, that sounds really... and it just kind of snowballed'.

This incident was clearly significant to Chris, and it seems likely that this accounted for the fact that the Student Voice policy (discussed in Chapter 6) referred to the colour of paint in the corridors as a 'major decision'. In this way,

Chris saw herself as not just building connections between the school and the Oakton community, but also contributing to a sense of community within the school.

> 'It started off in engaging people in taking action and engaging them in charity work and, and what that did at the time was it worked alongside where the school was at, at the time, alongside, you know, having a new Headteacher coming in, and it didn't work because I made it work, it worked because the timing, everything fit nicely together and the young people were looking for a sense of identity and belonging and their place in this school, and what their role was and what I offered them was something a little bit exciting and enriching and they all jumped on the bandwagon and it fell from there really'.

Identity and diversity

Mary, the Head if Citizenship in The Heath School, was very aware of how the agenda had shifted in Citizenship policy since the introduction of the first programmes of study. When asked to reflect on the purpose of the policy and how the school had implemented it, she argued:

> 'I think the political agenda, it has changed because of 9–11, we've got that and we've got bombs in London… the whole thing has changed and… yes it's still about getting us to vote, but I think now, well we've got the fourth pillar [identity and diversity] so it is changing, it isn't just about that political thing only anymore, and that's taken a bit of a back seat'.

Mary acknowledged that the dominant discourse had shifted from using Citizenship to tackle the problem of low voter turnout and youth apathy towards a vision of 'us all living together in tolerance and acceptance'. However, she was also adamant that she had been building a Citizenship programme which rigorously addressed the political literacy element and she would not review the balance of the school's provision to accommodate this policy development. This implied a clear understanding of shifting priorities for policy initiators, but an equally clear decision about largely ignoring those changes. For Mary, the school's provision had an internal logic, which was partly driven by its ethos, partly determined by a longer curriculum development cycle in which the school had always attempted to make space for teaching about an international dimension and partly shaped by her own sense of what the children needed (political literacy).

The response to this aspect of the agenda in Oak Park seemed less clear and less assertive. Katrina, the only black Citizenship teacher interviewed, argued that the main issue the school needed to address was not related to the students' sense of identity, rather it was about how they perceived others.

> 'Going back to the key concepts of Citizenship, I think in this school the understanding of not necessarily identity, but diversity in this school, I think is a major issue because that kind of understanding of the fact that not all immigrants that come to this country [Penny – yeh] are illegal immigrants… it's impossible if you are a member of the EU [laughs] you know, to be an illegal immigrant because your, you… it's kind of that understanding of diversity that a lot of the students here kind of don't understand'.

This is one of several points in the joint interview where Katrina raised issues related to ethnicity and racism. However, on several occasions Penny's reaction was to de-racialize the nature of the observation; for example, here Katrina was clearly opening up the distinction between EU citizenship and free movement in the context of the debate about immigration and the xenophobia she felt was often present in her classroom ('we always have discussions about immigration in my lessons, we always come back to immigration'), but Penny's next comment reverted to an easier more comfortable criticism of the children's parochialism:

> 'Even accents, I mean, Gemma [a student teacher] came to our school and she kind of had like a London accent and they couldn't get their head round it at all, they'd be like, they'd copy what she said, and I said, that's how the kids speak where I come from, I said, you know, they drop their T's, we'll do that next year, we'll catch up with the pace, with the kids [laughs]… sorry…'

They both drew on a range of examples from their teaching to illustrate the work they undertook in relation to diversity, including lessons about the lived experiences of British Muslims to tackle Islamophobia, and watching Hotel Rwanda to teach about conflict, the UN and human rights. This latter example was used to encourage the students to appreciate how conflicts may make it impossible for people to stay where they are, and to try to develop empathy for people who have to claim refugee status or who decide to migrate elsewhere. In trying to explain how she tackled this, Katrina expressed the difficulty she felt:

> 'I try not to suppress any of their opinions, I try to challenge, I don't always challenge, I then ask a question to the rest of the class, what do you think of this opinion, do you think this is always the case what are other cases I try to umm challenge [Penny – develop thinking] develop, yeh, I try to challenge… that one… that I can see, that I think is quite narrow minded or really, you know, quite negative views of the world around them, I'll try and challenge it, but umm, what is it, you know, we've got time constraints, there are always things…

I try not to, I really, really try not to umm get too much involved… some things are quite extreme in terms of their views and you try and challenge, try to get them to re-think, think about what they're actually saying, do they actually mean what's just come out of their mouth or are they, they haven't thought it through properly'.

This is one of the least coherent sections of her interview, and the uncompleted phrases indicate a lack of certainty, which presumably stems from a lack of clarity about how to tackle this in the classroom. It appears that Katrina felt that suppressing students' opinions would not be appropriate, and so she is left to challenge opinions, but this is then qualified and applied only to extreme views. This gives some idea of the difficulties involved for a young, inexperienced teacher trying to open up these issues and, having opened them up in the classroom, trying to bring them to some purposeful resolution.

Socio-economic diversity

These teachers' understanding of the local community and their account of diversity also touched on issues of class and socio-economic status. Katrina pointed out that the school's lack of diversity included socio-economic status as well as ethnicity, and Penny reflected on this in relation to the minority of students who did not share in the general affluence of the local area:

'And those students who do have that deprivation, you don't tend to, they don't tend to discuss it because they've got their own issues… and also they don't want to share because the rest of them either come from big houses or….'

Here the students from poorer families were presented as somehow cowed by their poverty and unable to articulate their experience. But Penny went on to argue that this was partly also due to a general lack of awareness of class:

'And there isn't that understanding, when we were children there was that understanding there was working class, there was middle class, there was upper class, there was all of that and there hasn't been, obviously the Labour government they're more about being equal, and so obviously that's pushed it out, but when they watch East Is East they have no idea about social class and stuff like that, and something that's really obvious to us'.

This theme, reflecting on students' general ignorance in relation to class, was also echoed in Katrina's comments:

'The students in this school particularly they kind of don't get that some people actually don't have any money at all, 'why can't they just go and buy some new shoes or some new clothes?', they don't get that actually some people can't because you know there is no money, there is no money, it's that kind of, the... free school meals in this school is less than 10 per cent, or less than, I don't know what the, I don't know the percentage at all, but it's it's very small in proportion to schools that are just in the direction of London'.[1]

These comments are also interesting in that the children were described once again as limited by their own experiences. The teachers feel the students lack the ability to understand the nature of diversity, partly because their school is generally homogenous, and partly because they lack the critical understanding required to put their own experiences in the broader context of Britain as a whole.

Implicit learning

Given the emphasis in Oak Park's school policies on the need to dispel ignorance about diversity and teach to support inclusion, it seemed reasonable to ask to what extent the teachers tackled these areas of ignorance in their teaching. In the conversation with Katrina and Penny, they agreed that class was not explicitly taught at all in the Citizenship curriculum:

'I think it's more implicit [Penny – yeh], I always try and refer back to it... implicitly, but it's not explicit in, this is... this is what real poverty, you know is like, or this is a diverse, diverse... you know what I'm saying?'. (Katrina).

This is important because in the preceding comments these two teachers had generally agreed that the students' understanding of class (and diversity in general) was limited, and Penny argued that the minority of students from poorer families felt alienated because of their socio-economic status. This would seem to be a legitimate area for teaching then, both to address students' lack of knowledge, and to attempt to build a more inclusive ethos. The Ajegbo Review

---

[1] This latter section is interesting because it betrays the fact that Katrina has a definite view of the school and its socio-economic profile, but she acknowledges that this is not rooted in factual knowledge. Her lack of knowledge about the actual proportion of students in receipt of free school meals does not interfere with her ability to make an argument about the students' families. In fact, the 2007 OfSTED report for the school indicates that the proportion of students eligible for free school meals is only just below the national average. Although of course this is likely to be considerably lower than the outer London boroughs with which Katrina draws the comparison, the level is likely to be above her estimate of 10 per cent.

argued that many teachers taught about diversity (largely religious and ethnic diversity) but often failed to engage with the lived experience of diversity. In this example, there seems to be a lack of attention paid to both the knowledge dimension, and to the lived experiences of students and others.

After Chris had raised issues relating to identity and multiculturalism, I asked her about the extent to which this area was covered in citizenship education. Her answer reflected the approach adopted above in relation to class:

'Well I mean, I suppose I'd like to think that through the teaching and learning it umm it embeds those sort of core skills of tolerance and of, umm, of understanding of open-mindedness, and I don't think it necessarily directly deals with those issues but I think for education if people make informed choices then so be it, but I think when informed choices aren't made that's when assumptions... are made, am I making myself sort of... [interviewer clears throat, well...] I'm just saying I don't think it directly deals with, I think it's too, it's a very difficult subject to directly deal with but I think through the skills, learning Citizenship through the type of education that you're giving, the using the right material umm you're building up understanding and like I say tolerance, yeh... [interviewer umm, do you...] from a non personal umm, I think with young people you've got to be careful to, to whilst making it a real situation, taking it away from them as well and giving them some more global issues to look at, and allowing them to have that understanding of tolerance and blah blah blah, and then using those skills to reflect maybe on more local situations or....'.

Chris was struggling in this answer to articulate her response, and her lack of confidence is evident in the pauses, the way she asks if she is making sense, and in the use of phrase 'blah, blah, blah' which indicates that she feels perhaps she is reverting to clichés or listing meaningless phrases. In fact, her answer clarified to some extent the assumptions underpinning the school's policy statements about the role of teaching in this regard – Citizenship was seen to be valuable not because it tackled the issues directly, but because it built a general outlook, and a set of skills for critically thinking about social issues, which, if successfully taught, could be applied to specific situations, such as those relating to diversity. This is more or less the approach supported by Bernard Crick (as discussed in Chapter 4), who encouraged teachers to avoid 'full frontal' assaults on racism, and to see citizenship education in the round, as having the capacity to 'to cure the disease as a denial of free and equal citizenship, not constantly to battle with the symptoms' of racism (Crick, 2000a: 132).

However, in adopting this approach it is equally clear that the school's Citizenship provision fell short of the Ajegbo Review's recommendations that teachers should pay attention to the lived experience of diversity in the UK. These teacher interviews indicate that the tensions in policy and academic circles about the relationship between Citizenship and community cohesion are also reflected in the classroom. In Chapter 6 I argued that teachers appeared to have identified social problems and then interpreted Citizenship as a means to correct the problems. In the discussion above it appears that the teachers had identified some specific issues relating to socio-economic status and other forms of inequality as areas for Citizenship to address, but they appeared to be reticent to follow this diagnosis through and to use Citizenship to tackle the issues head-on. Their reticence seems all the more remarkable when one considers the views of the students themselves (discussed in Chapter 7) who seemed quite keen for Citizenship to engage with some of the issues more directly. The final section of this chapter turns to consider what the young people in the case study schools had to say about diversity and community.

Students

The local community

As we saw from the discussion of the teachers' perceptions, Chris felt very strongly that, as a community school, Citizenship and community cohesion went hand in hand in Oak Park. She was a strong advocate of the idea that Citizenship should promote stronger links between the school and the community, and between the students and their community. This was reflected in one of the contributions in the very first meeting with the student research group:

> 'It's for us to get involved in community stuff, because we do involve a lot of the community, like when we're doing like voting the polling station is always in the school so it's kind of like the centre of the community and I think they try and teach us stuff based around community... and I think all the things they teach us are mostly relevant to us'. (Amelia, OP Meeting 1).

Whilst this particular example perhaps overstated the significance of the school hosting the local polling station during elections (this is a common arrangement) it did nevertheless reiterate Chris' point about the centrality of the school to the community. The point Amelia made in relation to being taught about the local community was also reflected in some of the interviews the student researchers conducted, where students felt this was valuable. One boy said he did not feel very involved in the community but that Citizenship made him think about doing so, 'because it kind of explains that the community is important', (OP Interviewee 1, Year 8), whilst another agreed 'it's taught me about my community and how it works' (OP Interviewee 8, Year 11). However, by the end of the research other students were voicing more sceptical arguments:

> 'I think as a whole school we should do more for our local community... because we *claim* to be this school that loves... that is at the heart of the community... but we don't actually do anything that actually helps our local community' (Claire, OP Meeting 5).

The school clearly does do something about community links, but the force of this student's views reflects that, for her at least, the rhetoric has outstripped the reality.

The global community

By contrast with the focus on local community evident in many of the conversation in Oak Park, students in The Heath School barely mentioned their local community. This was partly due to the context of the school – as a large school in a small town drawing on a very large catchment area, the local community was not particularly relevant to the students or the teachers. Coupled with the school's international ethos, this meant that young people were much more likely to talk about global citizenship and the global community, than they were to discuss local issues. Most of the examples of important topics involved national and international examples. For example, learning about rights was largely concerned with learning about rights violations and political action in other countries, learning about charities was often linked to specific crises in poorer countries, and students were more likely to mention the UN and EU than they were to discuss the UK or local government.

Racism

The case study in Oak Park yielded much more data because I was able to sustain my work with the students for much longer and because they had time to interview their peers about aspects of Citizenship. As a consequence, by the time of our final meeting the students appeared to be discussing their ideas quite freely which was reflected in the informal ways in which they talked about race and diversity.

'I can understand why a teacher would stop a student, because if you go into racial things, then yes it would have to be stopped [Robert – but it's still their opinion and you have to hear it out] but no, you can't... they should have their opinion to a certain extent, but you can't like go into racial... like all black people should be banned from the country or something, [Robert interrupts with inaudible comment] see Robert, that's what I'm saying... you can't shout out... if you say like I don't like the Conservatives because I don't agree with their policies or something, you can, that's an opinion... but if you go into a whole racial or some sort of discrimination sort of thing, you have to stop it there because you could offend people and they could get upset about it' (Tony, OP Meeting 5).

This echoes a point raised in the first meeting, that racism appears to serve as a marker for unacceptable behaviour – students generally seem to understand that this is an area where they may not go. This attitude was evident in the student survey results when they were asked if they thought teachers should sometimes stop students from expressing themselves during discussions in the Citizenship classroom. Whilst three quarters of students said this should never happen, many of those who said they thought it was acceptable cited being offensive as a common reason why students should be stopped from speaking, and the only specific examples of such behaviour mentioned racism.

Amelia used the discussions about race and religion in the student research group to share some of her personal experiences. Her only account of her own ethnicity occurred in the middle of a story about her father, where she noted 'he's not white or anything', which indicated a hesitance in the way she described herself. Here it was captured in this slightly odd formulation 'or anything' which seemed to soften the otherwise very clear sentence, and therefore somehow diffuse the statement that her father was not white. In an earlier meeting, when we were planning the questionnaire, Amelia said it would not be adequate to simply ask students to indicate whether they had a religion, because 'I'm a Muslim, but there's a scale: normal to extremist, we need to ask a question about where they are on the scale' (Amelia, OP Meeting 2). I noted this in my research journal as it seemed to indicate defensiveness about her identity. There is a similar discomfort about the following story, which Amelia recounted in one of the student research meetings:

'Certain people like Cara, I know she's only joking when she turns round and calls people a Paki because that's like, what she does [Robert – can she really talk?... her calling people a Paki...] no, she only calls her friends, so we know, and so like she names us each a different name, it is offensive, like for a stranger, they would turn round and punch her in the face... but because like, we're her friends we sort of know, but if someone said something like that in class, they would be in massive trouble...' (Amelia, OP Meeting 5).

On one reading, this reflects the ways in which taboo terms are often used informally among young people; even so there seems some discomfort about being called a 'Paki', even in jest – as Amelia points out this would attract a punch in the face anywhere else. But on the other hand it seems significant that the person who used these terms also appeared to be from a minority ethnic group, which might indicate this was an attempt to reclaim these harmful words.

To explore this possibility I mentioned the example of the reclaiming of the word 'nigger' and illustrated it with examples from my own teaching, where I had to discuss with some black students whether they could use the word (which was widely used within their friendship group) within the school. This elicited the following response from Tony:

'Black people, it really annoys me, like they call each other nigger and they don't get told off for it, and then if we say it, we get, we get, well we get expelled from the school, that's how seriously they take it [Robert – a black person is allowed to be racist to a white person] yeh, exactly and we're not allowed to do that and they just play the black card... they bring the whole history back and say, you used to use us as slaves' (Tony, OP Meeting 5).

This exchange between Robert and Tony is interesting because of the way several related ideas come cascading together. First Tony has misunderstood my example, which could be the fault of my explanation, but I think it is actually related to a simplistic reading of equality, which asserts that everyone must adhere to exactly the same rules at all times regardless of difference, rather than with regard to relevant differences. Robert then moves the conversation to another point entirely by arguing that a black person can get away with racism towards a white person, which is clearly different from the previous point in which a black person uses a word which is usually seen to be derogatory to black people. This then elicits another different point from Tony, when he claims not only are some black students allowed to be racist to their white peers, but they also play the race card, thus somehow pushing the burden of white guilt onto Tony and Robert's (white) shoulders. This kind of reasoning is discussed in Hewitt's study, 'White Backlash', in which individual stories about racial antagonism are interpreted as examples of white students being treated more harshly than minority ethnic students when those in authority become involved and punish the white students disproportionately (Hewitt, 2005). What is interesting about the comparison is that Hewitt's discussion focused on poor, white students' perceptions in the racially charged atmosphere of Greenwich in the shadow of Stephen Lawrence's murder and an active local BNP. Robert and Tony were in a relatively affluent, semi-rural, predominantly white area, yet the same perceptions persisted.

Amelia chose to respond to this complaint of unfair perceived treatment with a more concrete example:

> 'Sometimes like, they don't take punishment too far, like my brother, when he was in the school, someone was really... they were friends and they fell out and he decided to be really racist to him in front of the teacher and the teacher decided not to do anything, and so other students went to the Head of Year and complained and finally something happened, he got a day in isolation and I thought... what he said it wasn't reasonable, and in a way, I'm not saying everybody should be really punished, but they should know that if they go out into the streets and just start walking down the High Street and turnaround to say like an Indian person and say like "oh here you Paki" and punch them in the face...'. (Amelia, OP Meeting 5)

> '[Interrupting] Maybe that should be a lesson in Citizenship, err racial discrimination or something' (Tony).

> '... You should have lessons in, actually, racism' (Amelia).

> 'That should be a lesson in Year 7, that's the sort of relevance I'm talking about in Year 7' (Tony).

By providing this example from her own family's experience of the school, Amelia effectively undermined the point Robert and Tony had been making about white students somehow being at a disadvantage, and asserted a clear counter example where a minority ethnic student had suffered from racist abuse, but where the teacher had chosen not to treat it as a racist incident. Tony's swift agreement that something should be done indicated that the first exchange with Robert does not represent his view entirely.

Returning to the subject later, two other student researchers began to think about the importance of their context in this debate:

> 'The school is mainly white and we're always going to have... because we're in Oakton, and it's like, the best we can do is tell them that it's wrong I guess' (Mary, OP Meeting 5).

> 'I think sometimes it's hard for people in like places, like small communities, because like if you're somewhere in London, you'd have a different like

opinion, but I think it depends like where you are to teach racism. Racism can be taught quite easily if it's in a multicultural place where it's an everyday thing to see different people, yeh sometimes I think people dominate' (Shelley, OP Meeting 5).

In terms of the main focus of this research – exploring students' experiences of citizenship education – what seemed pertinent was the revelation that these students said they had not experienced any lessons about racism. There was ready agreement in the research group that the school should teach about racism and explicitly reinforce an anti-racist message through Citizenship, indeed the student researchers identified this as one of their recommendations to the senior management team when they presented their findings. It is particularly interesting that this appeared not to be a feature of the school's planned provision given that the policy documents, discussed in Chapter 6, positioned racism as an issue for teaching rather than discipline. However, it does indicate that the teachers' reticence to teach about inequality head-on (which emerged from their interviews) has indeed had an impact on the students, who felt this was an omission.

Multiculturalism

The research group's discussions of the student survey results and about racism and the school led them to identify this as an area for further investigation in the interviews. Consequently they agreed to approach the subject by stating that England is a multicultural country and asking participants how that affected them, with possible follow up questions asking for people's opinions about the advantages and disadvantages of multiculturalism. Several themes emerged from these responses. The most common response was a positive one, usually referring to the chance to learn from others about their culture and to broaden their friendship circles to include people who were different to themselves.

'Umm, you can make friends out of your culture and you can learn more about their cultures which is good for RE' (Interviewee 5, OP Year 11).

'We are in a diverse society and we learn about each other… we have better ideas of culture like food and religion' (Interviewee 7, OP Year 9).

'You get to meet new people' (Interviewee 9, OP Year 10).

These comments reflect the most frequent type of response, far more frequent than those who merely noted that multiculturalism was a fact of life, and those who implied that multiculturalism gave rise to problems.

Of those who cited specific disadvantages or who volunteered problems associated with multiculturalism, one mentioned that it is difficult to make friends with people from different cultures, another complained that having to be constantly aware of diversity 'becomes a bit too much all the time' (OP Interviewee 19, Year 9), and another complained that the English were not allowed to wave their flag. One is worth quoting at greater length:

> 'Well there's some people from other countries that have caused havoc in our communities if you know what I mean [laughs] you know the tubes blowing up, you know that's the disadvantages, the advantage is that [laughs] we've got them working in corner shops' (OP Interviewee 25, Year 9).

This interview was interesting because the interviewee was a friend of the interviewer and she clearly adopted a playful approach to the whole interview, for example using silly voices for different answers, especially when she was giving an extended or reasoned answer. It is difficult to read this extract in that context, and my sense from listening to the recording is that this reflected an exaggerated perspective that she was adopting for the interview; however, she was not presenting this answer as the opinion of someone else entirely. I therefore read it as a reflection of her own understanding, but expressed in a way that is intended to gain some comic effect – hence the frequent laughter whilst she is talking. The laughter is not reciprocated though, and clearly laughter also works in conversation as a way to sugar the pill, and de-emphasize the potential offensiveness of what is being said. Whilst this answer presents these views in a particularly stark light it does reflect other aspects of the responses more generally – she was not alone in referring to corner shops and ethnic restaurants, nor in linking diversity to immigration.

Some of the other answers also conflated 'multicultural society' with 'immigration', with several respondents referring to our overcrowded country, foreigners and people who come to our country, for example:

> 'Yes... it affects me because it shouldn't just be like me talking to people from Britain you should be talking to people from all over the world to see what their culture is like... Some people are rude... once there was this person came from a different country and that person was quite rude to me and I thought not everyone can be nice from other countries' (OP Interviewee 12, Year 7).

> 'We get people who are not meant to be over here' (OP Interviewee 22, Year 9).

As interviewee 12 implies, the connection between immigration and a multicultural society does not necessarily mean that children have negative views about diversity, but it does reinforce the binary division between 'us' (presumably white, English) and 'them' (multicultural Britain), as opposed to a more inclusive understanding, which simply accepts that 'we' are multicultural.

Where negative viewpoints were more evident, the respondents often mentioned employment, and these answers also fed off a 'them' and 'us' view of the world, which allows the conclusion that 'they' are taking 'our' jobs.

> 'I mean, there are less jobs available, but that's it really' (OP Interviewee 5, Year 11).

> 'Disadvantages, they take jobs of ours' (OP Interviewee 23, Year 9).

> '...of course it's becoming very crowded in England but I don't think that's a problem, people need to get out of their country and that's OK and people need jobs because everyone deserves the right to have a job and not to be discriminated against because they're not from England' (OP Interviewee 26, Year 9).

Unlike direct racism, this does seem to be an area the students have learned about in Citizenship classes. In our initial meeting, one of the research group explained how she had engaged with this area of debate:

> 'It's a bit like when we did the topic on asylum seekers, loads of people thought, oh yes, people coming over and stealing our jobs, and then we kind of like, because we gained a better understanding we were like, oh wait, that's not entirely true. And I think it does help... it's not there to change people's opinion – your opinion is whatever you think' (Shelley, OP Meeting 1).

However, by the end of their interviewing phase, the research group seemed rather disillusioned with the answers they had heard, and with the lack of understanding that seemed to be evident in much of their data.

In their discussion of this section of the interviews, the research group had the following exchange:

> 'I think people almost had, like an almost racist thing when it came to what are the disadvantages of them being here' (Claire, OP Meeting 5).

> 'It's like parents have said to them, they've taken our jobs, they've taken our jobs' (Mary).

> '... ignorance...' (Claire).

> 'I've sort of come to that conclusion where everyone's racist nowadays' (Robert).

> 'You could tell their opinion had been influenced by someone else because if

you like said, why do you think that, they'd be like, oh I don't know... like it's almost like... I don't know if it's the media or stuff like that...' (Claire).

These young people were clearly sensitive to some of the ways in which everyday racist assumptions informed many of the comments they heard during interviews.

They also remarked on the unexpectedly high number of references to take-aways and restaurants. Their engagement with this reflected their sense that there was something significant here, but also their inability to describe and analyse it fully:

'To be fair, not in a racist way, that is a really good thing, because people are accepting other cultures because they are eating their food, because otherwise if they weren't accepting them they would sort of say they wouldn't eat their food' (Claire, OP Meeting 5).

Once again, Amelia, as the only member of the research group to identify herself (albeit hesitantly) as a member of a minority ethnic group, brought some clarity to the discussion:

'I watched this documentary... and it was like a racist one and it was about this, two really like, there was two Pakistani people, they were married and they were like journalists and this 10 year old kid was walking up to this lady, running around her with his bike, like pushing her, punching her, like beating her up and I thought that's like a bit shocking... but that's not to say that he won't still go and eat Chinese and Indian food, that they haven't accepted the culture because they don't believe it's right for them to live there' (Amelia, OP Meeting 5).

Through this story Amelia makes a powerful point, that underlying racist assumptions can remain intact whilst a superficial engagement with cultural diversity is apparent. Because she is more attuned to the ways in which these assumptions have affected her and her family, she can highlight some of them for the others in the group.

From the above discussion it is evident that the student researchers felt there was a combination of ignorance, misunderstandings and negative attitudes that amounted to a kind of everyday low-level racism that was not being tackled by the school's Citizenship provision. Whilst some members of the group felt that they had personally benefitted from lessons where immigration, the Taliban and Islam were discussed openly, they recognized that this was largely due to their teacher, and was not a systematically planned element of the citizenship education programme. They argued that the responses of their peers in the interviews indicated there was a need for a more explicit approach to this area.

> 'I think like if religion were taught it would get over the terrorism thing and people would more understand that it's not just Muslims that are terrorists, you know there was that abductor guy going round taking the kids... all the parents in my little brother's school were going round their little kids saying any guy who is coloured who is like, who doesn't look normal and he's not from England you have to stay away from him and not go near him...and my dad, he's not white or anything, and my mum felt really sad that my dad would feel uncomfortable going to pick my brothers up, and I think that's really out of order that someone could say that to their children and think it's right, so I think if more religions are taught it can get over that terrorism and racism thing" (Amelia, OP Meeting 5).

Amelia's comments came after a lengthy discussion about the school's RE provision, and there was general consensus that religion was not taught in a way that interested students, nor which engaged with the real lives of people in Britain.

Conclusions

In the longitudinal survey it appears that there is general unanimity that tolerance of diversity can sit alongside a positive identity with the vast majority of respondents feeling some positive identification with England or Britain. However, the ICCS comparative case study data indicated that in some areas, especially attitudes towards migrant communities and trust in public institutions, citizenship may be experienced differently depending on ethnicity and religious belief. There is some evidence here that white young people and those from Christian backgrounds are more negative in relation to migrant rights and more likely to trust public institutions, whilst those from minority ethnic backgrounds are more positive about immigration and less likely to trust such institutions. Again, these findings echo differences in UK society at large.

The teacher interviews illustrate the complex ways in which the teachers in Oak Park have constructed their own understanding of Citizenship. In some important ways they resonate with aspects of the political agenda which informed the development of the Citizenship curriculum, but these teachers also espouse views which are at odds with some aspects of the official model.

Broadly speaking one can discern a general tendency towards a communitarian model of citizenship, and there is a significant focus in this school on developing Citizenship as part of a broader project in which the school aspires to be a community school, which implies internal developments to ensure a sense of community within the school, and a closer set of links between the school and other institutions, agencies and individuals outside. Whilst this falls short of the civic republican model, it does connect with other aspects of the model presented in the Crick Report, which adopted a rather general philosophical stance on the nature of citizenship, as opposed to a detailed engagement with the inequalities which shape citizens' lives. In Oak Park School, there is a tendency to treat 'the community' as a rather homogenous entity, whilst the other aspect of this discourse 'diversity' is often left implicit. The teachers are able to articulate some strong views about the students' experience and understanding of diversity, but they appear reticent about explicitly engaging with this as the main content of a lesson, and they also often demonstrate a lack of confidence about how to deal with it when these issues arise within the class.

The student research group were increasingly uncomfortable as they became aware of the low-level racism that was evident in their interviews. Whilst many students were able to talk in general terms of the benefits of multiculturalism, there was a tendency to elide multiculturalism with immigration. The student researchers felt quite strongly that the Citizenship curriculum should more proactively tackle prejudice and discrimination in lessons, but in neither of the schools was this discussed as a major area of work. The students in Oak Park shed some light on the ways in which the tensions between general commitments to principles of community and reciprocity can be undermined by a corrosive scepticism towards immigration. The students themselves came to the conclusion that reality was much more complicated in this regard than it seemed from first appearances. Whilst young people tend to profess they are committed to inclusive values, the ongoing negative attitudes towards immigration (and immigrants) implies there is a serious need for schools to address these issues. Whilst these schools partially responded in their Citizenship lessons, the young people felt there was room for improvement.

10

Active Citizenship

A range of factors influenced the introduction of citizenship education into the national curriculum but two of the most significant were the desire to promote higher levels of interest in politics among young people and higher levels of participation. For Blunkett and Crick, this was certainly the defining characteristic of their civic republican view, and they espoused the belief that, when properly inducted into citizenship, young people could come to understand the democratic imperative for them to participate and come to appreciate how this would lead to a more fulfilled life. It is fitting for this to feature as the final substantive chapter in this book and, as with the previous two chapters, we will start with an overview of the data about this theme, and then consider the view from the case study schools, starting with the teachers' views and ending with the young people.

Young people, participation and intentions

Eighteen–year-olds had good intentions with regards to their future participation with around 70 per cent in the longitudinal CELS survey saying they intended to vote in elections, raise money and volunteer in the future (Keating et al., 2010: 26). In the 2009 ICCS comparative survey 72 per cent said they intended to vote in national elections (68 per cent in 1999). Actual participation rates in elections were far below this, for example there was a 44 per cent turnout for 18–24 year olds in 2010 (Ipsos-Mori, 2010), but young people have been consistently less likely than older people to vote, indicating that when they become older they do indeed vote in greater numbers (Office for National Statistics, undated). The gap between young and old voters has varied over time but analysis of the 2010 election indicates that whilst the gap remained, the turnout increased more markedly for 18–24 year olds (7 per cent higher than 2005) than for all other age groups (Ipsos-Mori, 2010).

In the CELS longitudinal cohort, the final year's data looked at participation rates among 18-year-olds, who had been through secondary schooling since the introduction of citizenship education. The data tells us as much about changes over the period of adolescence as it does about the impact of citizenship education, with many measures dipping towards the end of secondary school. For these 18 year olds the most common form of political participation was signing a petition (59 per cent), with other forms of activity being much less common – attending a public meeting or rally (15 per cent), campaigning with others (12 per cent), contacting an MP or councillor (11 per cent). Perhaps more significantly, 29 per cent reported they had participated in none of these political activities. These low figures are reflected in independent national surveys of citizenship activity, which continue to indicate that young people participate less than other age groups (Taylor and Low, 2010).

Clearly though, remaining in school or college is a significant factor, as 48 per cent of CELS respondents said they had taken part in fundraising activities in school, whilst only 28 per cent said they had done so outside of school, work or training (Keating et al., 2010: 22). Participation in school councils rose for those staying on in school or college with 52 per cent of 18–year-olds reporting they had voted in school council elections, compared to 41 per cent of 16-year-olds and 45 per cent of 11–year-olds (Keating et al., 2010: 20). Whilst the majority of students reported participating in some sort of civic activity in school (voting, standing for election, supporting good causes), very few continued such involvement outside of school, with between 10–20 per cent reporting involvement with political or environmental organisations or campaigns.

The exception to the generally low levels of out of school engagement is young people's involvement with fund raising campaigns, where 46 per cent reported involvement (although for some their involvement was over a year before the survey, indicating this is not a regular commitment). Almost two in five reported some form of involvement in voluntary community groups, a figure which may also lend some support to the hypothesis that young people's engagement tends not to be overtly political (see Chapter 4 and Nelson et al., 2010: 88, Weller, 2007). This may reflect levels of interest, or feelings of low efficacy. In relation to efficacy, only 42 per cent agreed that they have political opinions worth listening to (Nelson et al., 2010: 82), and in relation to interest 59 per cent rarely or never spoke to parents about political issues, and 68 per cent rarely or never spoke with their friends about political issues (Nelson et al., 2010: 90).

Positive intentions to participate were generally correlated with high levels of civic knowledge and parental interest in social and political issues (Nelson et al., 2010: 96). However, overall the data indicates that activities such as voting and volunteering are supported much more highly than more 'activist' forms of citizenship such as joining a political party, campaigning, and attending meetings, which reflects the patterns in the general population (DCLG, 2011: 7). This reflects a tendency evident in both the CELS and ICCS research projects for young people to hold a more holistic definition of citizenship than merely political participation (Nelson et al., 2010: 50–2). The two most commonly supported characteristics of good citizenship were 'working hard' (94 per cent agreed) and 'obeying the law' (93 per cent), whilst voting (79 per cent) was seen as equally important to more general commitments such as promoting human rights (77 per cent) and protecting the environment (79 per cent). Despite the low levels of trust young people had in politicians, 81 per cent of ICCS respondents maintained that 'respecting government representatives' was an important characteristic of the good citizen. These findings would suggest that notions of the 'good citizen' still hold out over the 'active citizen', which in turn reflects Crick's discussion of the prevalent tendency to favour a de-politicised account of the 'good citizen' (Crick, 2000a: 2).

As this data demonstrates, there is more support for forms of involvement which are relatively undemanding but despite these figures the ICCS report's authors struck an optimistic note in their interpretation of this data:

> Pupils need to be given opportunities to participate in school and class decision-making processes and to take an active part in school life. Whilst it is important for schools to stress the importance of future adult engagement in political life, it is not imperative that pupils are encouraged to take part in too much out-of-school activity at the age of 14. It seems much more advantageous to pupils to develop an understanding of democratic process and of decision making through the secure environment of their schools and classrooms (Nelson et al., 2010: 112–3).

This is an argument which one may or may not support, but it certainly reflects the reality that opportunities for involvement are more easily provided *within* schools. Taken together with young people's propensity for low-demand forms of participation, this may well explain the low rates of out of school participation. The actual participation rates for 18-year-olds are considered in the CELS report discussed above, and this data indicates that levels of community engagement increase between the ages of 14 and 18, providing some support for the optimistic interpretation.

Teachers

I asked Chris to reflect on how her understanding of Citizenship had developed since the subject's introduction in Oak Park, and the active dimension emerged very strongly in her response:

> 'Initially my understanding was probably very, very small... I think, obviously it was to try and make people, in my understanding at the time, was to try and make people good citizens, engage them in their community and you know I suppose raise, you know, political apathy, to try and get people, literally, engaged more and to give them a level of education that allows them to do that'.

When she discussed how her thinking had developed over the years, Chris argued that she had come to appreciate the broader agenda for citizenship education:

> 'It was bigger than that, it's not just about knowledge is it? It's about giving them an experience and I think initially what came across was this is what they've got to learn and I think it takes... when you've got a subject like Citizenship it's actually very different from lots of subjects in the sense that it's very active. And I think initially it was another subject with another load of knowledge that we've got to teach and over time I think what's become really clear is that it's not just the teaching and learning, it's all the other things that go along side it'.

Chris described the tensions between knowledge and action and implied that, as she became more familiar with the subject, and more confident in leading Citizenship in school, she has been able to develop the active dimension. In this it appears active citizenship is different to identity and diversity in that Chris felt she had moved to a resolution – she wanted to promote a more active model of citizenship rather than a narrower knowledge based model.

By contrast, Jenny in The Heath School felt this was the weakest element of the school's provision. Whilst she was very active in organising Fair Trade events, and facilitating young people's campaigning and fundraising activities, she argued that 'we know we're quite strong on providing the lessons, and what we want to do is to be in a position to do the active stuff as well'. Jenny compared the school unfavourably to another school in the local authority, which had focused much more on active citizenship than the taught curriculum, and she felt that the active citizenship also provided a mechanism for bringing young people together.

Chris's earlier significant experiences in Oak Park were often apolitical and related to student voice, for example painting the classroom. When asked about the kinds of experiences she planned into the curriculum, Chris offered a much richer variety of experiential learning opportunities, including:

> 'Kids forming a pressure group on something and you know trying to campaign for change… kids forming a trade union and we give them fake scenarios and they get together and they campaign, umm, we do… voting, we have writing to MPS, we have… lots of different bits and pieces going on'.

These opportunities were planned into schemes of work, and most of these half-termly plans ended in some form of active application of the learning. Inevitably, many of these involved writing in class, but this demonstrates the ways in which teachers have to work within the constraints of the school curriculum.

Teachers were also willing to work beyond the curriculum in a variety of ways. All three Citizenship teachers in Oak Park mentioned a student-led project to establish a local youth club. Here Penny described what happened:

> 'I have a student in Year 11 who is one of the founding members of a charity… and they are a youth group created by youths, individuals, all young people, and myself and Chris have become a trustee… He's showed such commitment and dedication that he's already found a route in life where he wants to go and loves Citizenship… so that's always good'.

This was clearly a significant undertaking for all involved, and whilst the impetus for the action came from the student, the teachers' agreement to undertake the legal role of trustees was also necessary as part of the formalisation of the project into a charity. Chris explained that the student had secured local authority funding for a part-time youth worker and negotiated access to an existing building, but was lobbying now for a full-time youth worker and a dedicated building for this local provision. Whilst such projects are unlikely to characterise the formal Citizenship provision, it is noteworthy that the student had felt able to engage with the activity, and that the teachers had been prepared to invest the time and additional effort outside of their formal roles to support this programme. This illustrates that the commitment to active citizenship runs across a broad spectrum of activities, from minimal classroom engagement (writing letters, role plays etc) to significant opportunities to influence the community in enduring ways.

This spectrum of activities in the school also included other forms of participation, and Chris saw participation in broad terms:

> 'I think we are lucky in that we have active community members who like to engage in Citizenship – we are the only department in the school who has its

governor regularly coming in and talking to the kids. And through external, through other agencies we manage to bridge the gap between the school being a separate entity in comparison to the local community so for example the youth service, allowing them in means they meet their remit and we get that kind of, the gap minimised between what goes on outside of school and inside school. Getting kids engaged and stuff... But I also think that it's important that, as much as we can, we get the kids out, and that the local community come in'.

Whilst some of the activities Chris outlined in her interview were explicitly political, for example trips to parliament and meetings with the local MP, she located these within a broader concept of constructive engagement with community activities, so that setting up stalls for the local carnival, investigating local statistics, discussing crime with police officers, engaging with youth workers, participating in simulations of political activity, and engaging in real campaigning are all cited as examples of active citizenship. This is perhaps a much more communitarian concept of citizenship than the narrower 'political' engagement advocated by Crick, and the overlap between active citizenship and discussion of the community, community links, and the school as a community school were important in defining the agenda for Chris.

In The Heath School where this was not such an overt element of how the school worked, Jenny felt there were often very real obstacles for young people:

'We found this with the Youth Bank group, they've got into this position where they've been voted there and they think right, we can do things now, we can start making changes and then they start hitting brick walls, they start realising the amount of bureaucracy involved in things, they realise there's red tape, they realise they've got to get all sorts of people to agree things, that they've got to have meetings and they realise that logistics of things and the cost and I think these things put them off, and you know, we've got people running a project at the moment where they've just sort of hit a brick wall and there is not a single person that they've come across who thinks what they're doing is a bad idea or who objects to what they're doing, it is simply a case that they're, you know, it's finding time for it'.

It is interesting, given this sense of frustration, that one of the active citizenship projects being undertaken in the school at the time I was collecting data was a group of students campaigning to get a shelter erected near the local train station so the large numbers of students using the station to get home could be protected from the weather. Four years on I received a copy of the school newsletter which reported that the shelter had finally been built and pictured the young campaigners, who had by then left school. This illustrates in very real terms how difficult it is to align the timescale of some citizens' actions with the curriculum timescale.

Students

The research with the young people covered several dimensions relevant to active citizenship. First, the discussions within the student research groups touched on active learning and out of school learning, which seemed to motivate the students involved and gave them an opportunity to apply their learning in a new situation. Second, the research explicitly focused on formal forms of civic participation, for example actual voting in school elections and intention to vote in general elections. Third, the research considered broader forms of community activity and asked students to share information in relation to their community involvement.

In the initial meeting with the student research groups there was a significant difference between a broadly positive attitude towards involvement in general, and a more sceptical attitude towards formal citizen participation, such as voting. All the students in the initial meeting agreed that voting was one of the least significant indicators of 'good citizenship' and in the discussion about this decision they developed two arguments to support their opinion. First, they argued that voting was ultimately a personal decision and therefore it would not be appropriate for anyone to question it. Second, some argued that because of the high number of people who had little understanding of politics, it was better to allow them to opt out of elections – they felt this was actually the most responsible decision someone could make, as opting out of elections was felt to be more appropriate than casting a vote whilst being ignorant of politics and the parties' manifestoes. This initial discussion seemed interesting then in that the students were able to articulate and defend a coherent argument about active citizenship which embraced taking responsibility for improving local conditions, but which also seemed to adopt a fairly ambiguous stance in relation to participating in elections.

Students were asked about voting in school elections, and secondly if they thought they would vote in a general election once they turned 18 years of age (they were also given space to explain their latter answer). In Oak Park, just over three quarters of the students believed it was important to vote in school elections, and in The Heath School two thirds said they had voted in their elections. In Oak park, where the survey was distributed through the whole school, there was some correlation with age, and the number agreeing each year fell from a high of 86 per cent in Year 7 to 63 per cent in Year 10.[1] There was also a difference between boys and girls, with girls being slightly more likely to agree (83 per cent for girls and 70 per cent for boys) and less likely to disagree (4 per cent for girls and 16 per cent for boys).[2] There were no gender differences evident in The Heath School.

School councils

In The Heath School the role of the school council emerged from the original discussions as quite controversial and so the survey asked some follow-up questions about attitudes towards it. Most students felt it could be improved and the two most common suggestions included simply making sure it had more impact, and secondly making sure students heard about what it achieved. There was a general sense that it was not successful, and Jenny agreed that students were often frustrated by the apparent lack of impact and the timescales associated with making decisions in school. In Oak Park there was relatively little discussion of the school council in the student interviews and in considering why this was the case, the student researchers felt that it was because the council had a relatively low profile.

> 'No-one really mentioned it... the school council do do stuff, but I think they don't really do anything that really stands out to us' (Student researcher[3], OP Meeting 5).

This led quickly to a discussion of an example which the student research group felt quite strongly had brought the school council into some measure of disrepute:

> 'One incident that happened, was that you know this new uniform, yeh, we all voted on what school uniform we wanted, and we went for stuff like blue jumpers, black skirts and black trousers and we got red kilts [laughter from others in the group] and basically our opinion was totally ignored, even though the school council was promised that what we said would really matter... and it was a massive thing... Mr P [the old Headteacher] and Mrs C [Head

---

[1] The Kendall's tau-b correlation coefficient was a relatively low 0.158, which is still significant at the 0.01 level (2 tailed).

[2] The Kendall's tau-b correlation coefficient for gender was lower than that for age, 0.122, which is only significant at the 0.05 level (2 tailed).

[3] This student is not identified because it was sometimes difficult to identify who was talking from the recording of the session, because students talked so quickly over each other.

of Citizenship] had an argument about it [Tony – did they?] yeh, she tells me everything' (Mary, OP Meeting 5).

This provides an interesting counterbalance to the very positive story presented by Chris in her interview and it also highlights the difficulties in working with school councils. This example illustrates a trap identified by a range of authors and practitioners in this field. Starting from a theoretical perspective, analysing Article 12 of the UNCRC, Lundy has drawn attention to the need to incorporate listening and responding into any system for realising student voice (Lundy, 2007) and, starting from more practical concerns, Trafford has identified the same requirement for any Headteacher who aspires to introduce an element of student democracy into their school (Trafford, 2008). Here the value of such advice is underlined, as the experience of being asked and subsequently ignored has left a lasting impression that the school council was not effective.

This interpretation is supported by the exchange that followed this example:

'Student voice – there's nothing underneath it' (Billy, OP Meeting 5).

'Student voice, there's nothing there, because we don't have a voice... Like, I don't actually know anything that the school council is involved in... but I think that's to do with Miss L [the new Headteacher] as well, you know I don't think she cares about the school council as much' (Shelley, OP Meeting 5).

'I don't think they take the school council seriously really, it's like it's a joke in a way' (Amelia, OP Meeting 5).

It is noteworthy that citizenship education was not necessarily tainted in this discussion, because student voice/the school council was seen as separate from Citizenship, and because Chris was seen as someone who was championing student voice in the school as a whole, representing the spirit of Citizenship beyond the confines of the Citizenship class. Of course, the lesson that was learned from this was that she had failed in this significant example, and therefore the overall place of students and student voice remained a limited one in these students' understanding of the school.

Voting intentions

When we come to consider general election voting intentions the picture was slightly different. In Oak Park only just over half the students intended to vote, and of the remaining students they were almost equally split between those who had no opinion and those who had no intention of voting. In The

Heath School, the proportion intending to vote was slightly higher at around two thirds. However, both schools had lower results than the larger surveys of young people's voting intentions, which indicate about 70 per cent intend to vote. Indeed, the figures in Oak Park are nearer the actual turnout figure for first time voters. This unexpectedly low figure does seem significant given that these schools were in many regards successful Citizenship schools where Citizenship lessons were generally well received by most students who generally enjoyed their learning.

Those who said they would vote gave many reasons to justify their answer. Only very few mentioned narrow self interest (to get benefits) or specific policies (to elect a government which would not go to war). Most made general points concerning the importance of voting as the main way we get to have a say in who runs the country and they also mentioned the importance of voting for the general good of the country and the need to help choose a government which would improve things. There was some evidence from the interviews that Citizenship had helped students to think about their voting intentions:

'Yes, now I know how to vote… and what to look out for in a political party' (OP Interviewee 8, Year 11).

'If you didn't have Citizenship then you wouldn't know how to vote or what to do' (OP Interviewee 11, Year 8).

Clearly this kind of connection was intended by policy initiators when they introduced Citizenship, and tackling voter apathy occurred in many justifications for the subject. However, the case study data indicated many students did not make such a connection.

Of those students who said they would not vote, there were a range of reasons given. Some reflected the media caricature of the apathetic youth and simply said they could not be bothered, or were not interested in politics at all; others said they didn't understand politics well enough to make an informed decision. Several others gave a variety of reasons for their scepticism about politics and elections, with some saying elections do not really make much difference; one saying that they just did not like the competition between politicians; and some dismissing politicians as a group:

'All the government parties are crooks and just lead the country into debt! The government are a load of CROOKS!! – with no experience of what is like to live as a real average citizen' (OP Respondent 145).

'Because the Government are stupid making unrealistic laws and sending our troops into Afghanistan and the citizens don't want them there' (OP Respondent 76).

These types of response indicate that it was not simply apathy that led these young people to say they were unlikely to vote; but for many of them the decision not to vote was actually the result of a level of political literacy. They had simply decided that they knew enough about politics and politicians to believe that they were untrustworthy, and therefore it probably would not matter much which politicians were elected to power. This research was conducted in the aftermath of the MP's expense scandal, and this had obviously fuelled some of the scepticism, but there were other reasons given as well, indicating that this willingness to dismiss politicians had more complicated causes. It also demonstrates that effective citizenship education can enhance political literacy, but does not necessarily challenge the political scepticism that many people feel as a result of their knowledge. The problem of voter turnout then is deeper than mere apathy and often reflects a more active and determined rejection of politics.

Turning to the broader dimension of active citizenship, the student co-researchers adopted different approaches in their surveys. In The Heath School they were interested in finding out what types of responsible actions students had undertaken, whilst in Oak Park they adopted a more open-ended approach. The list the students devised in The Heath School reflected the kinds of activities that had been promoted in classes: a third of students claimed to have bought a fair trade product; slightly fewer than half the students had ever signed a petition; only about 18 per cent had volunteered; 60 per cent had sponsored someone; 68 per cent recycled and 65 per cent switched off lights to save electricity. In Oak Park students were asked if Citizenship provided them with the chance to get involved in the community, and secondly if they felt they had sufficient opportunities to get involved. The findings from these two questions show that this is one of the least well developed dimensions of students' experiences – 29 per cent of students felt Citizenship gave them opportunities to get involved in the community and only a third felt they had enough opportunities to do so.

The relatively small number of students agreeing to these two questions illustrates the difficulties involved for the school in setting up opportunities for genuine community involvement for large numbers of students. In fact when one turns to the examples provided by the students in Oak Park who said that Citizenship had provided them with the chance to get involved in the community, one gains an appreciation of just what varied activities had been planned within the Citizenship programme. Several types of participation came up repeatedly, involving the youth centre and voluntary work in an old people's home. However, other examples that were mentioned by one or two students reflected a much wider range of active projects, which included: visits to parliament, visits to 11 million (the Children's Commissioner's office), eco-schools, fund-raising, army cadets, sports clubs, a party in the park and even clearing the graveyard. This range indicates the Citizenship department was facilitating a range of opportunities for engaging students in community-based projects, although the general nature of some of the examples might lead us to question the extent to which they all enabled students to apply specifically Citizenship knowledge and skills.

Some of the practical issues relating to such planning are hinted at in the interviews. Some active projects are much more easily planned into lesson times, so the Youth and Philanthropy Initiative (YPI), for example, requires students to make a case for funding to go to a cause they want to support. This kind of project directly links to the skills of advocacy in the programme of study for Citizenship, and can be seen as a self-enclosed project, which is relatively easy to build into lessons:

'… because of the YPI – charities… we can help our community and it's fun and active' (OP Interviewee 23, Year 9).

Another student indicated that the requirements of the GCSE course also provided a useful structure for ensuring that everyone had some form of active citizenship experience:

'We had to do active citizenship for our coursework so we had to get involved in the community' (OP Interviewee 6, Year 11).

However, as we have seen in previous chapters, some teachers have begun to argue that the GCSE requirement is actually fairly limited, and that the kinds of experiences that are accepted by the examination boards are not particularly demanding or active and may in fact be fairly superficial (Wright, 2011). This might be reflected in the following comment in response to a question exploring whether Citizenship had helped to promote community engagement:

'I don't think it has, like we did the games and another group did the community thing down the valley, so we had different things to do' (OP Interviewee 17, Year 10).

This appears to indicate that the teacher had to organise groups in order to manage the active citizenship dimension, and that some groups ended up doing more community based activities than others.

Whilst it is evident that the Citizenship department in the school planned and facilitated a wide variety of opportunities for community participation, the students seemed to feel they would like more. This demonstrates one of the enduring challenges to implementing Citizenship in a way which promotes the active dimension envisaged in the programme of study – the logistics of community involvement are simply very demanding. The other data in this section demonstrates that even when Citizenship is taught by well qualified teachers and is generally perceived positively by students, there is only a very weak correlation between these factors and future voting intentions. Given that Oak Park was a school with well-established Citizenship provision, it seems significant that voting intentions should have remained so much lower than can be seen in other surveys, and this at least signals the possibility that more Citizenship will not necessarily mean more voters, although it may lead to better informed non-participation.

Conclusion

In relation to active citizenship, it appears that young people overall favour low-demand forms of participation, and even in school minimal forms of engagement are favoured, for example voting in class elections and donating money. Whilst significant numbers of young people claim they are willing to vote (70 per cent plus intended to vote in both national reports), the general election data for 2010 indicates actual turnout remains significantly short of such figures. Similarly, actual and intended participation rates outside of school remain low for 14- and 18-year-olds, indicating that good intentions and good habits established in school do not necessarily lead on to high levels of community involvement. This evidence needs to be seen in relation to other pressures on children, and so perhaps we should not be surprised that relatively few teenagers are politically active in their communities, given the pressures on them to attend school or college, succeed in examinations and prepare for work or further study. The ICCS authors certainly favour this interpretation, and refocus their analysis on the significance of school to induct young people into some form of active citizenship. Here though the results are perhaps not as positive as one might expect with half of students still failing to engage in minimal forms of participation such as voting in school elections or contributing to fund raising efforts.

Oak Park appears to offer an impressive variety of opportunities for young people to get involved. As with the broad approach to 'community', these activities seem to be more aligned with a communitarian model than with the more focused civic republican model favoured by Crick. Participation seems to be valued more because of the connections it achieves between individuals, and between them and the community, than for its contribution to political literacy. Hence, starting a youth centre and painting a classroom appear as archetypal examples of valuable activities. Although the teachers also cite other examples of activities, which are more overtly political, there appears to be no imperative to enhance or interrogate these other non-political experiences, to turn them into political literacy learning opportunities. By contrast, The Heath School has not addressed active citizenship in such a thorough way and there is more responsibility on the students to organise their own activities.

Students generally appeared to desire more opportunities to engage in community activities. This reflected the practical difficulties in providing opportunities within a school structure. Even so there was some evidence that individual projects could be harnessed for several different types of Citizenship learning, and Oak Park's involvement in the local youth club illustrated how teachers were trying to use this as a resource for different kinds of participation and classroom learning. Given the difficulties inherent in planning community based learning there is a need to make the most of in-school opportunities for active engagement and participation. In this regard it is significant that, whilst the teachers in both schools spoke highly about the school council, the students perceived it as problematic. The older they got, the less likely they were to think voting in school elections was important and there was also evidence of some scepticism about the extent to which the school management really wanted to listen to the student voice.

11

New Labour, New Citizens?

To what extent did New Labour's intentions succeed?

It has been the contention of this book that at the heart of the Labour government's domestic policy agenda there was a core set of ideas about the role of citizens. Whilst the analysis of exactly what attributes and actions would characterise this citizen developed over time, and varied slightly between different departments and politicians, Chapter 3 outlined a number of observations, which are summarised below.

Rights, responsibilities and participation

Whilst the government enshrined citizens' rights in UK legislation with unprecedented clarity, there was an emphasis on responsibilities. Conceptualisations of citizens' responsibilities were influenced by an attempt to define a Third Way approach to welfare reform, and thus embodied a mixture of personal responsibility for one's own welfare and that of one's family; and a larger responsibility to become a responsible consumer of welfare services, and to form part of a virtuous cycle in which consumer-citizen choice and voice would drive service improvements. This dimension to talking about responsibilities took on a moral tone, and reflects a communitarian and Christian Socialist tradition within New Labour. However, thinking about responsibilities also extended into participation in the civic realm and informed a range of initiatives inspired to empower people to become active citizens. This strand of thinking reflected a civic republican influence in New Labour thinking, which was particularly espoused by Crick and Blunkett in the Department for Education and the Home Office.

Community and diversity

At the root of the philosophical traditions mentioned so far sits the notion of the community – sometimes perceived as a moral community from which citizens derive their rights and responsibilities, and sometimes a polity through which individuals realise their potential. Thus the relationship between citizen and community became significant as a site of policy work. Thinking about the relationships between individuals and communities and between separate communities inevitably generated tensions, especially in the wake of the acts of terrorism and civil unrest during the Labour government's second and third terms. This led to an acknowledgement that whilst individuals construct their identities from the resources available to them in the communities they feel they belong to, politicians wanted to promote an additional layer of identity, which would more proactively bind the British together. The language shifted away from a community of communities (where public funds supported internal community strengthening initiatives) and towards a national project, where communities were open to one another and where individuals' hybrid identities would include a variety of allegiances, including to the nation (where public funds supported bridge building projects between communities). These developments indicate that Crick and Blunkett's civic republican intentions for Citizenship tended to become lost in the general shift towards a more overtly communitarian stance in government policy.

A vision for citizenship education?

In education policy we saw that these influences were evident in the policy documents which sought to shape citizenship education and we also saw, in the transition from Crick to Ajegbo discussed in Chapter 4, how the emphasis shifted from the initial focus on rights responsibilities and active citizenship within communities towards a more overt concern with mutual understanding, bridge building between communities and a greater emphasis on identity. If one were to attempt to simplify these agendas one might characterise Crick's vision as being largely informed by an abstract *political philosophical model* of Britain as a polis with active citizens engaging with one another regardless of social differences; whilst Ajegbo's more *sociological model* recognised the socially constructed nature of identity and sought to encourage citizens to engage with others with regard to their differences. Regardless of this significant shift in emphasis however, Ajegbo was careful to stress that he aimed to add a dimension to Crick's original model of citizenship education, rather than replace it entirely. In fact all the major elements of the initial Crick curriculum stayed in place and were simply added to with a more explicit requirement to teach about identity and diversity.

From vision to reality

Having surveyed the debates about these agendas and examined the evidence about citizenship education in practice, we are able to say something now about what happened to the vision in reality, and what impact it had. In short, did the imagined new citizen emerge over the decade in question?

The national longitudinal evidence indicates that where citizenship education is taken seriously in schools it does have a positive impact on how young people feel about citizenship and their intentions to participate. However, the broader discussion of the national evidence demonstrated that the government's intentions have not been generally met on a national scale and there appear to have been minimal changes in attitudes or knowledge in the period overall. Crick's rallying cry to make citizenship education the path to change the political culture of the nation has not been achieved. The survey data indicates that, over the period in which Citizenship was introduced, young people have become less respectful of politicians, are no more likely to intend to vote, and whilst there are significant numbers of young people who are 'active' there are relatively few who are politically active, or active in the civic realm.

But perhaps the overall picture should not be a surprise – education has rarely, if ever, taken on the role of political revolutionary agent. As Bernstein urged us to remember, education cannot compensate for society (Bernstein, 1971b), and there may well have been more than a measure of hubris in some of the claims made for citizenship education in the early days. The first reason for Citizenship's failure to have the intended impact relates to the difficulties of implementing curriculum change. On the national level there was still a great variation between schools in the quality and extent of provision and in my local case studies the reasons for some of this variation are evident. These issues are discussed in more detail in the following section.

The second reason why curriculum innovation may not lead to wholesale predictable changes in citizenship may relate to the fact that schooling is only one source of formative influences on young people. It may simply be more likely that education plays a supportive role in either reinforcing existing social values and norms, or supporting changes during periods of transition in broader society (Anderson, 2006). Following this line, one might expect the impact of citizenship education to more effectively mirror the overall impact of New Labour's broader attempt to construct new citizens. Simply put, if the overall project failed to take hold in the broader political culture, it seems unlikely that schools would be able to buck this trend entirely. Although this aspect has not been tested specifically in this research, the case study revealed that teachers (Chapter 6) and young people (Chapter 7) talked about other factors outside of school as being important in shaping young people's attitudes. The opinion poll evidence discussed also indicated that significant shifts are taking place in society in relation to attitudes towards citizenship, some of which are antithetical to New Labour's idealised version.

If one views the policy of citizenship education from these two perspectives, then the mixed picture that emerges is far from a policy failure, rather it illustrates the variety of ways in which policy chimeras encounter the complexities of social reality and are shaped and re-shaped by circumstances. I turn now to consider what the preceding analysis suggests about the process of curriculum reform, and what lessons emerge that could inform future developments in relation to citizenship education.

Thinking about citizenship education as an example of policy implementation

In this section I explore some of the issues arising when politicians take a contested construct such as citizenship and attempt to fit it into a school curriculum. I discuss these conclusions under three sub-headings:

- Staff and school variation
- Subject status
- Curriculum policy

Staff and school variation

Teachers create their own vision

The teachers in this study all had rather different ideas about what Citizenship was, and what it was for. In a subject such as Mathematics, this might be acceptable, because ultimately there are some relatively uncontested knowledge and skills to teach, and these can be tested in national assessment regimes. In

Citizenship, where everything is inherently more contested and contestable, there is value I think in working through some of the key debates and in clarifying what positions are desirable. One teacher I spoke to felt political knowledge was important in and of itself, another felt that a feeling of self-worth and inclusion was vital, and another that a sense of community should drive their work. Clearly these different starting points will shape their interpretation of the curriculum they encounter, the teaching style adopted and thus shape the experience of the subject for young people.

The national surveys at the beginning of the implementation of Citizenship indicated that whilst the vast majority of teachers claimed they understood the purpose of the new subject, very few had read beyond the very short programme of study (Kerr, 2003). Given that this document did nothing more than list areas of knowledge and skills to be taught and made no attempt to explain why, or to put it into a broader context of policy, social change, or broader educational reforms, one must assume that the teachers' certainty reflected either a lack of concern about the broader purpose, or a happiness that they had constructed their own meaning from it. Certainly this latter interpretation is supported by the conversations I had with teachers during this research.

School ethos influences the vision

In the schools I visited this connection between Citizenship and school ethos was positive, which presumably reflects the fact that both places were selected because the subject was taken seriously. The Head of Department in Oak Park school was also responsible for community cohesion policy, and she clearly interpreted Citizenship as one dimension in that broader policy. Similarly, the Head of Citizenship in The Heath School was also coordinator for the international dimension and saw it as one part of a broader commitment to engaging students with the wider world. These joint responsibilities thus reflected the ethos of the schools, and such positions seem to signify the seriousness with which each school approached Citizenship. In each school this strong link to the ethos was also evident in teacher talk and in policy documentation, demonstrating a consistent approach to aligning Citizenship with the ethos. The extent to which this was apparent in the experiences of the students however was varied. For example, in The Heath School students knew that the school had a strong international ethos, indeed that was why many of the children were there, but whilst many students in Oak Park school were aware of a claim to be a community school they were less clear what this meant and less likely to identify this as a defining characteristic of their Citizenship provision.

Teachers respond to the local context

All the teachers I spoke to made generalisations about the young people in the school, often linked to judgements about their parents or local area, and these informed their views about what kind of citizenship education was suitable. In Oak Park there was some consensus in the department that children lived in a local 'bubble' and that Citizenship could broaden their understanding of the society around them. In The Heath School staff had different views on the nature of their students but spoke about Citizenship as a response to the deficits they perceived.

Subject status

The struggle for curriculum space

It seems clear that what Crick called the 'strong bare bones' of the programmes of study were not sufficiently strong to provide a consistent shape to citizenship education in schools. This reflects the weak conceptualisation of the practical implications in the Crick report and the failure to robustly address some of the issues relating to implementing Citizenship in a crowded curriculum (as discussed in Chapter 5). There is a continuing tension between the broader idea of citizenship education and the narrower project of Citizenship as a school subject, and the latter has certain rules and expectations attached. According to Bernstein these rules are important in school because they determine the status of a subject, the resources available and clarify the unique contribution of each lesson. Citizenship education was introduced into a strongly classified and framed existing curriculum, in which clear boundaries existed between subjects, which were themselves reinforced by specialist training and subject associations, and by a widely accepted pecking order, in which Maths, English and Science enjoyed greater status and resources – and especially curriculum time. The bare bones approach, and the ambivalence about whether Citizenship joined other subjects in the timetable as an equivalent subject (albeit one which would inevitably be lower down the pecking order) or whether it could be delivered through or alongside other subjects, replicated many of the problems which had been noted in earlier, failed cross-curricular initiatives (Whitty et al., 1994).

The NFER longitudinal evaluations clearly record the debate about whether citizenship education should happen in specialist classes or through other classes, and eventually evidence emerged that discrete provision was more likely to have successful outcomes. But in many ways the lack of certainty was difficult to overcome, and still at the end of the first decade of implementation many schools did not have discrete provision. Oak Park school reflected this uncertainty in two ways. First the staff interviews demonstrated that the subject had still not achieved any sense of stability within the curriculum, and not only had it been clustered into departments with an ever-changing group of other subjects, but even at the relatively late stage of this research it was about to be merged with PSHE within a broader Humanities faculty. Secondly, the confusion was also evident in the students' responses, as many of the examples of Citizenship lessons they cited were actually unrelated to the Citizenship programmes of study, instead often drawing on content associated with PSHE.

The impact of becoming a subject

The issue of status is not easily resolved because the transformation of citizenship education into a tightly defined school subject also seems to bring with it certain other restrictions. There is a risk of a trade-off between the broader aspirations of citizenship education and the narrowing influence of conforming to curriculum constraints. School subjects are taught in discrete time slots, and in Citizenship this was rarely more than one period a week, and was often less. In Oak Park school, even with a short course GCSE in Citizenship, formal Citizenship classes ended at the end of Year 10, to ensure they did not encroach on the core business of getting higher status GCSEs in Year 11. But the problem of being squeezed by higher status subjects is not the only one. Being a subject in the curriculum means adhering to the general requirements for being inspected like any other subject and that requires a focus on the evidence of learning, which hardened in OfSTED advice into a focus on the quality of written work in Citizenship (Ofsted, 2004a, 2006). Similarly, at the beginning of the implementation phase Crick called for the subject to avoid text books, but publishers and educational organisations set about producing text books to accompany the subject's new status. Research into these text books indicates they tend towards relatively low-level tasks and stay within fairly limited and conservative conceptions of citizenship (Davies and Issitt, 2005). Being a subject therefore came with other expectations, and once one places text books, exercise books, a teacher and thirty students in a classroom, the experience of school Citizenship is already to a large extent defined for the students.

The foregoing demonstrates the kinds of pressures that came to bear on Citizenship as it became a school subject, but it is important to recognise that in the case study schools many of the students thought Citizenship lessons were actually rather different to this characterisation. The student research group spoke repeatedly about the ways in which their Citizenship classes were different because they did not feel undue assessment pressure and because there was a productive focus on discussion as a major teaching strategy. These students recognised however, that this placed demands on the teacher and as the data from Oak Park shows, only one teacher appeared to be exceptional in the students' eyes.

The challenge of community participation

The other important aspect of this process of becoming a school subject relates to the most distinctive element of the programmes of study – the entitlement to some form of active citizenship. School subjects are largely designed to be self-enclosed and are often associated with specialist spaces. Science, the subject, is conducted in science laboratories, as is real life science; PE is conducted in the gym or field, which is where people conduct their normal sporting activities. Citizenship, the school subject, is largely conducted in rather plain rooms, whereas the exercise of active citizenship is envisaged as taking place in the public realm – in the community. In short, schools are simply not generally designed to engage routinely with out-of-school, real-life, community-based activities. Where they do so, they are often specific projects, either defined by a specific time frame or a specific group of young people. But one could argue that to do full justice to the requirement for participation, Citizenship demands more routine access to community-based experiences. This was reflected in the description of Citizenship as both a 'subject and more than a subject' (Ofsted, 2006) but this poses very basic organisational problems for schools.

The NFER national surveys illustrate the problem both in the low levels of participation children record in their responses, but also unwittingly in the fact that the researchers range far beyond what would normally be considered a 'citizenship' act. Similarly, although it is evident from Oak Park school that some teachers spend a significant amount of time and effort organising out of school experiences for students, the survey data illustrates that a third or fewer say they participate in community activities or that the school provided them with sufficient opportunities for this. And those examples offered in the survey and interviews reflected a wide range of activities, few of which exemplify the kinds of actions normally identified as active citizenship – for example, participation in after school clubs and sporting activities.

Curriculum policy

Blunkett has given some indication that he became aware of some of these problems:

> 'Perhaps, looking back, we should have been more "directive" – we opted for a light-touch rather than making it plain that we wanted Citizenship taught in all schools and that was the law' (Blunkett, 2009: 3).

And this may well be one of the conclusions to draw from the implementation of citizenship education, although it is not inevitable that this is the only interpretation arising from this analysis. In essence it seems there are two routes a government can take in determining curriculum policy. The first is to embrace what Ball has referred to as the 'writerly' nature of some policy (Ball, 2010, Bowe et al., 1992) and allow teachers the space and freedom to tailor the curriculum to their context. On this reading, the government intention behind citizenship education might simply be to promote greater discussion of citizenship, and enhance young people's understanding of citizenship and politics. It could not seek to promote a particular form of citizenship, because the local interpretations would be diverse and reflect competing and contradictory views. Government would therefore have to withdraw to some extent from specifying what the purpose and shape of Citizenship would be and accept a multiplicity of forms of citizenship education. There are some recent curriculum policies which might be seen as falling into this category: for example, the introduction of Personal Learning and Thinking Skills (PLTS) left teachers with significant scope for determining how the area could be defined, where it would fit within the curriculum and broader life of the school and who might teach it (Braun et al., 2010).

The second approach is to follow Blunkett's instinct, and is reflected in the 'deliverology' ethos he established at the Department for Education. On this reading, the government might decide to close down the possibilities for interpretation as far as possible and to render citizenship education much more of a 'readerly' policy (Ball, 2010). In their discussion of Ball's early use of these distinctions, Hatcher and Troyna argued that by controlling assessment, and thus determining the content, curriculum policy was much more determined by government than first appeared to be the case to Ball (Hatcher and Troyna, 1994). Ball has recently characterised much of curriculum policy in these terms, especially where the curriculum area is closely aligned with the Standards debate, which is seen as providing a master-narrative through which all decisions must be justified (Ball, 2010).

Whilst the levers of control (assessment and OfSTED) were used to enforce a degree of conformity with other school subjects, they were not obviously used to reinforce the key ideas that had informed the original vision for Citizenship. Thus OfSTED guidance reflected the nature of being a 'respectable school subject' as much as it dwelled on the distinctive nature of active citizenship learning. Similarly, whilst the GCSE exam specifications eventually included 60% of assessment linked to active citizenship, the requirements of such action were ill-defined and allowed young people and teachers to conspire in demonstrating minimum compliance, rather than exploring genuine action (Wright, 2011). If one were to adopt a 'deliverology' perspective and thus seek to exert greater control over the subject it would be necessary to ensure these levers of control were more clearly aligned with the policy vision for Citizenship. Otherwise it seems inevitable that the general discourse of 'Standards' will determine the key messages that shape implementation at school level.

Citizenship for the Big Society?

The change of UK government in 2010 shifted the discursive context and led to new political themes being played out, which will inevitably influence citizenship education. Before taking office Michael Gove, the new coalition government's Secretary of State for Education, bemoaned the fact that school staff 'are being turned into social workers with requirements to cut obesity, promote community cohesion and ensure children become good citizens' and he pledged to 'strip down the 'politically motivated' curriculum forced on state schools and allow staff to focus on teaching' (Paton, 2009). This scepticism about citizenship education fits in with a more general commitment to tackle educational inequalities through 'traditional, successful, tried and tested approaches to teaching' and a rejection of theory and ideology (Conservative Party, 2007: 16). This rhetoric sits uneasily with community based learning and the flexible child-centred education which so often form part of active citizenship education.

On the other hand, David Cameron's Big Society speech shortly after he became Prime Minister asserted that government 'must foster and support a new culture of voluntarism, philanthropy, social action' (Cameron, 2010a). A few months later in his party conference speech he reiterated that, 'citizenship isn't a transaction in which you put your taxes in and get your services out. It's a relationship – you're part of something bigger than you, and it matters what you think and feel and do' (Cameron, 2010b). This is a formulation which could have been lifted from Osler and Starkey's model of citizenship as feeling, practice and status (Osler and Starkey, 2005b) and, as the Big Society vision is worked through in policy, education is likely to have a role in promoting this agenda. Annette's analysis of work supported by the Department for Communities and Local Government under the Labour government to promote lifelong learning of active citizenship skills demonstrated many of the principles that Cameron was promoting – devolved decision-making, community empowerment, individual and group action (Annette, 2009, Mayo and Annette, 2010). One of the most contentious questions that has arisen in relation to the Big Society concerns whether it represents a state withdrawal from certain areas of provision on the assumption that individuals and groups will simply fill the gap, or whether there might be a strategy to ensure that local capacity is nurtured and structures established in which 'philanthropy', 'voluntarism' and 'social action' can thrive.

One action that has followed from the Big Society rhetoric is the establishment of National Citizen Service (NCS) for 16-year-olds, which includes opportunities for young people to participate in community voluntary projects through placements with charities and social enterprises (Cabinet Office, 2010). Interestingly the briefing documents for potential bidders applying to run this programme made reference to radical traditions in community education such as Freire and Alinsky, which indicates that it could well serve as a continuation of communitarian approaches to citizenship. If the NCS is successful and is extended to include more than the few thousand participants in the pilot phase, this model could set a template for the kinds of preparatory activity that schools might be encouraged to pursue. The evidence discussed in this book points towards the likelihood that this model would be fairly well received by teachers and young people who seem generally more comfortable with a citizenship education which promotes 'good' citizenship activities such as helping others, raising money and volunteering, as opposed to a more critically oriented 'political' citizenship, such as that advocated by Crick in the civic republican tradition.

In addition the new coalition government has started to review the nature and place of citizenship education in the curriculum. If the requirement to promote active citizenship were completely removed it would deter many schools from investing the necessary time, effort and expertise required to provide such opportunities for participation. Many would find it irresistible to return to the core curriculum on which they were being assessed. However, it is also possible that a statutory aim or entitlement without a compulsory curriculum may lead to a more pragmatic active citizenship education, which could more explicitly embrace the full range of experiences rather than attempt to exclude some valuable activities on the grounds of political purity. The discussion of the nature of active citizenship in Chapter 4 indicated that there may be some advantage in embracing activities which promote the virtues of citizenship through school-based activities. This would involve being clearer about the purposes of such activities and being explicit about how such virtues could relate to democratic participation beyond the school (in both a spatial and temporal sense). This approach recognises that schools may not be sufficiently powerful social institutions to overcome the prevailing societal problems associated with mistrust of politicians and scepticism about the way democracy works, but perhaps they can nurture the kinds of underlying attitudes, skills and knowledge that support democratic citizenship, and also provide young people with some school-based and community-based experiences which provide glimpses of what empowered, responsible, collaborative citizenship looks and feels like. This kind of citizenship education is described by McCowan (2009) as 'pre-figurative' which recognises that schools can help to generate resources for young people to draw on when the opportunities arise in society for greater participation. Perhaps the Big Society affords us an opportunity to bring greater clarity between school-based activities and the theoretical rationale for the subject? If so, there are three recommendations I would draw from this book which could usefully inform future Citizenship policy development.

(1) Staffing and status

Specialist teachers make a significant difference to the quality of citizenship education. It is essential that government, when thinking about how to promote citizenship education, should rigorously address this dimension of implementation. Given this it seems significant that teacher training has failed to supply enough specialist teachers for each secondary school in England (Hayward and Jerome, 2010). Similarly, school managers should note that without such specialist teachers, many students will feel they are wasting their time, and the potential benefits of the subject may well be lost. Whilst school management may make the judgement that this is not a priority for staff development (because OfSTED and other quality assurance systems do not address it explicitly), there should be greater awareness that the time and money spent on non-specialist citizenship education is not the cheap option, but is actually loading the odds against the subject having any real value at all.

In relation to the subject's status, whilst the longitudinal evaluation project concluded that high profile assessment of Citizenship promotes better outcomes, there was some evidence in the student data from my case studies that students were actually appreciative of the fact that their Citizenship teachers were not overtly focused on GCSE scores, unlike other subjects. This holds out the possibility for schools that students may not necessarily need to have everything of value translated into GCSE systems to be valued. This chimes with Osler's work with young people, where she found many secondary students were able to articulate the ways in which exam pressure affected staff and students, and to critique this (Osler, 2010b).

(2) Central or local control

The government should be clearer on what is non-negotiable in citizenship education and what is open to local interpretation. Blunkett and Crick were clear on some features which were closely aligned to civic republicanism, but this was not followed through in detail. It would be possible to align OfSTED regulations and exam specifications with a clear national curriculum, to ensure greater coherence. I suspect though, having seen how teachers in the case study schools interpreted Citizenship in the light of their own values, that teachers would always re-interpret the curriculum to introduce some inconsistencies. This may well be the case where the vision of Citizenship is overtly politicised, and linked to wider policy reforms which are genuinely debatable political issues. This was certainly the case in research I undertook with student teachers in relation to teaching Britishness, where they eschewed models of teaching to promote particular notions of identity (Jerome and Clemitshaw, 2012).

The alternative would be to formalise procedures around the local interpretation of the curriculum, and to embrace the inevitable variability that would arise from this, whilst introducing an element of democratic accountability. Whilst Blunkett favoured the tightening of control, Crick argued that policy makers should accept the 'postcode lottery' as a concomitant of local accountability and responsiveness.

> To hell with the post-code lottery argument, I say; diversity is a price worth paying for liberty, community and local democracy (Crick, 2010: 24).

It may well be that embracing such local variation would require a new form of local accountability, perhaps through a Citizenship version of the local SACREs that determine appropriate Religious Education content.[1] Schools have demonstrated that they are able to work beyond the confines of the school itself to fulfil broader responsibilities, not least through the Community Cohesion policy, and such local boards may well build on these approaches.

(3) Curriculum in context

Any government initiative which seriously sets out to 'change a political culture' (as the Crick report claimed) should take seriously the constant cry for joined up government. I have argued above that it would be naive to expect a single hour a week in the secondary school curriculum to achieve this, and this is especially so when one acknowledges the logistical constraints faced by teachers trying to plan active citizenship experiences. It would seem inconsistent if the Cameron government were to undermine the curriculum contribution to replace it with a community based NCS (Cameron, 2009), and it would be more coherent to align the NCS with school Citizenship to ensure the experiences connected up school and community-based provision.

Schools are well positioned to provide a basic entitlement to learning *about* citizenship, and may well be able to provide some opportunities for learning *through* citizenship experiences. But young people have varied needs and varied opportunities to learn through citizenship experiences and schools cannot meet them all. If some young people need more opportunities for participation organised outside of the limited options available to them in their normal lives, it would make perfect sense to have a broader suite of opportunities on offer. This provides an opportunity for NGOs and education charities to provide wider experiences than could be provided by schools alone (Davies et al., 2009), but there are also implications for local authorities as well as the NCS organized at national level. Given the scale of the challenge it would seem unlikely that one school-based initiative could provide sufficient educational experiences to help all young people in their journey towards full citizenship, but schools could be well placed to act as a conduit to other forms of provision in local communities.

---

[1] This suggestion derives from a conversation with Karl Sweeney, a local authority advisory teacher for Citizenship, PSHE and RE and a member of the Council for the Association for Citizenship Teaching.

A final thought

The introduction of Citizenship as a new subject in the national curriculum has provided a valuable case study, both of a government's efforts to shape the ideal citizen, and of the nature of curriculum reform. The decade long struggle to understand, initiate and improve Citizenship in schools has provided observers with some useful insights into both the political project and the school subject. If the coalition government is serious about deepening our democracy through promoting citizenship then I believe these insights should be addressed seriously. Whilst it is important to establish a clear vision for Citizenship which can demand popular support, it is also worth noting the apparent receptiveness of teachers and young people to a broadly communitarian model, which emphasises good behaviour, moral responsibility and helping others. Acknowledging the existing comfort zone also helps us identify a foundation to build on, as well as identifying the areas where guidance and support may need to be more explicit if we wish to move beyond it.

The practicalities of curriculum reform also require clear thought about how to create a subject with status, a framework which responds to local conditions and a clear connection to wider community experiences. Whilst we should remain cautious about the impact of a single educational reform, there is evidence from national research that, when taught well, Citizenship can help young people develop a sense of efficacy and the case studies reported here indicate that there is an appetite for citizenship education among teachers and many young people. Therefore there are grounds for remaining optimistic that citizenship education *could* contribute to a broader political project to support democratic citizenship.

References

Adams, P. and Calvert, M. (2005) A square peg in a round hole: citizenship education and problems with 'curriculum' – the English secondary school problem, *Learning Beyond Cognition – Biennial Conference of the European Affective Education Network*, The Danish University of Education, 30 June – 2 July 2005.

Advisory Group on Citizenship (1998) Education for Citizenship and the Teaching of Democracy in Schools (London, Qualifications and Curriculum Authority).

Ai, J. C. O. (1998) Civics and Moral Education in Singapore: lessons for citizenship education?, *Journal of Moral Education*, 27(4), pp. 505–24.

Ajegbo, K. (2007) Curriculum Review: Diversity and Citizenship (London, Department for Education and Skills).

Alderson, P. (1999) Human rights and democracy in schools do they mean more than 'picking up litter and not killing whales?', *The International Journal of Children's Rights*, (7), pp. 185–205.

—(2000a) Citizenship in Theory and Practice: Being or Becoming Citizens with Rights, in D. Lawton, J. Cairns and R. Gardner (eds) *Education for Citizenship* (London, Continuum).

—(2000b) Practising democracy in two inner city Schools, in A. Osler (ed) *Citizenship and Democracy in Schools: Diversity, Identity, Equality* (Stoke on Trent, Trentham).

—(2008) *Young Children's Rights: Exploring Beliefs, Principles and Practice* (London, Jessica Kingsley).

Anderson, B. (2006) *Imagined Communities, 2nd Edition* (London, Verso).

Andrews, R. (2004) Theorising the Third Way: Stakeholding, Active Citizenship and Democratic Renewal, *Political Studies Association Conference*, Lincoln University

Annette, J. (2000) Education for citizenship, civic participation and experiential and service learning in the community, in D. Lawton, J. Cairns and R. Gardner (eds) *Education for Citizenship* (London, Continuum).

—(2003) Community, politics and citizenship education, in A. Lockyer, B. Crick and J. Annette (eds) *Education for Democratic Citizenship: Issues of Theory and Practice* (Aldershot, Ashgate).

—(2005) Faith schools and communities: communitarianism, social capital and citizenship, in R. Gardner, J. Cairns and D. Lawton (eds) *Faith Schools: Consensus or Conflict?* (Abingdon, RoutledgeFalmer).

—(2008) Community involvement, civic engagement and service Learning, in J. Arthur, I. Davies and C. Hahn (eds) *The Sage Handbook of Education for Citizenship and Democracy* (London, Sage).

—(2009) 'Active learning for active citizenship': Democratic citizenship and lifelong learning, *Education, Citizenship and Social Justice*, 4(2), pp. 149–60.

Apple, M. (2008) Keynote address, *International Centre for Education in Democratic Citizenship Annual Conference 'Civic Society, Democracy and Education'*, Birkbeck College, University of London, 14 June 2008.

Aronovitch, H. (2000) From Communitarianism to Republicanism: On Sandel and His Critics, *Canadian Journal of Philosophy*, 30(4), pp. 621–48.

Arthur, J., Davies, I. and Hahn, C. (eds.) (2008) *Sage Handbook of Education for Citizenship and Democracy* (London, Sage).

Audigier, F. (2000) Basic concepts and core competencies for education for democratic citizenship *Project on Education for Democratic Citizenship* (Strasbourg, Council of Europe, Council for Cultural Co-operation).

Bailey, L. (2010) Young conservatives: Pupils views shift to the Right as they head towards adulthood, *Daily Mail,* 23rd November 2010.

Ball, S. J. (1994) *Education reform, A Critical and Post-Structural Approach* (Buckingham, Open University Press).

—(1999) Labour, Learning and the Economy: a 'policy sociology' perspective, *Cambridge Journal of Education*, 29(2), pp. 195–206.

—(2006/1993) What is policy? Texts, trajectories and toolboxes, in S. Ball (ed) *Education Policy and Social Class. The selected works of Stephen J. Ball* (London, Routledge).

—(2007) *Education plc: Understanding private sector participation in public sector reform* (Abingdon, Routledge).

—(2008) *The Education Debate* (Bristol, Policy Press).

—(2010) Policy subjects and policy actors – towards a theory of enactments' in two parts *Policy futures: from the global to the local (CeCeps Seminar Series)* (Institute of Education, University of London).

Barber, B. R. (2003) *Strong Democracy: Participatory Politics for a New Age* (London, University of California Press).

Barker, R. and Anderson, J. (2005) Segregation or cohesion: Church of England schools in Bradford, in R. Gardner, J. Cairns and D. Lawton (eds) *Faith Schools: Consensus or Conflict?* (Abingdon, RoutledgeFalmer).

Bauman, Z. (2008) *Does Ethics Have a Chance in a World of Consumers?* (London, Harvard University Press).

BBC (2006a) *Three rebels 'back school plans'*, BBC News on-line, available at http:// news.bbc.co.uk/1/hi/uk_politics/4789684.stm [accessed 25 November 2008]

—(2006b) *Faith Schools Quota Plan Scrapped*, BBC News on-line, available at http:// news.bbc.co.uk/1/hi/education/6089440.stm [accessed 25 November 2008]

Beckett, F. (2007) *The Great City Academy Fraud* (London, Continuum).

Bellamy, R. (2008) *Citizenship: A Very Short Introduction* (Oxford, Oxford University Press).

Benton, T., Cleaver, E., Featherstone, G., Kerr, D., Lopes, J. and Whitby, K. (2008)

Citizenship Education Longitudinal Study (CELS): Sixth Annual Report. Young People's Civic Participation In and Beyond School: Attitudes, Intentions and Influences (DCSF Research Report 052) (London, Department for Children, Schools and Families).

Bernstein, B. (1971a) On the classification and framing of educational knowledge, in M. Young (ed) *Knowledge and Control* (London, Collier-Macmillan).

—(1971b) Education cannot compensate for society, in B. Cosin (ed) *School and Society* (London, Routledge and Kegan Paul).

Biesta, G. and Lawy, R. (2006) From Teaching Citizenship to Learning Democracy: Overcoming individualism in research, policy and practice, *Cambridge Journal of Education*, 36(1), pp. 63–79.

Birzéa, C. (2000) Education for Democratic Citizenship: A Lifelong Learning Perspective *Project on Education for Democratic Citizenship* (Strasbourg, Council of Europe, Council for Cultural Co-operation).

Blair, T. (2010) *A Journey* (London, Hutchinson).

Bland, D. and Atweh, B. (2007) Students as researchers: engaging students' voices in PAR *Educational Action Research*, 15(3), pp. 337–49.

Blunkett, D. (2000) *Extracts: David Blunkett's speech on education,* Report of Labour Party Conference Speech, Brighton,available on-line at http://www.guardian.co.uk/politics/2000/sep/27/labourconference.labour3 [accessed 28 February, 2012]

—(2001) *Politics and Progress: Renewing Democracy and Civil Society* (London, Politico's Publishing).

—(2003) Towards a Civil Society (London, IPPR).

—(2005) *A New England: An English identity within Britain,* Speech to the Institute for Public Policy Research IPPR, 14th March 2005, (London, IPPR).

—(2009) Why citizenship must be a priority for the future of education, *Citizenship News,* February, 2009 (London, Learning and Skills Improvement Service).

Bowe, R., Ball, S. and Gold, A. (1992) *Reforming Education and Changing Schools: case studies in policy sociology* (London, Routledge).

Braun, A., Maguire, M. and Ball, S. J. (2010) Policy enactments in the UK secondary school: examining policy, practice and school positioning, *Journal of Education Policy*, 25(4), pp. 547–60.

Brennan, T. (1981) *Political Education and Democracy* (Cambridge, University of Cambridge).

Brighouse, H. (2005) Faith-based schools in the United Kingdom: an unenthusiastic defence of a slightly reformed status quo, in R. Gardner, J. Cairns and D. Lawton (eds) *Faith Schools: Consensus or Conflict?* (Abingdon, RoutledgeFalmer).

—(2006) *On Education* (Abingdon, Routledge).

Brown, G. (2006) The Future of Britishness *Keynote speech delivered to the Fabian New Year Conference, 'Who do we want to be? The future of Britishness'*, Imperial College, London, 14th January 2006.

—(2008) *Earned Citizenship* article on the Prime Minister's website, available on-line at http://www.pm.gov.uk/output/Page14625.asp [accessed 22 March 2008].

Burnett, J. and Whyte, D. (2004) *New Labour's new racism*, article published by the Institute of Race Relations, available on-line at http://www.irr.org.uk/2004/october/ak000008.html [accessed 30 March 2008].

Butler, T. and Robson, G. (2003) *London Calling: The Middle Classes and the Re-making of Inner London* (Oxford, Berg).

Cabinet Office (2010) *National Citizen Service 2011 Pilot Specification*, published by the Cabinet Office posted on-line by the London Work Based Learning Alliance: http://wblalliance.org.uk/10resources/NCS%20SPECIFICATION%20AND%20EOI%20QUESTIONS.pdf [accessed 7 November 2010].

Callan, E. (1997) *Creating Citizens: Political Education and Liberal Democracy* (Oxford, Oxford University Press).

Cameron, D. (2009) *The Big Society*, speech delivered on 10 November 2009, available on-line at http://www.conservatives.com/News/Speeches/2009/11/David_Cameron_The_Big_Society.aspx [accessed 11 August 2011].

—(2010a) *Big Society Speech*, Liverpool, 19 July 2010, available on-line at: http://www.number10.gov.uk/news/big-society-speech/ [accessed 11 August 2011].

—(2010b) David Cameron's speech to the Tory conference: in full, Report of the Prime Minister's Speech, Conservative Party Conference, Birmingham, 6 October 2010, available on-line at http://www.guardian.co.uk/politics/2010/oct/06/david-cameron-speech-tory-conference [accessed 11 August 2011].

Cantle, T. (2008) *Community Cohesion: A New Framework for Race and Diversity. Second Edition.* (London, Palgrave Macmillan).

Carlini, A. and Barry, E. (undated) 'Hey, I'm nine not six!' A small-scale investigation of looking younger than your age at school, Research Report published on-line by the Open University, Children's Research Centre, available at http://childrens-research-centre.open.ac.uk/research.cfm [accessed 8 January 2009].

Carvell, J. (2000) Poverty no excuse for failure, says Blunkett, *The Guardian,* 2nd March 2000, available on-line at http://www.guardian.co.uk/uk/2000/mar/02/schools.news1 [accessed 11 August 2011].

Children Schools and Families Committee (House of Commons) (2008a) Testing and Assessment, Vol. 1, HC169-1 (London, The Stationery Office).

—(2008b) Testing and Assessment, Vol. 2, Oral and written evidence (London, The Stationery Office).

Clarke, C. (1999) House of Commons Hansard Debates, Column 1099, 20 July 1999, published on-line at: www.publications.parliament.uk [accessed 11 August 2011].

Clarke, J. (2005) New Labour's citizens: activated, empowered, responsibilized, abandoned?, *Critical Social Policy*, 25(4), pp. 447–63.

Cleaver, E., Ireland, E., Kerr, D. and Lopes, J. (2005) Citizenship Education Longitudinal Study: Second Cross-Sectional Survey 2004. Listening to Young

People: Citizenship Education in England (DfES Research Report 626) (London, Department for Education and Skills).

Codd, J. A. (1988) The construction and deconstruction of educational policy documents, *Journal of Education Policy*, 3(3), pp. 235–47.

Coffield, F., Steer, R., Allen, R., Vignoles, A., Moss, G. and Vincent, C. (2007) *Public Sector Reform: Principles for improving the education system* (London, Institute of Education, University of London).

Cogan, J. J. and Derricott, R. (1998) *Citizenship for the 21st Century: An international perspective on education* (London, Routledge).

Commission on Integration and Cohesion (2007) *Our Interim Statement* (London, Department for Communities and Local Government).

Conservative Party (2007) *Raising the bar, closing the gap: An action plan for schools to raise standards, create more good school places and make opportunity more equal,* Policy Green Paper 1 (London, Conservative Party).

Cook Sather, A. (2002) Authorizing students' perspectives: towards trust, dialogue, and change in education, *Educational Researcher*, 31(4), pp. 3–14.

—(2007) Resisting the Impositional Potential of Student Voice Work: Lessons for liberatory educational research from poststructuralist feminist critiques of critical pedagogy, *Discourse: studies in the cultural politics of education*, 28(3), pp. 389–403.

Couldry, N. (2010) *Why Voice Matters: Culture and Politics After Neoliberalism* (London, Sage).

Covell, K. and Howe, R. B. (2008) Rights, Respect and Responsibility: Final Report on the County of Hampshire Rights Education Initiative (Sydney, Nova Scotia, Canada, Children's Righst Centre, Cape Breton University).

Covell, K., Howe, R. B. and McNeil, J. K. (2008) 'If there's a dead rat, don't leave it'. Young children's understanding of their citizenship rights and responsibilities, *Cambridge Journal of Education*, 38(3), pp. 321–39.

Crick, B. (1978) *Political education and political literacy: the report and papers of, and the evidence submitted to, the Working Party of the Hansard Society's 'Programme for political education'* (London, Longman).

—(1982) *In Defence of Politics* (Harmondsworth, Penguin).

—(2000a) *Essays on Citizenship* (London, Continuum).

—(2000b) Introduction to the new curriculum, in D. Lawton, J. Cairns and R. Gardner (eds) *Education for Citizenship* (London, Continuum).

—(2002a) *Democracy: A very short introduction* (Oxford, Oxford University Press).

—(2002b) *A Note on What Is and What Is Not Active Citizenship,* available on-line at http://www.post16citizenship.org/files/033_BernardCrick_WHAT_IS_CITIZENSHIP.pdf [accessed 28 September 2008].

—(2002c) Education for Citizenship: The Citizenship Order, *Parliamentary Affairs*, (55), pp. 488–504.

—(2002d) Citizenship must begin to replace ethos in the classroom *The Independent – Education*, 27 September 2002.

—(2003) The English citizenship order 1999: context, content and presuppositions, in A. Lockyer, B. Crick and J. Annette (eds) *Education for Democratic Citizenship: Issues of Theory and Practice* (Aldershot, Ashgate).

—(2010) Civic republicanism and citizenship: the challenge for today, in B. Crick and A. Lockyer (eds) *Active Citizenship: What Could it Achieve and How?* (Edinburgh, Edinburgh University Press).

Cunningham, F. (2002) *Theories of Democracy: A Critical Introduction* (Abingdon, Routledge).

David, T., Tonkin, J., Powell, S. and Anderson, C. (2005) Ethical aspects of power in research with children, in A. Farrell (ed) *Ethical Research with Children* (Maidenhead, Open University Press).

Davies, I. (2003b) *What subject knowledge is needed to teach citizenship education?*. Available on-line at: *www.citized.info/pdf/commarticles/Ian_Davies2.pdf* [accessed 2 March 2008].

Davies, I., Evans, M. and Reid, A. (2005a) Globalising Citizenship Education? A Critique of 'Global Education' and 'Citizenship Education', *British Journal of Educational Studies*, 53(1), pp. 66–89.

Davies, I., Flanaghan, B., Hogarth, S., Mountford, P. and Philpott, J. (2009) Asking questions about participation, *Education, Citizenship and Social Justice*, 4(1), pp. 25–39.

Davies, I., Gregory, I. and Riley, S. (2005b) Teachers' perceptions of citizenship in England, in W. O. Lee and J. T. Fouts (eds) *Education for Social Citizenship: Perceptions of Teachers in the USA, Australia, England, Russia and China* (Hong Kong, Hong Kong University Press).

Davies, I. and Issitt, J. (2005) Citizenship education textbooks in England, Canada and Australia, *Comparative Education*, 41(4), pp. 389–410.

Davies, L. and Yamashita, H. (2007) School Councils, School Improvement: The London Secondary School Councils Action Research Project (London, School Councils UK and Centre for International Education and Research).

DCLG (2011) Citizenship Survey: April – September 2010, England. Cohesion Research Statistical Release Number 14 (London, Department for Communities and Local Government).

DCSF (2008) Working Together: Listening to the voices of children and young people (London, Department for Children, Schools and Families).

DfEE (1999) Learning To Succeed: A New Framework for Post-16 Learning (London, DfEE).

de Leeuw, E. (2008) Self-administered questionnaires and standardized interviews, in P. Alasuutari, L. Bickman and J. Brannen (eds) *The Sage Handbook of Social Research Methods* (London, Sage).

Deacon, A. (1994) Justifying workfare: the historical context of the workfare debates, in M. White (ed) *Unemployment and Public Policy in a Changing Labour Market* (London, PSI).

—(2000) Learning from the US? The influence of American ideas upon 'new labour' thinking on welfare reform, *Policy and Politics*, 28(1), pp. 5–18.

Denscombe, M. (2007) *The Good Research Guide: for small-scale social reserach projects, Third Edition* (Maidenhead, Open University Press).

Deuchar, R. (2006) 'Not only this, but also that!' Translating the social and political motivations underpinning enterprise and citizenship education into Scottish schools, *Cambridge Journal of Education*, 36(4), pp. 533–47.

Dewey, J. (1997/1938) *Experience and Education* (New York, Touchstone).

Diamond, P. and Giddens, A. (2005) The new egalitarianism: economic inequality in the UK, in A. Giddens and P. Diamond (eds) *The New Egalitarianism* (Cambridge, Polity Press).

Driver, S. and Martell, L. (2006) *New Labour* (Cambridge, Polity Press).

Dryzek, J. (2000) *Deliberative Democracy and Beyond: Liberals, Critics, Contestations* (Oxford, Oxford University Press).

Dunn, A. and Burton, D. (2011) New Labour, communitarianism and citizenship education in England and Wales, *Education, Citizenship and Social Justice*, 6(2), pp. 169–79.

Dunne, M., Pryor, J. and Yates, P. (2005) *Becoming a Researcher: A research companion for the social sciences* (Maidenhead, Open University Press).

Dürr, K. (2004) The All-European Study on Pupils' Participation in School – The School: A Democratic Learning Community. *Education for Democratic Citizenship 2001–2004* (Strasbourg, Council of Europe).

Edexcel (2009) Examiners' Report Summer 2009 (Citizenship) available on-line at: www.edexcel.com [accessed 10 January 2012].

Edwards, R., Nicoll, K., Solomon, N. and Usher, R. (2004) *Rhetoric and Educational Discourse: Persuasive Texts?* (London, RoutledgeFalmer).

Ekholm, M. (2004) Learning democracy by sharing power: the student role in effectiveness and improvement, in J. Macbeath and L. Moos (eds) *Democratic Learning: The challenge to school effectiveness* (London, RoutledgeFalmer).

Etzioni, A. (1993) *The Spirit of Community: Rights, Responsibilities and the Communitarian Agenda* (New York, Crown Publishers).

Fairclough, N. (1989) *Language and Power* (London, Longman).

—(1992) *Discourse and Social Change* (Cambridge, Polity).

—(2000) *New Labour, New Language?* (London, Routledge).

—(2001) *Language and Power (2nd edition)* (London, Longman).

Faulks, K. (2000) *Citizenship* (Abingdon, Routledge).

—(2006b) Rethinking citizenship education in England: Some lessons from contemporary social and political theory, *Education, Citizenship and Social Justice*, 1(2), pp. 123–40.

Fielding, M. (2004a) 'New Wave' Student Voice and the Renewal of Civic Society, *London Review of Education*, 2(3), pp. 197–217.

—(2004b) Transformative approaches to student voice: theoretical underpinnings, recalcitrant realities, *British Educational Research Journal*, 30(2), pp. 295–311.

Fisher, P. (2011) Performativity, well-being, social class and citizenship in English schools, *Educational Studies*, 37(1), pp. 49–58.

Flutter, J. and Rudduck, J. (2004) *Consulting Pupils: What's in it for schools?* (London, RoutledgeFalmer).

Fontana, A. and Frey, J. H. (2003) The interview: from structured questions to negotiated Text, in N. K. Denzin and T. S. Lincoln (eds) *Collecting and Interpreting Qualitative Materials* (London, Sage).

—(2005) The interview: from neutral stance to political Involvement, in N. K. Denzin and Y. S. Lincoln (eds) *The Sage Handbook of Qualitative Research, Third Edition* (London, Sage).

Foucault, M. (1988a) Politics and reason, in L. D. Kritzman (ed) *Michel Foucault. Politics, philosophy, culture: Interviews and other writings, 1977–1984* (New York, Routledge).

—(1988b) *Politics, philosophy, culture: Interviews and other writings, 1977–1984* (New York, Routledge).

—(1991) Governmentality, in G. Burchell, C. Gordon and P. Miller (eds) *The Foucault Effect: Studies in Governmentality* (London, Harvester Wheatsheaf).

Frazier, E. (2008) Key perspectives, traditions and disciplines: overview, in J. Arthur, I. Davies and C. Hahn (eds) *The Sage Handbook of Education for Citizenship and Democracy* (London, Sage).

Gamarnikow, E. and Green, A. (1999) The Third Way and Social Capital: Education Action Zones and a new agenda for education, parents and community?, *International Studies in Sociology of Education*, 9(1), pp. 3–22.

—(2000) Citizenship, education and social capital, in D. Lawton, J. Cairns and R. Gardner (eds) *Education for Citizenship* (London, Continuum).

—(2005) Keeping the faith with social capital, in R. Gardner, J. Cairns and D. Lawton (eds) *Faith Schools: Consensus or Conflict?* (Abingdon, RoutledgeFalmer).

Gardner, R., Cairns, J. and Lawton, D. (eds.) (2005) *Faith Schools: Consensus or Conflict?* (Abingdon, RoutledgeFalmer).

Gewirtz, S. (2001) Cloning the Blairs: New Labour's programme for the re-socialization of working-class parents, *Journal of Education Policy*, 16(4), pp. 365–78.

Giddens, A. (1998) *The Third Way: The Renewal of Social Democracy* (Cambridge, Polity Press).

—(2002) The Third Way Can Beat the Far Right, *The Guardian,* 3 May 2002. Aavailable on-line at: *www.guardian.co.uk/politics/2002/may/03/eu.thefarright* [accessed 10 January 2012].

Gillborn, D. (2006) Citizenship education as placebo, *Education, Citizenship and Social Justice*, 1(1), pp. 83–104.

Gilroy, P. (2004) *After Empire: Melancholia or Convivial Culture?* (Abingdon, Routledge).

Lord Goldsmith (2008) Citizenship: Our Common Bond (London, Ministry of Justice)

Gordon, C. (1991) Governmental rationality: an introduction, in G. Burchell, C.

Gordon and P. Miller (eds) *The Foucault Effect: Studies in Governmentality* (London, Harvester Wheatsheaf).

Gray, J. (1986) *Liberalism* (Milton Keynes, Open University Press).

—(1997) *Endgames: Questions in Late Modern Political Thought* (Oxford, Polity).

Gunter, H. M. and Chapman, C. (2009) A decade of new labour reform of Education, in C. Chapman and H. M. Gunter (eds) *Radical Reforms: Perspectives on an Era of Educational Change* (London, Routledge).

Habermas, J. (1999) *The Inclusion of the Other: Studies in Political Theory* (Cambridge, Polity).

Hahn, C. (1998) *Becoming Political: Comparative perspectives on citizenship education* (Albany, State University of New York Press).

Hall, S. (2003) New Labour's Double-Shuffle, *Soundings*, (24), pp. 10–24.

Halstead, J. M. and McLaughlin, T. (2005) Are faith schools divisive?, in R. Gardner, J. Cairns and D. Lawton (eds) *Faith Schools: Consensus or Conflict?* (Abingdon, RoutledgeFalmer).

Hand, M. and Pearce, J. (2009) Patriotism in British Schools: Principles, practices and press hysteria, *Educational Philosophy and Theory*, 41(4), pp. 453–65.

Hannam, D. (2001) A pilot study to evaluate the impact of the student participation aspects of the citizenship order on standards of education in secondary schools (London, Community Service Volunteers).

—(2003) 'Participation and responsible action' for all students – the crucial ingredient for success, *Teaching Citizenship*, (5), pp. 24–33.

Happold, F. C., Hoyland, W. F., Deed, B. L., Sharp, C. H. C., Dobinson, C. H., Frampton, R. and Hahn, K. (1937) *Experiments in Practical Training for Citizenship* (Letchworth, The Garden City Press).

Harris, D. E. (2002) Classroom assessment of civic discourse, in W. C. Parker (ed) *Education for Democracy: Contexts, Curricula, Assessments* (Greenwich, Connecticut, Information Age Publishing).

Hart, R. (1992) *Children's Participation: from Tokenism to Citizenship* (Florence, Italy, UNICEF/International Child Development Centre).

Hatcher, R. and Troyna, B. (1994) The 'Policy Cycle': A Ball by Ball Account, *Journal of Education Policy*, 9(2), pp. 155–70.

Hayward, J. and Jerome, L. (2010) Staffing, Status and Subject Knowledge: What does the construction of citizenship as a new curriculum subject in England tell us about the nature of school subjects?, *Journal of Education for Teaching*, 36(2), pp. 211–25.

Heater, D. (2001) The history of citizenship education in England, *Curriculum Journal*, 12(1), pp. 103–23.

—(2004) *A History of Education for Citizenship* (London, RoutledgeFalmer).

Henn, M. and Foard, N. (2011) Young People, Political Participation and Trust in Britain, *Parliamentary Affairs*, 65(1), pp. 47–67.

Hennessy, P. (2000) *The Prime Minister: The office and its holders since 1945* (London, Allen Lane).

Hewitt, R. (2005) *White Backlash and the Politics of Multiculturalism* (Cambridge, Cambridge University Press).

Home-Office (1998) Race Relations Forum: Terms of Reference, available on-line at http://www.nationalarchives.gov.uk/ERORecords/HO/415/1/pubapps/rrf.htm [accessed 5 May 2008].

—(2009) Borders, Citizenship and Immigration Bill, HL Bill 15, (London, Home Office).

House of Commons Education and Skills Committee (2007) Citizenship Education. Second report of session 2006–07. (London, The Stationary Office).

Howe, R. B. and Covell, K. (2010) Miseducating children about their rights, *Education, Citizenship and Social Justice*, 5(2), pp. 91–102.

Ipsos-Mori (2009) Trust in Professions annual survey available on-line at: http://www.ipsos-mori.com/researchpublications/publications/publication.aspx?oItemId=1305 [accessed 15 January 2011]

—(2010) How Britain Voted in 2010 available on-line at: http://www.ipsos-mori.com/researchpublications/researcharchive/poll.aspx?oItemId=2613&view=wide [accessed 3 January 2011].

Ishay, M. R. (2008) *The History of Human Rights: from ancient times to the globalization era* (Berkeley and Los Angeles, University of California Press).

Isin, E. and Nielsen, G. (eds.) (2008) *Acts of Citizenship* (London, Zed Books).

Jerome, L. and Algarra, B. (2005) Debating debating: a reflection on the place of debate within secondary schools, *Curriculum Journal*, 16(4), pp. 493–508.

Jerome, L. and Clemitshaw, G. (2012) Teaching (about) Britishness? An investigation into trainee teachers' understanding of Britishness in relation to citizenship and the discourse of civic nationalism, *Curriculum Journal*, 23(1), pp. 19–41.

Jerome, L. and Shilela, A. (2007) Thinking about Diversity and Citizenship as if power, inequality and political struggle mattered: A Response to the Ajegbo Review *Education for Democratic Citizenship: Multiculturalism and National Identity Conference organised by the International Centre for Education for Democratic Citizenship*, Birkbeck, London, 13 July 2007.

Jochum, V., Pratten, B. and Wilding, K. (2005) *Civil Renewal and Active Citizenship: A guide to the debate* (London, National Council for Voluntary Organisations).

Jones, K. (2003) *Education in Britain: 1944 to the present* (Cambridge, Polity).

Jordan, B. (2005) New Labour: choice and values, *Critical Social Policy*, 25(4), pp. 427–46.

Keating, A., Kerr, D., Benton, T., Mundy, E. and Lopes, J. (2010) Citizenship Education in England 2001–2010: Young people's practices and prospects for the future, Research Report DFE-RR059 (London, Department for Education).

Keating, A., Kerr, D., Lopes, J., Featherstone, G. and Benton, T. (2009) Embedding Citizenship Education in Secondary Schools in England (2002–08): Citizenship Education Longitudinal Study Seventh Annual Report, DCSF Research Report 172 (London, Department for Children, Schools and Families).

Keddie, A. (2008) Engaging the 'maximal' intentions of the citizenship curriculum: one teacher's story, *Cambridge Journal of Education*, 38(2), pp. 171–85.

Kellett, M. (2005a) *How to Develop Children as Researchers* (London, Paul Chapman).

—(2005b) Children as active researchers: a new paradigm for the 21st century? *ESRC National Centre for Research Methods, Review Paper (NCM/003)*, available on-line at http://www.ncrm.ac.uk/publications/methodsreview/ MethodsReviewPaperNCRM-003.pdf [accessed 5 May 2008].

Kellett, M., Forrest, R., Dent, N. and Ward, S. (2004) 'Just Teach Us The Skills Please, We'll Do The Rest': Empowering Ten-Year-Olds as Active Researchers, *Children and Society*, 18(5), pp. 329–43.

Kennedy, H. (2004) *Just Law: The changing face of justice and why it matters to us all* (London, Chatto and Windus).

Kerr, D. (1999) Changing the Political Culture: the Advisory Group on Education for Citizenship and the Teaching of Democracy in Schools, *Oxford Review of Education*, 25(1/2).

—(2000) Citizenship education: an international comparison, in D. Lawton, J. Cairns and R. Gardner (eds) *Education for Citizenship* (London, Continuum).

—(2003) Citizenship Education in England: The Making of a New Subject, *Online Journal for Social Science Education*, (2).

Kerr, D., Lines, A., Blenkinsop, S. and Schagen, I. (2002) England's Results from the IEA International Citizenship Education Study: What Citizenship and Education mean to 14 year olds (Slough, National Foundation for Educational Research).

Kerr, D., Cleaver, E., Ireland, E. and Blenkinsop, S. (2003) Citizenship Education Longitudinal Study First Cross-Sectional Survey 2001–2002, Research Report RR416 (Slough, NFER/DfES).

Kerr, D., Smith, A. and Twine, C. (2008) Citizenship education in the United Kingdom, in J. Arthur, I. Davies and C. Hahn (eds) *The Sage Handbook of Education for Citizenship and Democracy* (London, Sage).

Kisby, B. (2006) New Labour and Citizenship Education, *Parliamentary Affairs*, 60(1), pp. 84–101.

—(2009) Social capital and citizenship lessons in England: Analysing the presuppositions of citizenship education, *Education, Citizenship and Social Justice*, 4(1), pp. 41–62.

Kivisto, P. and Faist, T. (2007) *Citizenship: Discourse, Theory and Transnational Prospects* (Oxford, Blackwell).

Kiwan, D. (2008) *Education for Inclusive Citizenship* (London, Routledge).

Klein, D. B. (1999) The Ways of John Gray: A Libertarian Commentary, available on-line at http://lsb.scu.edu/~dklein/papers/gray.html [accessed 22 March 2008].

Klein, G. (1993) *Education Towards Race Equality* (London, Cassell).

Korten, D. C. (1995) *When Corporations Rule the World* (West Hartford, Connecticut, Kumarian Press).

Kundnani, A. (2005) The Politics of a Phoney Britishness, *The Guardian,* 21 January 2005

Kymlicka, W. (1995) *Multicultural Citizenship: A liberal theory of minority rights* (Oxford, Oxford University Press).

—(2002) *Contemporary Political Philosophy: An Introduction* (Oxford, Oxford University Press).

Leenders, H., Veugelers, W. and De Kat, E. (2008) Teachers' views on citizenship education in secondary education in The Netherlands, *Cambridge Journal of Education*, 38(2), pp. 155–70.

Leighton, R. (2004) What you give is what you get: a preliminary examination of the influence of teacher perceptions of the role of citizenship education on its delivery, status and effectiveness in schools *British Sociological Association Annual Conference*, University of York, 22 – 24 March 2004.

Lemke, T. (2007) An indigestible meal? Foucault, governmentality and state theory available on-line at: www.thomaslemkeweb.de/publikationen/IndigestibleMealfinal5.pdf [accessed 10 January 2012].

Lemos, G. (2005) *The Search for Tolerance: Challenging and changing racist attitudes and behaviuour among young people* (York, Joseph Rowntree Foundation).

Lewis, M. (2003) Review of PGCE Course Handbooks, available on-line at http://www.citized.info/pdf/commarticles/Review_of_PGCE_Citizenship.pdf [accessed 5 May 2009].

Liégeois, D. (2005) Democracy at School – School governance, school environment and local community: towards democratic schooling in Europe (Strasbourg, Council of Europe).

Lincoln, Y. S. and Guba, E. G. (1985) *Naturalistic Enquiry* (London, Sage).

Lister, R. (2001) New Labour: a study in ambiguity from a position of ambivalence, *Critical Social Policy*, 21(4), pp. 425–47.

Lister, R., Smith, N., Middleton, S. and Cox, L. (2003) Young people talk about citizenship: empirical perspectives on theoretical and political debates, *Citizenship Studies*, 7(2), pp. 235–53.

Lukes, S. (2005) *Power: A Radical View (Second Edition)* (Basingstoke, Palgrave Macmillan).

Lundy, L. (2007) 'Voice' is not enough: Conceptualizing Article 12 of the United Nations Convention on the Rights of the Child, *British Educational Research Journal*, 33(6), pp. 927–42.

MacNaughton, G. and Smith, K. (2005) Transforming research ethics: the choices and challenges of researching with children, in A. Farrell (ed) *Ethical Research with Children* (Maidenhead, Open University Press).

MacPherson, W. (1999) The Stephen Lawrence Inquiry: Report of an Inquiry by Sir William MacPherson (London, Home Office).

Manley Scott, P., Baker, C. R. and Graham, E. L. (eds.) (2009) *Remoralizing Britain? Political, Ethical and Theological Perspectives on New Labour* (London, Continuum).

Marshall, T. H. (1964) *Class, Citizenship and Social Development* (Garden City, NY, Doubleday).

Maylor, U. (2010) Notions of diversity, British identities and citizenship belonging, *Race, Ethnicity and Education*, 13(2), pp. 233–52.

Mayo, M. and Annette, J. (eds.) (2010) *Taking Part? Active Learning for Active Citizenship, and beyond* (Leicester, National Institute of Adult and Continuing Education (England and Wales)).

McClintock, A. (1995) *Imperial Leather: Race, Gender and Sexuality on the Colonial Contest* (London, Routledge).

McCormack, J. (2011) Information + consumer choice = oppression: Towards a Freirean conception of tenant empowerment in social housing, *Citizenship, Society and Social Justice: new agendas? The 5th annual conference of the International Centre for Education for Democratic Citizenship*, Birkbeck College, London, 1 July 2007.

McCowan, T. (2008) Curricular transposition in citizenship education, *Theory and Research in Education*, (6), pp. 153–72.

—(2009) *Rethinking Citizenship Education: A curriculum for participatory democracy* (London, Continuum).

McGhee, D. (2005) *Intolerant Britain? Hate, citizenship and difference* (Maidenhead, Open University Press).

—(2008) *The End of Multiculturalism: Terrorism, Integration and Human Rights* (Maidenhead, Open University Press).

McLaughlin, M. (2008) Beyond 'misery research' – new opportunities for implementation research, policy and practice, in C. Sugrue (ed) *The Future of Educational Change* (Abingdon, Routledge).

McLaughlin, T. (2000) Citizenship Education in England: The Crick Report and Beyond, *Journal of Philoshopy of Education*, 34(4), pp. 541–70.

McNay, L. (1994) *Foucault: A Critical Introduction* (Cambridge, Polity).

Mead, N. (2010) Conflicting concepts of participation in secondary school Citizenship, *Pastoral Care in Education*, 28(1), pp. 45–57.

Meier, A. R., Cleary, F. D. and Davis, A. M. (1952) *A Curriculum for Citizenship: A total school approach to citizenship education. A Report of the Citizenship Education Study* (Detroit, Wayne University Press).

Mensa (2007) Dorling Kindersley Survey Results available on-line at: http://www.mensa.org.uk/cgi-bin/item.cgi?ap=1&id=395 [accessed 14 January 2012].

Mill, J. S. (1859/1990) On liberty, in S. M. Cahn (ed) *Classics of Western Philosophy* (Indianapolis, Hackett).

Morris, L. (2007) New Labour's Community of Rights: Welfare, Immigration and Asylum, *Journal of Social Policy*, 36(1), pp. 39–57.

Morrow, R. A. and Torres, C. A. (2002) *Reading Freire and Habermas: Critical Pedagogy and Transformative Social Change* (New York, Teachers College Press).

Mouffe, C. (2005) *On The Political* (Abingdon, Routledge).

Myers, J. P. (2009) Learning in politics: Teachers' political experiences as a pedagogical resource *International Journal of Educational Research*, 48(1), pp. 30–9.

NCSR (2010) British Social Attitudes 26th Report – Public support for new benefit rules for lone parents (Press Release), published by the National Centre for Social Research and available on-line at http://www.natcen.ac.uk/media-centre/press-releases/2010-press-releases/british-social-attitudes-26th-report--public-support-for-new-benefit-rules-for-lone-parents [accessed 15 January 2011].

Nelson, J., Wade, P. and Kerr, D. (2010) Young People's Civic Attitudes and Practices: England's outcomes from the IEA International Civic and Citizenship Education Study (ICCS), Research Report DFE-RR060 (London, Department for Education).

Newman, J. (2001) *Modernising Governance: New Labour, Policy and Society* (London, Sage).

Niemi, R. G. and Junn, J. (1998) *Civic Education: What Makes Students Learn* (New Haven, Yale University Press).

Nozick, R. (1974) *Anarchy, State and Utopia* (New York, Basic Books).

Office for National Statistics (undated) Voting turnout: by age and gender: Social Trends 32, available on-line at http://www.statistics.gov.uk/STATBASE/ssdataset.asp?vlnk=5204 [accessed 3 January 2011]

Ofsted (2003) Update 43, on-line newsletter, downloaded from: www.ofsted.gov.uk [accessed 4 April 2005].

—(2004a) Ofsted subject reports 2002/03: Citizenship in secondary schools (HMI1991) (London, Office for Standards in Education).

—(2004b) Initial teacher training for teachers of citizenship 2003/04: Overview report (HMI 2299) (London, Office for Standards in Education).

—(2005a) Citizenship in secondary schools (HMI 2335) (London, Office for Standards in Education).

—(2005b) Initial teacher training for teachers of citizenship 2004/05: Overview report (HMI 2486) (London, Office for Standards in Education).

—(2006) Towards Consensus? (London, Office for Standards in Education).

—(2009) Professional development for citizenship teachers and leaders (Ref 070253) (London, Office for Standards in Education).

—(2010) Citizenship established? Citizenship in schools 2006/09 (London, Office for Standards in Education).

Olssen, M. (2004) From the Crick Report to the Parekh Report: multiculturalism, cultural difference and democracy – the re-visioning of citizenship education, *British Journal of Sociology of Education*, 25(2), pp. 179–92.

Olssen, M., Codd, J. and O'Neill, A.-M. (2004) *Education Policy: Globalization, Citizenship and Democracy* (London, Sage).

Osler, A. (ed) (2000a) *Citizenship and Democracy in Schools: Diversity, Identity, Equality* (Stoke on Trent, Trentham).

—(2000b) The Crick Report: difference, equality and racial justice, *The Curriculum Journal*, 11(1), pp. 25–37.

—(2010a) Teacher interpretations of citizenship education: national identity, cosmopolitan ideals, and political realities, *Journal of Curriculum Studies*, 43(1), 1–24.

Osler, A. (2010b) *Students' Perspectives on Schooling* (Maidenhead, Open University Press).

Osler, A. and Starkey, H. (1996) *Teacher Education and Human Rights* (London, David Fulton).

—(2000) Citizenship, human rights and cultural diversity, in A. Osler (ed) *Citizenship and Democracy in Schools: Diversity, Identity, Equality* (Stoke on Trent, Trentham).

—(2003) Learning for Cosmopolitan Citizenship: theoretical debates and young people's experiences, *Educational Review*, 55(3), pp. 243–54.

—(2005a) Study on the advances in civic education in education systems: good practices in industrialised countries, in V. Espinola (ed) *Education for Citizenship and Democracy in a Globalized World: a comparative perspective* (New York, Inter-American Development Bank).

—(2005b) *Changing Citizenship: Democracy and Inclusion in Education* (Maidenhead, Open University Press).

—(2005c) Education for Democratic Citizenship: a review of research, policy and practice 1995–2005, *Research Papers in Education*, 24(4), pp. 433–66.

Ozga, J. (2000) *Policy Research in Educational Settings: Contested terrains* (Buckingham, Open University Press).

Parker, W. C. (1987) Teachers' mediation in social studies, *Theory and Research in Social Education* 15(4), pp. 1–22.

Parker, W. C. and Hess, D. (2001) Teaching with and for discussion *Teaching and Teacher Development*, 17(3), pp. 273–89.

Paton, G. (2009) Teachers being turned into social workers, warns Michael Gove*Telegraph*

Perczynski, P. (1999) Citizenship and Associative Democracy *European Consortium of Political Research, Annual Joint Sessions, 'Innovation in Democratic Theory' Workshop*, Mannheim, Germany, 26–31 March 1999.

Perry, R. P. (1977) Educational Seduction: The Effect of Teacher Reputation on Student Satisfaction and Learning, *American Educational Research Association*, New York, 4–8 April 1977.

Phelan, S. (2001) *Sexual Strangers: Gays, lesbians and dilemmas of citizenship* (Philadelphia, Temple University Press).

Phillips, A. (1998) *The Beast in the Nursery* (London, Faber and Faber).

Plant, R. (1990) Citizenship and rights, in R. Plant and N. Barry (eds) *Citizenship and Rights in Thatcher's Britain: Two Views* (London, Institute of Economic Affairs Health and Welfare Unit).

PMSU (2006) The UK Government's Approach to Public Service Reform – A discussion paper (Prime Minister's Strategy Unit, Cabinet Office).

Power Inquiry (2006) The Power Inquiry (York, The Power Inquiry).

Power, S., Whitty, G., Gewirtz, S., Halpin, D. and Dickson, M. (2004) Paving a 'third way'? A policy trajectory analysis of education action zones, *Research Papers in Education*, 19(4), pp. 453–75.

Punch, K. F. (2009) *Introduction to Research Methods in Education* (London, Sage).

Putnam, R. (2000) *Bowling Alone: The Collapse and Revival of American Community* (New York, Simon and Schuster).

Pykett, J. (2007) Making citizens governable? The Crick Report as governmental technology, *Journal of Education Policy*, 22(3), pp. 301–19.

—(2010) Personalised governing through behaviour change and re–education, *Political Studies Association Conference*, Edinburgh, 29 March – 1 April 2010.

Pykett, J., Saward, M. and Schaefer, A. (2010) Framing the Good Citizen, *The British Journal of Politics and International Relations*, 12(4), pp. 523–38.

QCA (2000) Citizenship Programmes of Study (Key Stage 3 and 4) (London, Qualifications and Curriculum Authority).

—(2001) 'Getting involved: extending opportunities for pupil participation' in Schemes of Work for key stage 3 (QCA/01/776) (London, QCA).

—(2007) Citizenship Programmes of Study (Key Stages 3 and 4) (London, Qualifications and Curriculum Authority).

Rapport, N. and Overing, J. (2000) *Social and Cultural Anthropology: The key concepts* (London, Routledge).

Rawls, J. (1971) *A Theory of Justice* (London, Oxford University Press).

Rowe, D. (2005) The development of political thinking in Year 8 and 9 students: an English perspective, *International Journal of Citizenship and Teacher Education* 1 (1), pp. 97–110.

Rudduck, J., Chaplain, R. and Wallace, G. (1996) Pupil voices and school improvement, in J. Ruddock, R. Chaplain and G. Wallace (eds) *School Improvement: What Can Pupils Tell Us?* (London, David Fulton).

Runneymede Trust (2000) *The Future of Multi-Ethnic Britain: the Parekh Report* (London, Profile Books).

Schweisfurth, M. (2006) Education for global citizenship: teacher agency and curricular structure in Ontario schools, *Educational Review*, 58(1), pp. 41–50.

Sears, A. (2009) Children's understandings of democratic participation: lessons from civic education, in M. Print and H. Milner (eds) *Civic Education and Youth Political Participation* (Rotterdam, Sense).

Sim, J. (2008) What does citizenship mean? Social studies teachers' understandings of citizenship in Singapore schools *Educational Review*, 60(3), pp. 253–66.

Smith, R. M. (1997) *Civic Ideals: Conflicting Visions of Citizenship in US History* (New Haven, Yale University Press).

Smithers, A. and Robinson, P. (2008) The Good Teacher Training Guide 2008 (Buckingham, University of Buckingham).

Spencer, S. (2007) Immigration, in A. Seldon (ed) *Blair's Britain 1997–2007* (Cambridge, Cambridge University Press).

SSAT (2007) Annual Report 2006–7 (London, Specialist Schools and Academies Trust).

Stark, S. and Torrance, H. (2005) Case Study, in B. Somekh and C. Lewin (eds) *Research Methods in the Social Sciences* (London, Sage).

Starkey, H. (2007) Teaching and Learning about Human Rights, *Teaching Citizenship*, (18), pp. 10–14.

—(2008) Education for citizenship, diversity and 'Britishness' 1997–2007, in T. Whitton (ed) *Le New Labour et l'identité britannique* (Clermont Ferrand, Observatoire de la Société Britannique No.5).

Stedward, G. (2000) New Labour's education policy, in D. Coates and P. Lawler (eds) *New Labour in Power* (Manchester, Manchester University Press).

Straw, J. (1999) House of Commons Hansard Debates, Column 767, 29 March 1999, published on-line at: www.publications.parliament.uk [accessed 11 August 2011].

Sunderland, C. (2003) Exploring Citizenship in PGCE, available on-line at: *www.citized.info/pdf/commarticles/Chris_Sunderland.pdf* [accessed 5 May 2008].

Talisse, R. (2005) *Democracy After Liberalism: Pragmatism and Deliberative Politics* (Abington, Routledge).

Taylor-Gooby, P. (2009) *Reframing Social Citizenship* (Oxford, Oxford University Press).

Taylor, E. and Low, N. (2010) 2008–09 Citizenship Survey: Empowered Communities Topic Report (London, Department for Communities and Local Government).

Torney-Purta, J. and Klandl-Richardson, W. (2002) An assessment of what fourteen year olds know and believe about democracy in twenty eight countries, in W. C. Parker (ed) *Education for Democracy: Contexts, Curricula, Assessments* (Greenwich, Connecticut, Information Age Publishing).

Torney-Purta, J., Lehman, R., Oswald, H. and Shulz, W. (2001) *Citizenship and Education in Twenty-Eight Countries: Civic Knowledge and Engagement at Age Fourteen* (Amsterdam, International Association for the Evaluation of Educational Achievement).

Townsley, E. (2001) 'The Sixties' Trope, *Theory, Culture and Society*, 18(6), pp. 99–123.

Toynbee, P. and Walker, D. (2005) *Better or Worse? Has Labour Delivered?* (London, Bloomsbury).

Trafford, B. (2008) Democratic schools: towards a definition, in J. Arthur, I. Davies and C. Hahn (eds) *The Sage Handbook of Education for Citizenship and Democracy* (London, Sage).

Trivers, H. (2010) UNICEF Rights Respecting School Award and Hampshire County Council's Rights, Respect, Responsibility programme: empowering or controlling young people? (unpublished Masters dissertation) *Institute of Education* (London, University of London).

Trowler, P. (2003) *Education Policy* (London, RoutledgeFalmer).

Vaughan, R. (2010) Good news for Gordon: teachers back Labour, *The Times Education Supplement,* 15 January 2010.

Vincent, C. and Martin, J. (2005) Parents as citizens: making the case, in G. Crozier and D. Reay (eds) *Activating Participation: Parents and teachers working towards partnership* (Stoke on Trent, Trentham).

Walkington, H. and Wilkins, C. (2000) Education for critical citizenship: The impact of teachers' world-view on classroom practice in the teaching of values, *The School Field*, 11(1/2), 59–78.

Wallerstein, I. (1995) *After Liberalism* (New York, The New Press).

Walzer, M. (1997) *On Toleration* (London, Yale University Press).

Watts, M. (2006) Citizenship education revisited: policy, participation and problems, *Pedagogy, Culure and Society*, 14(1), pp. 83–97.

Weller, S. (2007) *Teenagers' Citizenship: Experiences and Education* (Abingdon, Routledge).

White, C., Bruce, S. and Ritchie, J. (2000) *Young People's Politics: Political interest and engagement amongst 14–24 year olds* (York, Joseph Rowntree Foundation).

White, H. (1973a) *Metahistory: The historical imagination in nineteenth-century Europe* (Baltimore, The Johns Hopkins University Press).

White, J. P. (1973b) *Towards a Compulsory Curriculum* (London, Routledge and Kegan Paul).

Whitty, G. (2002) *Making Sense of Education Policy* (London, Paul Chapman).

Whitty, G., Rowe, G. and Aggleton, P. (1994) Discourses in cross-curricular contexts: limits to empowerment, *International Studies in Sociology of Education*, 4(1), pp. 25–42.

Whitty, G. and Wisby, E. (2007) Real Decision Making? School Councils in Action, Research Report DCSF-RR001 (London, DCSF).

Wilkins, C. (1999) Making 'Good Citizens': the social and political attitudes of PGCE students, *Oxford Review of Education*, 25(1), pp. 217–30.

Williams, F. (2004) What Matters is who Works: Why Every Child Matters to New Labour. Commentary on the DfES Green Paper Every Child Matters, *Critical Social Policy*, 24(3), pp. 406–27.

Wood, J. (2006) Defining active citizenship in English secondary schools, *Reflecting Education*, 2(2), pp. 23–37.

—(2009) Young People and Active Citizenship: An Investigation. Unpublished PhD Thesis. *Health and Life Sciences* (Leicester, De Montfort University).

Woodward, V. (2004) Active Learning for Active Citizenship (London, Home Office, Civil Renewal Unit).

Worley, C. (2005) 'It's not about race. It's about the community': New Labour and 'community cohesion', *Critical Social Policy*, 25(4), pp. 483–96.

Wright, J. (2011) Slacktivism or Activism?, *Teaching Citizenship*, (31), pp. 18–21.

Wringe, C. (1984) *Democracy, Schooling and Political Education* (London, George Allen and Unwin).

Young, I. M. (2000) *Inclusion and Democracy* (Oxford, Oxford University Press).

Index